Sidney Webb, Harold Cox

The Eight Hours Day

Sidney Webb, Harold Cox

The Eight Hours Day

ISBN/EAN: 9783337848415

Printed in Europe, USA, Canada, Australia, Japan

Cover: Foto ©Suzi / pixelio.de

More available books at **www.hansebooks.com**

THE EIGHT HOURS DAY.

By SIDNEY WEBB, LL.B.,

Lecturer on Economics at the City of London College and Working Men's College;

AND

HAROLD COX, B.A.,

Late Scholar of Jesus College, Cambridge.

LONDON:
WALTER SCOTT, 24 WARWICK LANE,
PATERNOSTER ROW.

PREFACE.

THE following work is an attempt to put together in accessible form as much information as possible concerning the Eight Hours Movement. The authors recognise that a complete history is beyond their powers, but they venture to think that, at the present time, a convenient account of that movement, in its historical, economic, and social aspects, will be of service to politicians and the public. The bibliography at the end of the volume may facilitate the research of other students of what bids fair to be the most important industrial movement of the close of the century. Additions to, or corrections of, that bibliography will be thankfully received.

A small portion of the work appeared in two articles in the *Nineteenth Century* and the *Contemporary Review* respectively, and is reproduced by permission of the proprietors of those magazines.

4 PARK VILLAGE EAST,
  LONDON N.W., *4th April* 1891.

CONTENTS.

CHAPTER I.

	PAGE
INTRODUCTION	1

CHAPTER II.

THE GROWTH OF THE EIGHT HOURS MOVEMENT—

(*a*) THE GENERAL SCOPE OF THE MOVEMENT	12
(*b*) THE MOVEMENT IN GREAT BRITAIN	13
(*c*) THE MOVEMENT IN AUSTRALIA	38
(*d*) THE MOVEMENT IN THE UNITED STATES AND CANADA	44
(*e*) THE MOVEMENT IN OTHER COUNTRIES	55

CHAPTER III.

FACTS OF TO-DAY RELATING TO THE HOURS OF LABOUR	66

CHAPTER IV.

THE PROBABLE ECONOMIC RESULTS OF AN EIGHT HOURS DAY—

PAGE

1. THE DIFFICULTY OF THE PROBLEM . . 93

2. THE RESULT OF PREVIOUS REDUCTIONS IN THE HOURS OF LABOUR. 94

3. THE THEORETIC RESULTS OF A GENERAL REDUCTION OF THE HOURS OF LABOUR IN ALL TRADES 103

4. THE ECONOMIC RESULTS OF AN EIGHT HOURS DAY IN PARTICULAR INDUSTRIES. . . 122

CHAPTER V.

SANITARY AND SOCIAL RESULTS OF AN EIGHT HOURS DAY 139

CHAPTER VI.

THE QUESTION OF OVERTIME . . . 153

CONTENTS.

CHAPTER VII.

HOW AN EIGHT HOURS DAY CAN BE OBTAINED—

- (*a*) VOLUNTARY ACTION BY EMPLOYERS . . 165
- (*b*) BY MEANS OF TRADE UNION COERCION . 167
- (*c*) BY LEGISLATION . . . 177

CHAPTER VIII.

ENGLISH PRECEDENTS FOR LEGISLATIVE ACTION . . 191

CHAPTER IX.

PRACTICAL PROPOSALS . . . 212
- I. PARTIAL PROPOSALS 214
- II. GENERAL PROPOSALS . . . 229

CHAPTER X.

CONCLUSION 238

APPENDIX.

I. HOURS OF LABOUR IN DIFFERENT TRADES . . 244

II. LETTERS, ETC., RECEIVED FROM FIRMS WHICH HAVE ALREADY ADOPTED AN EIGHT HOURS DAY . 254

APPENDIX—*continued.*

	PAGE
III. REPORT ON THE SWISS LEGISLATION REGULATING THE HOURS OF ADULT LABOUR	265
IV. PUBLICATIONS RELATING TO THE EXISTING FACTORY LEGISLATION AND THE EIGHT HOURS BILL	268
INDEX	273

THE EIGHT HOURS DAY.

CHAPTER I.—INTRODUCTION.

THE EIGHT HOURS DAY.

"WHEREAS it is desirable for the general welfare of the community that the hours of Daily Labour should be such that workmen may have a reasonable time at their own disposal for recreation, mental culture, and the performance of social and civil duties: And whereas it would be conducive to this end to declare by law the proper duration of a Day's Labour."

The above is the preamble of a bill introduced into the parliament of Queensland on June 26th, 1890, by Sir S. W. Griffith, Q.C., the Colonial Premier. It expresses concisely the motives which inspire the advocates of an Eight Hours Bill. The demand for shorter hours of labour has arisen among the working classes, not so much from the conviction that their present hours are injurious to health—though that in many cases is the fact,—not so much from the theory that shorter hours mean higher wages—though that theory is in the main sound,—but from the strongly-felt desire for additional opportunities for recreation and the enjoyment of life. Just as it was the growing wealth and intelligence of the middle classes which forced on the Reform Bill of 1832, so now it is the wider education, the increased prosperity, of the operatives and artisans of England which make them demand some relief from the irksomeness of their daily labour. Incidentally such a measure may lead to higher wages; incidentally it may benefit the workman's health; and both these considerations probably present themselves to each man's mind when he begins to think out the question. But the real force which gives vitality to the Eight Hours Movement is the spontaneous longing for a brighter, fuller life.

Men and women who toil for wages are everywhere growing tired of being only working animals. They wish to enjoy, as well as to labour; to pluck the fruits, as well as dig the soil; to wear as well as to weave. They are eager for opportunity to see more of the great world in which they live—a world of which many of them now for the first time hear from books. They want to see their friends who live at a distance; to go to the plays about which the papers talk; to have holidays and visit pleasant places. Nor is it only these comparatively facile forms of amusement that now attract the multitude. Peripatetic lecturers are daily scouring the country inspiring young men and women of every class with a new-born taste for the facts of science, or with a new-born appreciation of the beauties of literature. On all sides there is an expansion of life. New possibilities of enjoyment, physical, emotional, intellectual, are daily opening for the masses. New aspirations are daily surging up. We need not wonder then that this generation is no longer content to live as its fathers and mothers lived. They were content to work and to eat and to sleep, and when worked out to lay themselves down and die. What else could they find in life? To them reading and writing were cabalistic arts, and a journey of twenty miles suggested recklessness tainted with impiety. To such men as these—and the race is not yet extinct—a holiday is not a boon but a bore, and Sunday is the day most hated in the week.*

But the last representatives of this race are now to be found only in remote villages. The younger generation of villagers, and every generation of townsfolk, are eager to enjoy the world around them. They realise that life is large and many-sided, and they pant to taste of its sweets. Hence in all classes the demand for leisure grows keener and keener. Both men and women are growing daily more conscious of the cruelty of a system which

* One of the writers of this book has often heard a labourer of his acquaintance, a man still in the prime of life, remark, "I yäte Sunday more 'n any day in the week."

condemns them to a barely broken round of monotonous toil. Everywhere they begin fiercely to rebel against this system, and nerve themselves to prepare for its overthrow.

"Work we will," they say in effect, if not in words, "for we know that work is the condition of life. But we demand in return the wage for our work. Not mere money wage—for that by itself is useless—but the power and opportunity to enjoy the advantages which the labour of all of us has created."

This vague demand has found formal expression in the agitation for an Eight Hours Day. Not that there is anything sacred in the figure eight. Any other unit would do as well for the rough purposes of political agitation. But "eight" has forced itself to the front, as will be explained later on, largely from historical and sentimental considerations. And so we, the writers of this book, take up that figure as symbolising the popular demand for a shorter working day. That demand we propose, in the pages that follow, to examine in all its bearings.

Without attempting to write a history, we shall show how the contemporary Eight Hours Movement has grown out of the struggle for the Ten Hours Law and the Nine Hours Day. We shall show how the workmen's organisations have, at each recurring opportunity, successfully struggled to reduce their hours of labour, by law, by strikes, by the sanction of public opinion, or by any other means that came to hand.

We shall give particulars of the parallel movement which has gone on in the other countries of the industrial world. These particulars, whether in the case of the United Kingdom or in those of other nations, will be far from forming a complete record even of this one phase of the history of the working classes. Our aim has been merely to collect, in conveniently accessible form, such facts as we have been able to discover without pretence of research.

We have further endeavoured to show by facts the almost total absorption by work of the present life of the masses. Many of these facts are already commonly known.

Every one knows, or ought to know, that omnibus drivers and conductors work fourteen to sixteen hours a day, that the drivers and guards on many of our railways are often on duty for fifteen or eighteen hours at a stretch, and that the sweated tailors at the East End of London, who make the clothes that the West End wears, are sometimes kept bent over their work in a poisonous atmosphere for sixteen hours out of the twenty-four. But these cases, to which public attention has been attracted, are not really exceptional. There are thousands of men and women engaged in almost every variety of manual occupation who when they get up in the morning know that they must go through ten to twelve hours of heavy labour before they can rest again.

Some women, it is true, are protected from their own weakness, or from the tyranny of employers, by the Factory Acts. But these Acts only apply to certain specified occupations. Barmaids, shopgirls, waitresses in eating-houses and bread shops, hospital nurses, laundresses, and charwomen are all outside the scope of the factory law. It will be found that in most of these occupations the working day is twelve or thirteen hours.

In the preparation of this book we have taken pains to collect positive information as to the hours of labour in various occupations. Unfortunately, there are many gaps in the statement we are able to present. But the particulars collected are sufficient to prove that the demand for a shorter working day is not based on a fictitious grievance.

After the facts, the economics! The hours of labour may be shamefully long, but what would be the economic result of any reduction of them? That question we have set ourselves to answer in considerable detail.

It will be shown that the almost universal experience of the past indicates that a shortening of the hours of labour is compatible with a maintenance of the present aggregate product of labour. The workman, in many cases, but not in all, produces as much in ten hours as in twelve, in eight hours as in ten. Whether through greater energy, greater steadiness, or greater speed of work; whether through improved machinery or better methods of production; whether by diminished friction, fewer losses, or a rise in quality, experience shows that, in the arithmetic of labour, as in that of the Customs, two from ten is likely to produce, not eight, but even eleven.

In some cases, however, the worker's product will be less in eight hours than in ten or twelve. Especially is this the case in the services rendered by the workers on our means of communication, the staff of our railways, tramways, omnibuses, etc. We shall, however, show that this result is likely to be economically advantageous, not disastrous, to the community. Although millions of men and women are being daily overworked, to the detriment of their own health and the enfeeblement of the next generation, the productive power of the nation is not exercised to the full. For side by side with those who are overworked are others doing no work at all. Many of these are only too anxious to take their share of the work of the community; but they are not allowed to do so. Our industrial system can find no place for them; or rather, the place which they should take is occupied by the extra hours of those already in employ.

And hence results the commercial deadlock which in a more or less aggravated form is always present. On the one hand are manufacturers complaining that they cannot sell their goods. On the other, are hungry men walking the streets asking only for the means to buy these goods. The means to buy is rightly refused except in return for work done. The opportunity to work is wrongly refused because others are overworked. By reducing the hours of labour room will, in some industries, be made for more workers. A shortening of the hours of the myriad of manual labourers in public employment, and of the whole staff of the railways and tramways—to say nothing of other occupations—would undoubtedly have the result of transferring from irregular to full employment many thousands of those who can find no work to do. And hence, although the output of each individual may in some cases be diminished, the output of the nation may even be increased.

The result of the shortening of hours upon the rate of wages will be shown to be almost universally beneficial to the wage earner, and not always injurious to the capitalist. But some loss of profit there may easily be—a price for the benefit of the great mass of the community which we trust that shareholders will be not unwilling to pay.

In the various chapters of the book the bogie of foreign competition will be found fully dealt with, and the danger, real or imaginary, to each trade assessed at its proper value. And here parenthetically we may point out that from the first Factory Act in 1802 down to the present day, every single proposal for an improvement in the condition of factory operatives has been met with the cry that it will ruin our trade. The folly of this cry has been proved by facts over and over again. Each upward step taken by the working classes of this country has been followed by an improvement in our foreign trade. This is, indeed, exactly what a wider view of the workings of commerce would lead us to expect. An improvement in our workers is at least as important to our national wealth as an improvement in our machines; and every increase in our national wealth means an increase in our foreign trade. The workers, moreover, are not only sellers of labour, but buyers of commodities. Much of what they buy comes from abroad, and consequently an increase in their spending power means an increase in the national imports. This increase can, in the long run, only be paid for by increased exports.

We show, therefore, that a reduction in the hours of labour is not only economically possible, but also economically desirable; that it may give us, as a nation, a larger gross income, and that a larger percentage of this income would go to pay workers, and less to the maintenance of an idle class at either end of the social scale.

But though we have devoted a relatively large space to the economic results of an Eight Hours Day, we do not hold that these advantages are so important as the improvement of social and individual health that would follow a reasonable reduction in the hours of labour. We contend that a community in which some members are overworked while others can get no work at all is *ipso facto* unhealthy. Such a contrast entails a feverish unrest on all the individuals affected by it. They can never know what the enjoyment of life means. Those who are in work have not the leisure for healthy recreation; those who are out of work have not the spirit. The former are working anxiously, almost phrenziedly, lest they should be thrown out into the bottomless gulf of No-Work; the latter with equal anxiety wearily beat the streets in search of work.

Equally serious, as we shall have to point out, is the effect of long hours of labour on the physical health of the individual. The human body needs frequent change of surroundings, change of exercise, to keep it in perfect condition. A man, and still more a woman, will suffer from protracted occupation at one particular task, even if that task in itself is healthy enough. And of all the manual work done in an advanced industrial community to-day, how much is healthy in its nature or done under healthy conditions?

We may however safely assume that the majority of our readers will be ready to admit beforehand that the long hours so generally worked in many trades inflict serious evil both on the social health of the community, and on the physical health of the individual. But what, we shall be asked, is your remedy for this concomitant of civilisation? How do you propose to obtain an Eight Hours Day? We answer at once—By Act of Parliament; and we devote a large part of the present volume to justifying this answer.

That the individual workman cannot by himself secure an Eight Hours Day for himself is a proposition which should need no proof, but of which the full significance is not often realised by the average journalist or doctor, member of Parliament or lawyer, over whose industry the Juggernaut of the Industrial Revolution has not passed. In any highly evolved industry the individual workman has necessarily lost his power of arranging his own daily life, and has become a unit in a vast industrial army, over the hours of labour of which he has no more control than over the tides.

It is to obtain some protection for his individual life that the workman, incredible as this may seem to the apostles of "free labour," joins with his fellows in a Trade Union. Can he effectively secure an Eight Hours Day by this additional weapon?

We show both from the history of past struggles, and from the facts of to-day, that this method of industrial democracy is equivalent to private war—a mere relic of barbarism, costly and even dangerous to the nation in its operation. The instance of the Scotch Railway Strike shows how little it is to be relied upon to do what is required. In this case a powerful union of railway workers, backed up by large funds, ordered a simultaneous strike on three railways. The moment chosen was so timed as to cause the maximum of inconvenience to the companies. The men's ground of complaint was one which specially appealed to public sympathy. They complained that they were kept at work for usually 14 hours a day, and sometimes 19 or 20 hours. They asked not for an Eight Hours Day, but for ten hours. The strike lasted for five weeks. It was supported by large subscriptions from trade societies not directly involved in the quarrel, and from many private persons. At the end of the five weeks the men made complete submission.

After this there will probably be, in the United Kingdom, less talk than there was before of the power of combinations of workmen. We have, however, in a subsequent chapter fully examined the suggestion that the men should trust to their trade unions to win them the Eight Hours Day. We have shown that only a small proportion of the working classes belong to any trade society at all. That even where the societies are strong they have been unable to put down the admitted evil of overtime work. And finally, that a majority of the trade unionists in the kingdom have formally declared that they prefer an Act of Parliament to the so-called free action of their own societies.

Moreover, we contend that the non-combatant public has a right to be consulted in this matter. If an Eight Hours Day is to be won by trade unionists, it can only be won after a series of strikes, each involving enormous discomfort and loss to the whole community.

On these grounds, among others, we contend that even were it possible to obtain an Eight Hours Day by trade union action, an Act of Parliament would still be preferable.

To those who urge that this proposal involves a new departure in English policy, we reply by enumerating some of the striking precedents of such legislation. It is commonly asserted that Parliament has never yet regulated the hours of labour of adult males. We show that, as a matter of fact, the hours of labour of adults have been subject to rigid regulation for the last forty years. And we prove by quotations which admit of no criticism, that Parliament knew beforehand that these regulations would apply to men as well as to women, and that it has repeatedly renewed and confirmed them with that knowledge. Further, we produce an immense mass of precedents from foreign countries and our own colonies. We demonstrate the falsity of the common assertion that the Eight Hours Day in Australia is independent of legal sanction. Not one only, but several Acts exist in the Colony of Victoria for the limitation of the hours of labour of adults male and female. And these Acts are not declarations of the normal day such as have been placed upon the Statute Book in several American States; they are effective laws carrying penalties for their breach.

Neither considerations of practical expediency, nor precedents ancient or modern, convince the man who starts with the dogma that the regulation of the hours of labour is outside the proper functions of the State. For his benefit we have endeavoured to show that the legal prohibition of overwork is on the same juristic level as the legal prohibition of fraud or assault; and that it does not at any rate differ in essence from other legislation carrying out the express desires of a majority of the nation. Such legislation, moreover, by its restrictions upon the tyranny set by economic conditions in a society still largely individualistic in its basis, is calculated positively to increase the liberty of the great majority of the nation.

It may, however, be admitted that the demand, which has marked the present century, for a more general regulation of the hours and conditions of labour, does represent a marked advance upon previous conceptions of the sphere of legislation. Such an extension of collective activity is, it may safely be asserted, an inevitable result of political Democracy. When the Commons of England had been granted the right to vote supplies, it must have seemed an unwarrantable extension that they should claim also to redress grievances. When they passed from legislation to the exercise of control over the Executive, the constitutional jurists were aghast at their presumption. The attempt of Parliament to seize the command of the military forces led to a civil war. Its authority over foreign policy is scarcely two hundred years old. Every one of these developments of the collective authority of the nation over the conditions of its own life was denounced by great authorities as an illegitimate usurpation. Every one of them is still being resisted in countries less advanced in political development. In Russia, it is the right to vote supplies that is denied; in Mecklenburg, it is the right freely to legislate; in Denmark, it is the control over the Executive; in Germany, it is the command of the army; in Austria, it is the foreign policy of that composite Empire. In the United Kingdom and the United States, where all these rights are admitted, the constitutional purists object to the moral competence of the people to regulate, through their representatives in Parliament, the conditions under which they work and live. Although the tyranny which keeps the tram-car conductor away from his home for 17 hours a day is not the tyranny of king, or priest, or noble, he feels that it is tyranny all the same, and seeks to curb it as he best can. The step which these Anglo-Saxon communities are taking unavowedly, and often unconsciously, a smaller Republic expressly enshrines in its Constitution. The Swiss Federal Constitution, which we quote in a following chapter, explicitly declares the competence of the legislature to enact statutes "relating to the duration of the work which may be imposed upon adults."

But assuming that it is granted that Parliament may legitimately regulate the hours of labour, how practically do you propose to proceed? This very pertinent question we have answered in a subsequent chapter. We seek no legislative symmetry. We are anxious only that that should be first done which most needs doing and is most practicable. The hours of labour in some occupations constitute a scandal which ought not to go a day unremoved. If the conditions are such that an immediate Eight Hours Day is inapplicable, let us begin with nine hours or ten hours.

In other occupations the hours of labour are already relatively short. The cotton operatives, for example, have by law a week of 56½ hours. No one contends that this is oppressive. Undoubtedly a shorter week would be better for the operatives, and, as we show, the profits of the trade could probably bear the reduction. But till the operatives themselves make an effective demand for a 48 hours week, there is no reason for Parliament to trouble to help them to it.

In other cases, although a shortening of the hours of labour is urgently needed, legislative action does not appear to be at present practicable. For the workers in these unfortunate trades we can suggest only organisation among themselves, and the pressure of public opinion. Much, too, might be done for them by the efficient carrying out of improved factory legislation, and a more sustained sympathy from the rest of the working population; and, after a short time, experience in other cases may show how the strong arm of the law could be successfully brought to bear upon the hours in these unfortunate industries.

In the meantime there are whole groups of industries to which an Eight Hours Day might at once be granted by law, with the enthusiastic support of the great majority of those concerned. The hours of all public employés might be shortened by way of example to other employers. The working day of the miner, the railway or tramway worker, and the shop assistant, might be reduced without fear.

We seek, however, to go further. We think that it might be left to the workers in each industry, bearing in mind the risk to their own wages involved, to decide whether the normal working day in that industry should be reduced. This principle of "Trade Option," introduced as a novelty into the draft Eight Hours Bill of the Fabian Society in 1889, but since discovered, in principle, in the Victorian Factory Act of 1885, appears to afford the best practicable means of combining a recognition of the desirability of an Eight Hours Day with that of the right of the workers to settle for themselves the conditions under which they will work.

It may not be improper to explain, in conclusion, that we claim for the Eight Hours Bill no virtue as a panacea. It will not make the three-hooped pots to have ten hoops, nor endow us with a new heaven and a new earth. It will do little to remedy the evils caused by the great disparity of incomes, or by the individual ownership of the means by which the worker lives. It will not restore to social health a "submerged tenth" wasted by the demoralisation of extreme poverty, or the results of drink and disease. But if it secures for millions of tired workers an hour or two of leisure which would otherwise have been spent in toil ; if it enables many who would otherwise have plodded the daily round of monotonous labour to obtain access to some share in that larger life from which they are now relentlessly excluded ; if it protects the future generations of the race from physical degeneration or mental decay ; if it makes brighter the lives of those who have toiled that a small class among us might have education, and holidays, and culture ; if it accomplishes only partially some of these great ends, an Eight Hours Bill will be no mean achievement even of the greatest statesman, and no unfitting close to the century of the Factory Acts.

CHAPTER II.

THE GROWTH OF THE EIGHT HOURS MOVEMENT.

(*a*) *The General Scope of the Movement.*

WHAT is commonly known as "The Eight Hours Movement," now agitating alike England, the Western part of the Continent of Europe, and the United States, represents, in the main, nothing more precise than a desire for a shorter working day. As was said above, there is no magic in the number eight, which marks it out as the proper number of hours of daily labour; nor is there any reason for assuming that this or any other number of hours should be universally adopted in all occupations and in all countries.

The history of the Eight Hours Movement is therefore a record of the modern striving for shorter hours of labour, and we shall see that much of the most effective work to bring about an actual Eight Hours Day has been done under the guise of other demands. Further, in following the history of the Eight Hours Movement, we shall find it impossible to draw any distinction between the agitation for an Eight Hours Day and that for an Eight Hours Bill. This distinction is too subtle for the average artisan. As long as he gets a shorter day he is generally indifferent how he gets it. To the average English, American or Continental artisan, it has always seemed perfectly natural to utilise the power of the law, whenever he can, to secure that which he regards as essential to the well-being of his class. It is true that some of the older English Trade Unionists now share with the Continental Anarchists a rooted objection to State action in the matter of the hours of adult male labour. But this objection was not always apparent. Many of these men, or their fathers, fought side by side with Lord Shaftesbury to secure the passing of the Factory Acts. The zeal which they threw into the struggle was largely inspired by the confessed hope that laws intended primarily for women and children would curtail the hours of labour of men also.

There is, it need hardly be said, nothing new in a general demand for a reduction in the length of the working day. Ever since the wage-earning class has been able to make its voice heard in society at all, it has protested against the length of its daily toil. The proposition that the hours of labour might be and ought to be reduced has been periodically discussed for more than three-quarters of a century.

In Great Britain the Eight Hours Movement is the legitimate descendant of the agitation which resulted in the Ten Hours Bill of 1847, and of the succeeding Nine Hours Movement in various skilled handicrafts. In the United States an "Eight Hours Day" appears to have formed the chief aspiration of the workers' organisations ever since the great start made in manufacturing industries at the end of the war. On the Continent of Europe, although an Eight Hours Law was one of the most cherished aspirations of 1848, the present movement dates chiefly from the formation of the "International" in 1864, and derives its inspiration primarily from the writings of Karl Marx. The particular form which the movement takes, and the manner in which its demands are formulated, necessarily vary according to the political and industrial conditions of each country, and of each trade. And although the older "International" mooted the question, the Eight Hours Movement did not become consciously international in character until the International Trade Union Congress at Paris in 1883. For a systematic history of the movement adequate materials hardly yet exist, and in the present chapter we make no pretence to do more than record, in convenient form, some of the chief incidents in its course.

(*b.*) *The Movement in Great Britain.*

We have been unable to trace the origin of the feeling that Eight Hours constitutes, in some mysterious way, the "natural" or fitting length of the working day. It is well known that the "three eights" have been one of the leading aspirations of the

English artisan for, at any rate, fifty years.* The common tradition, which assigns the origin of the idea to Alfred's division of his time into eight hours work, eight hours sleep, and eight hours recreation and study, is somewhat fanciful. Much more probable is the theory that the equal threefold division of the 24 hours has, of itself, commended the idea of the eight hours work as specially reasonable. The following common rhyme, in which the idea is embodied—

> "Eight hours to work, eight hours to play,
> Eight hours to sleep, eight 'bob' a day,"

is perhaps of Australian origin, as it does not seem that an aspiration for wages of eight shillings a day has yet so much as entered the heads of any considerable section of English workmen. Mr. George Howell suggests that this fourth eight may have been added merely to complete the rhyme.

A more suggestive origin for the ideal of an Eight Hours Day is found in the practice of the fifteenth century. The late Professor J. E. Thorold Rogers states emphatically of that golden age that "it is plain that the day was one of eight hours."† But it appears that overtime was worked. At p. 175 of his useful little volume, we find the following :—

"I stated in a previous chapter that the day was one of eight hours' work, and grounded my opinion on the fact that winter wages were reckoned to be payable only in the months of December and January, and from the fact that extra hours, sometimes as many as forty-eight in the week, are frequently paid for by the King's agents when hurried work was needed. . . . The artisan who is demanding at this time an eight hours day in the building trades, is simply striving to recover what his ancestor worked by four or five centuries ago."

Those who have any experience of the length of time that traditions linger among an illiterate class will not think it altogether fanciful to suppose that the modern ideal of an Eight Hours Day is the half-forgotten survival from a long-cherished memory of a former shorter day.

---

* *The Conflicts of Labour and Capital*, by George Howell, M.P., ch. vi. sec. 30 (p. 302 of 1878 edition).

† J. E. Thorold Rogers, *Work and Wages* (abridged edition, p. 28).

The golden age did not, however, endure for long after the close of the fifteenth century. By the close of the reign of Elizabeth, the artisan and labourer seem to have sunk into a condition of industrial subjection far worse than anything recorded in the fourteenth or fifteenth centuries. By the end of the seventeenth the working week consisted of at least 72 hours.* But whatever be the ultimate origin of the Eight Hours dream, it has certainly been in the minds of Trade Unionists in England ever since the repeal of the Combination Laws in 1824, and has recurred at every season of reviving industrial prosperity since that time.

And even before this date a serious proposal to reduce the hours of factory labour to eight hours was apparently made by Robert Owen in 1817.† At that date, when even children were kept at work in the textile mills for fifteen or sixteen hours a day, the proposal of an Eight Hours Day must have seemed simply absurd. Robert Owen instituted a regular working day in his mills at New Lanark, of ten and a half hours nett, and he lived to see an even shorter day made universal in the textile industry.

At the beginning of the present century the ordinary working day of the English artisan appears to have varied from 11 to 14 hours. In the new industries, such as the textile manufactories, the employers, being free from traditions, often exacted a still longer day. The London bookbinders were working 12½ hours a day (14 less meal-times) in 1780, when a Trade Union was formed to obtain a reduction of an hour a day.‡

This movement became successful in 1786. King George the Third was the first employer to accord the boon, which he did to the "finisher" in the Royal Library. The "second hour" was

---

* "On April 9th, 1684, the magistrates of Warwick met at the county town, and assessed the wages for the year under the Act of Elizabeth. . . . The hours of labour are defined between March and September to be from five in the morning until between seven and eight at night—*i.e.*, 14½ hours, from which 2½ hours are to be allowed for meals. . . . From the middle of September till the middle of March he is to work from daylight till night."

† In 1834 Robert Owen asserted in *The Crisis*, iii. 188, that in August 1817 he advertised eight hours as a just day's labour. (Quoted in Sargent's *Robert Owen and his Philosophy*.) In 1818 Owen presented a petition to the Congress of Aix-la-Chapelle, for international factory legislation.

‡ *Social Science Assoc. Report on Trade Societies*, 1860, p. 93.

gained in 1794, and another half-hour about 1810, after an unsuccessful strike in 1806. Eighty years ago, therefore, the London bookbinders had won for themselves the Ten Hours Day.

Other workers, especially in the new industries, were by no means so fortunate. The stocking-makers of Leicester, who did not combine until 1817, were still working 14 to 15 hours a day in 1819.* The London coopers were working 13 hours a day in 1825,† and the master silk-weavers of Macclesfield at the same period attempted to increase the hours from 11 to 12 a day. This attempt was, however, successfully resisted by the men on the ground of the probable injury to their children who worked with them.‡

The history of the Factory Acts is briefly given elsewhere. These affected at first only the textile districts, but the increased power obtained by Trade Unions after the repeal of the Combination Laws led to the growth of a Ten Hours Movement in London and elsewhere, which more than kept pace with the agitation for the Ten Hours Bill in Lancashire and Yorkshire. In 1837, the Glasgow cotton-spinners had a strike which caused a Parliamentary inquiry. Adults were then still working 69 hours a week, and the object of every Union was said to be "to procure the passing of a Ten Hours Bill." §

By this time the Dublin carpenters had already brought their hours down to 63 per week, and the printers and painters in that city absolutely refused to work more than 60.‖ The Ten Hours Day seems to have become general in the London handicrafts some time before this period.

The practice of lengthening the day by means of overtime was, however, very general. It was to enforce a genuine Ten Hours Day, by the abolition of systematic overtime, that the "Amalgamated Society of Engineers" was formed. To this society was due the great strike and lock-out of 1851-2. Here the men had ultimately to surrender at discretion, but the strike did much to call the attention of working men all over the kingdom to the question of reduction of hours.

---

* Parliamentary Report on Combinations, 1824, summarised in *Soc. Sci. Assoc. Report*, 1860, p. 362.

† *Ibid.*, p. 372.   § *Ibid.*, pp. 391, 393, 400.
‡ *Ibid.*, p. 360.   ‖ *Ibid.*, pp. 405, 422, 427.

GROWTH OF THE MOVEMENT.

In the textile trades the Ten Hours Law had recently been made effective. The reduction of hours was usually from 69 to 60, and this reduction had been followed by a positive increase of wages.* Other trades began to move in the same direction. The Glasgow cloth-lappers struck in 1851 for a reduction of hours from 64 to 58 a week; they compromised on 62. In 1858 they returned to the charge, and gained two more hours, in both cases without reduction of wage.†

A much more important event was the opening of the Nine Hours Movement, in 1853, by the London building trades, who had long enjoyed a Ten Hours Day. The actual conflict did not begin until 1858. By this time the Australian Trade Unions had won their Eight Hours Day. And it was, as far as we can trace, on this occasion that the Eight Hours Day was first spoken of as the real goal of an English strike. The immediate demand was, however, only for a Nine Hours Day, plus a Saturday half-holiday. After six months' struggle the men surrendered.

Other trades had, in the meantime, been more successful. The West Yorkshire coal-hewers seem to have reduced their hours from 10 in 1844, and 9 in 1853, to 8 per day in 1858,‡ but the other workers in the mines, including boys of ten years old, still worked a Ten Hours Day. A similar system prevailed also in the South Yorkshire mines.§ The Glasgow masons struck in 1853 for a reduction of hours from 60 to 57 a week. They were successful, and gained at the same time a rise of wages amounting to over 8 per cent. Next year the Glasgow shipwrights successfully made the same demand.‖ At the time of the inquiry into Trade Societies by the Committee of the Social Science Association in 1860, the majority of artisans were still working 60 hours a week.¶ Some, however, such as the London and Liverpool tailors, and the London bakers, had still nominally a Twelve Hours Day, which was often exceeded.** A few trades were more fortunate.

---

* Statements of Preston Master Weavers and Weavers' Strike Committee, 1853, pp. 223, 225 of *Soc. Sci. Assoc. Report*, 1860.
† *Soc. Sci. Assoc. Report*, p. 276.   ‡ *Ibid.*, p. 32.
§ *Ibid.*, pp. 45, 268, 269.   ‖ *Ibid.*, p. 285.
¶ *E.g.*, joiners (*Report*, p. 297), painters (p. 298), ship joiners (p. 298), potters (p. 282), compositors, sometimes 59 hours only (pp. 84, 125).
** *Soc. Sci. Assoc. Report*, pp. 138, 295, 300.

The Glasgow painters were on strike for 57 hours,* and the railway spring-makers at Sheffield, a specially laborious trade, worked only nine hours a day.†

The prosperous state of trade and these successive reductions led, about 1860, to a revival of the "Nine Hours Movement." At the back of this was undoubtedly the Eight Hours aspiration, for at the masons' strike at Huddersfield in 1860 a reduction of hours from 57½ to 51½ was claimed.‡ No great progress was however made at that date, although the formation of the "International" in 1862, and its growing influences over English Trade Union leaders until 1871, kept the subject constantly before the minds of labour leaders.

During the depression of trade which followed the disastrous commercial crisis of 1866, the movement for a shorter day was not pressed. It was, however, never forgotten, and many men in the shipbuilding yards on the Tyne struck in 1866 for a Nine Hours Day. With returning prosperity, the old ideal of the Eight Hours Day seems once more to have entered vividly into the minds of working men.

At the Trade Union Congress held at Birmingham in 1869 (Wednesday, August 25th), Mr. Swain, of Manchester, read a paper in favour of a further reduction of the hours of labour, urging the claims of health, mental cultivation, and physical recreation, and showing that production had increased at an accelerated rate after the previous reductions. He said: "The question would of course naturally arise, Would the same rate of wages be retained after the decrease of the hours of labour? The reply was that the price of labour, like other commodities, would be regulated by supply and demand, and as shorter time would employ more hands, there was no reason to suppose that the price of labour would be lowered." Mr. Kane (Darlington) moved the following resolution:—"That it is the firm conviction as well as the duty of the trade representatives at this Congress to aid every fair and honourable movement which has for its object the shortening of the hours of labour, believing that it will aid in promoting morality and the physical and intellectual power of workmen, and assist in finding employment for the unemployed." This was seconded by Mr. Bailey (Preston), and *carried unanimously*, as

* *Soc. Sci. Assoc. Report*, p. 291.   † *Ibid.*, p. 575.   ‡ *Ibid.*, p. 335.

was also an addendum to the effect that eight hours should be the standard day's labour for the working classes throughout the United Kingdom.

Two years later, at the Congress held in London in 1871, Mr. Bailey (Preston) read a paper on the same subject, urging the same claims, and showing that since the passing of the Ten Hours Law, factory work had so increased in intensity that the hours of labour had again become excessive, and dangerous to life and health. The following resolution was *unanimously carried:*— "That the productive powers and the skill of the operatives of this country have arrived at a state of perfection which guarantees that eight hours labour a day will answer all the commercial, national, and domestic requirements of the population; and that, moreover, such a reduction is necessary on sanitary and moral grounds."*

It is interesting to notice that in all these instances the movement for an Eight Hours Day came from representatives of the Northern Trade Unions, and that special reference was made to the textile trades, in which a shorter day is now represented to be impracticable.

The result of this revival of feeling was a great outburst of strikes towards the end of 1869. Mr. G. Phillips Bevan gives the following statistics of the number of strikes occurring in the United Kingdom for the next ten years:—†

	Number of Strikes.	Time spent on Strike.
1870	30	68 days.
1871	98	279 ,,
1872	343	988 ,,
1873	365	1093 ,,
1874	286	812 ,,
1875	245	684 ,,
1876	229	952 ,,
1877	180	759 ,,
1878	268	1621 ,,
1879 (to 1st Dec. only)	308	1774 ,,
	2352	9027 = 54,163 working days.

* Quoted in the pamphlet by John Burns, L.C.C., *The Liverpool Trade Union Congress* (1890).

† "The Strikes of the Past Ten Years," by G. Phillips Bevan (read 20th January 1880). See *Journal of the Royal Statistical Society*, March 1880.

Most of the strikes in 1871 and 1872 were caused by the demand for a Nine Hours Day and a Saturday Half-holiday. The great strike of the building trades in London in the latter year was specially remarkable for the vigour with which the movement for shorter hours of labour was carried on. By the end of 1872 these demands had been granted to most of the skilled artisans. This 54 hour week (11 hours, less 1½ hours for meals, for 5 days, with 7 hours, less half-an-hour for a meal, on Saturday) resulted, indirectly, in a new Factory Act.

The textile trades had for over twenty years enjoyed their Ten Hours Day under legal protection, but the reduction of hours in other industries caused the proposal of a Nine Hours Bill in the Trade Union Congress of 1872, brought forward by the representatives of the textile unions, the majority being adult male operatives. This bill remained a subject of agitation in Lancashire and Yorkshire until the reduction of hours to 56½ per week by the Act of 1874.

It is worth notice that this movement for a legal reduction of the hours of work in textile mills was mainly carried on by the male operatives, to whom the Factory Acts profess not to apply. But the men's Trade Unions were keenly aware how successfully their own hours had been reduced by the Ten Hours Bill, and they felt that the best, and indeed the only practicable, way of attaining a further reduction was by another law. But the state of feeling in the House of Commons at that time, with the economics of the "Manchester School" still dominant among the Liberal Party, made it utterly hopeless to attempt to limit by law the hours of men. Mr. Thomas Ashton, J.P., then and now one of the leaders of the spinners, has since often explained how the men accordingly "skulked behind the women's petticoats," and vigorously promoted the Nine Hours Bill for women and children, being well aware that its operation must virtually secure the same hours for the male operatives. By these skilful tactics, the economic conscience of the House of Commons was appeased, although neither the manufacturers, nor the economists, nor indeed even the legislators themselves, could ignore that the result was, in effect, the same as if the bill had applied in express terms adult male labour.

The Eight Hours Day did not cease to be one of the leading ideals of English working men, but no definite steps were taken to promote its attainment during the depression of 1877-80. Philanthropists continued spasmodically to ask for a shorter day for particular workers. Mr. Reaney and other devoted enthusiasts vainly endeavoured to soften the hearts of tramway directors, that they might let their men go after less than sixteen hours' labour. The Duke of St. Albans, in 1877, introduced a bill to restrict the excessive hours of railway servants. This found, however, no support, and was abandoned. The Trade Unions had, indeed, enough to do to maintain, even nominally, the Nine Hours Day which they had won. In 1878 and 1879 a general effort was made by the employers in many trades to restore the Ten Hours Day, causing a great number of strikes, and much bitterness of feeling. The question of a further reduction was next raised by the Socialists. This party became formally organised in England in 1881, after practically over twenty years of quiescence. The advocacy of an Eight Hours Law by Karl Marx in *Das Capital*, first published in 1867, had not attracted any attention in England; nor had the French edition of 1875 much greater success. It was the formation of the Democratic Federation in 1881 (afterwards called the "Social Democratic Federation") which brought the ideas of Marx to the front in England. Mr. Hyndman put forward "a curtailment of the hours of labour, eight hours being the working day," as a part of an immediately practicable Democratic programme.* Jevons, in his *State in Relation to Labour*, published in 1882, refers to the widespread feeling in favour of an Act limiting the working day in all industries whatsoever.

An Eight Hours Bill did not, however, at first form any part of the explicit programme of the Social Democratic Federation. By 1884, however, they were advocating a restriction of the hours of all public servants to eight per day. By 1886 the idea of a general Eight Hours Bill had so far progressed as to warrant its express inclusion in the general programme.

In the meantime the apathy of the officials of the older Trade Unions had caused the formation of other Labour Associations in imitation of the American organisations. The Knights of Labour gradually spread in the Black Country, and one of their proposals was an Eight Hours Day. The "National Labour Federation" was formed on Tyneside in 1886 for the special purpose of securing

* *England for All* (London: E. W. Allen, 1881), pp. 84, 110.

this boon, but opinion was found to be not yet ripe for a strike, and the Federation devoted itself to other objects.

Public opinion among the working class began now, however, rapidly to turn in favour of a general Eight Hours Movement. This result was due largely to the energetic labours of Mr. Tom Mann, now President of the Dockers' Union, whose pamphlet in 1886 was one of the earliest separate publications on the subject. In 1887 a Conference of London Trade Unionists was called, under Socialist auspices, to discuss the question. As a result of this conference the question was made the subject of debate at the Trade Union Congress at Swansea in September of the same year. Mr. Swift, of Manchester, the delegate of the Steam Engine-makers' Society, proposed a resolution in favour of a further reduction of the working hours, to be brought about, "as far as adult males are concerned, by increased combination, assisted by the Government, reducing the hours of labour in all Government works to eight hours per day." To the resolution Mr. William Parnell, of London, the delegate of a Cabinetmakers' Society, moved the following amendment :—"This Congress is of opinion that the best way of providing permanent work for the vast number at present out of employment is by a general reduction of the hours of labour, and believes that the only effectual means of obtaining the same is by national and international political action, and therefore instructs the Parliamentary Committee to further the passing of an Eight Hours Labour Bill by all legitimate means in its power." The debate extended over two days, at the end of which the amendment was rejected by 76 votes to 29. A second amendment was then moved by Mr. Charles Drummond, secretary and delegate of the London Compositors' Society, "instructing the Parliamentary Committee to obtain a plebiscite of the members of the various Trade Unions of the country upon the question." This amendment, almost without discussion, was carried with two dissentients. The original resolution (Mr. Swift's) was then voted upon and rejected by 84 votes to 11. Finally, Mr. Drummond's amendment was put as a substantive motion and unanimously adopted.*

During the same year the question was raised in the House of Commons in the discussion upon the Government bill to amend

* *Report of Trade Union Congress, Swansea,* 1887.

GROWTH OF THE MOVEMENT.

the Coal Mines Regulation Act. Although the coal-hewers of South and West Yorkshire had enjoyed a nominal Eight Hours Day as early as 1858, the vast majority of workers in coal-mines (including youths) were underground for 9, 10, and even 11 hours a day. The feeling among them in favour of a legal limitation of hours was growing very fast. A motion was made in Committee by Mr. S. Williamson, Liberal member for Kilmarnock, and seconded by Mr. J. H. C. Hozier, Conservative member for South Lanarkshire, to add a clause forbidding the employment of miners underground for more than eight hours a day. The matter failed to excite the interest of the House; the "labour members" declined to vote on the plea that they had received no "mandate" from their constituents; and the motion was rejected by 159 to 104.* The "mandate" was soon to come.

At this time the agitation for an Eight Hours Bill formed the main topic of *The Labour Elector*, a weekly journal edited by Mr. H. H. Champion, which attained a considerable circulation among the members of the younger labour organisations. Mr. Cunninghame Graham, M.P., who had been elected for Lanark in 1886, lent his aid to the movement, which now began to attract the attention of political workers.

An Eight Hours Bill for Miners was introduced into the House of Commons by Mr. Graham in 1888, 1889, and 1890, but failed each session to secure a favourable place at the ballot for opportunities.

In March 1888 the Huddersfield Town Council, which is the only public authority directly administering its own tramways, reduced the hours of work of its tramway servants to eight per day on the ground of convenience.

The Parliamentary Committee of the Trade Union Congress had, in the meantime, issued a circular of inquiry, as directed by the Swansea Congress, but they took upon themselves to accompany it with arguments and warnings against any Eight Hours Bill. The result was that a comparatively small proportion of Trade Unionists answered the inquiry. The textile trades, in particular, stood aloof through the enmity of their leaders to the question.

The Returns, as they appeared in the Parliamentary Committee's

* *Hansard's Parliamentary Debates*, vol. 319, pp. 899-912.

Report laid before the Congress at Bradford in September 1888, were as follows:—

NAME OF SOCIETY.	Are you in favour of an eight hours limit of the day's work—total 48 hours per week?		Are you in favour of Parliament enforcing an eight hours day by law?	
	Yes.	No.	Yes.	No.
London Amalgamated Society of Upholsterers	17	15	6	28
Amalgamated Society of Lithographic Printers	197	337	138	375
National Union of Boot and Shoe Makers	1,039	177	276	238
United Tinplate Workers and Gas Meter Makers' Protection and Friendly Society of Edinburgh and Leith	39	..	..	..
United Operative Masons' Association, Scotland	350	..	250	..
Associated Blacksmiths, Scotland	263	..	199	..
Associated Iron Moulders, Scotland	358	928	..	..
Scottish National Operative Tailors' Trade Protection and Benevolent Society	242	70	241	106
London Society of Compositors	1,125	2,098	560	2,566
Amalgamated Society of Railway Servants, Scotland	775	146	260	..
French Polishers' Society, Edinburgh	127	..	119	8
London Saddle and Harness Makers' Friendly and Protection Society	66	81	37	97
Leicester Amalgamated Hosiery Union	588	5	588	7
Associated Carpenters and Joiners, Scottish	653	..	560	..
Amalgamated Society of House Decorators and Painters	101	168	57	186
Operative Stonemasons' Friendly Society	472	14	399	165
Women's Protective and Provident League	42	49	23	43
Ironfounders' Association, England	..	..	..	..
Amalgamated Society of Carpenters and Joiners	11,966	..	9,209	..
Stirlingshire Miners	4,300	..	4,300	..
Bookbinders' and Machine Rulers' Consolidated Union—Edinburgh Branch	..	..	5	..
	22,720	4,097	17,267	3,819

The Parliamentary Committee somewhat disingenuously summed up the situation in the following terms :—

"In summarising the whole of the Returns, it is almost impossible to give a definite opinion as to which way the balance lies, as the number of votes returned is so small; and it is, consequently, open for any one to put the opinion of those members who have not voted on which side they choose. A perusal of the Returns will, however, we think, be sufficient to satisfy any unprejudiced person that the time is not yet ripe for commencing (1) an agitation for an Eight Hours Day."

The Congress did not, however, accept this view of the case, nor were its members satisfied with the way in which the proceedings had been managed by the Parliamentary Committee. They therefore passed a resolution instructing the committee to take a fresh plebiscite, leaving out all the irrelevant and side questions, and asking simply—(1) Are you in favour of an Eight Hours Working Day? (2) Are you in favour of it being obtained by Act of Parliament? This resolution was carried by 42 votes to 22.

As if in answer to the somewhat discouraging result of this inquiry, a large demonstration in favour of an Eight Hours Day was held in the Birmingham Town Hall, in October 1888, under the auspices of local Trade Unionists and the Knights of Labour. The subject was, moreover, hotly debated at the International Trade Union Congress in London, in November 1888, when the following resolution was proposed :—

" This Congress is of opinion that, owing to the concentration of capital, and the relative weakness of trade unions in proportion to the number of workers, it is impossible to further reduce the hours of labour without the aid of the State, and that in every case eight hours should be the maximum number of hours worked."

The representatives of the older English Trade Unions made an attempt to prevent the resolution being discussed, and themselves took no part in the debate. Mr. Mawdsley, a member of the Parliamentary Committee, moved the previous question, on the ground that a plebiscite, taken within the ranks of the trade unions, had resulted in an uncertain result; but he did not say anything for or against the principle involved. This motion was defeated. Then an amendment was proposed to the effect that an Eight Hours Day should be enforced by law, but only for State and municipal contracts. Had this been carried, it would have shelved the resolution before the Congress, and therefore the foreign delegates, while approving of the amendment as far as it went, voted against it. The English delegates adopted the amendment by 23 votes to 12, but it was lost by five nationalities to one. Nevertheless, the fact remains that the whole of the foreign delegates, and the great majority of the English delegates, agreed that for all work done for the State or the municipalities the duration of the day's work should be limited by law to eight hours. M. Tortellier then introduced a second amendment, declaring that it was childish to expect legislators (who, to maintain their privileges, were interested in crushing the working classes) to pass beneficial laws reducing the hours of labour. This amendment was lost by four nationalities against two, and by 46 votes against 34. Then came the voting on the original resolution quoted above. This was carried by four nationalities against two. Thirty-one English delegates voted against, and only eleven in favour. The other nationalities (with the exception of the only Italian delegate) were unanimously in favour; and as there were 17 French, 10 Belgians, 9 Dutch, 2 Danes, and 11 English, this made four nationalities and 49 votes in favour of an Eight Hours Bill; two nationalities and 32 votes against.*

During the year 1888 the movement received a very great impetus from the growth of the "New Unionism." The new sense of solidarity in the ranks of labour, which was so marked a feature of the match-makers' strike in 1888, led to the formation and rapid extension of Trade Unions among workers who were either unskilled or who had, for other reasons, hitherto been without organisation. As these unions were formed usually under the prevailing Socialist influence, and especially through the exertions of Messrs. John Burns and Tom Mann, most of them adopted an Eight Hours Bill as a part of their programme. One of the most flourishing of these new unions, the "Gasworkers and General Labourers' Union," demanded, in November 1888, a reduction of their hours from twelve to eight per day. In nearly all the gasworks in the United Kingdom this reduction was conceded without a strike, and in many cases was accompanied by a slight increase in wages. Such a signal success gave an immense impetus to the general Eight Hours Movement. But within a year an event occurred which showed how precarious was an Eight Hours Day depending only on Trade Union sanction. The directors of the South Metropolitan Gas Company, in November 1889, in the course of a fierce struggle with their workmen, suddenly restored the twelve hours day. And when the struggle was over, continued to work on this system. Many Trade Unionists who had before held aloof from the agitation for an Act of Parliament, now began to recognise the necessity of obtaining some more permanent sanction for the Eight Hours Day than the vote of a trade society.

Another of the new societies was the "General Railway Workers'

* *A Critical Essay on the International Trade Union Congress*, by Adolphe Smith. (London: A. Smith, 19 Barclay Road, Walham Green, S.W.)

Union." This quickly grew to be an organisation of great influence. There had existed for many years an "old" union, the "Amalgamated Society of Railway Servants." But this had become apathetic, and had dwindled in numbers. Its officers had for some time opposed any restriction by law of the excessive hours of railway men, and had frowned upon the Eight Hours Movement. The new union was expressly formed with the object of promoting a bill to limit the hours of railway workers, a programme which proved so attractive to the men that in a very few months the new society had more than twice the membership of the old one. The result was that the old union changed its tactics, and established friendly relations with its younger rival. Both societies now press for an Act of Parliament limiting the hours of ordinary railway workers to 60 per week, and those of signalmen to 48 per week.

In February 1889 the question suddenly became of vital interest to politicians. At an interview with a deputation of his constituents, representing the Newcastle Labour Electoral Association, Mr. John Morley declared that he was "dead against" any restriction by law of the hours of adult male labour. This declaration he repeated at a subsequent interview, and in his speech to the Eighty Club in November 1889.* It is to be noted, however, that in the course of the interview Mr. Morley expressed himself prepared, upon adequate cause shown, to support a measure restricting the hours of railway workers. But when a motion with this object was made in the House of Commons, in January 1891 (see page 36), Mr. Morley absented himself from the debate and the division.

In January 1889 Mr. John Burns was elected to the London County Council, on a programme which included an Eight Hours Day for all public servants. The early reduction of the hours of nearly all the workmen in the employment of the Council proved that public opinion even amongst the so-called "moderates" was rapidly progressing.

During 1889, accordingly, the subject of an Eight Hours Bill was, for the first time in England, recognised as "good copy" for the monthly reviews, and it was brought before the English reading public by no fewer than five articles in various magazines, the first in date being that in the *Nineteenth Century* for July

* Report of Eighty Club Dinner, November 1889.

1889, by one of the present writers. The growing "social compunction" as to the excessive hours of labour found expression even in the legislation of 1889. Lord De La Warr had, during successive years, induced the Board of Trade to obtain from the railway companies a voluntary return of the number of cases of excessive hours.* This was now made obligatory. By the Railways Regulation Act of this year (52 and 53 Vic. c. 57), railway companies were required to report annually to the Board of Trade the number of cases in which railway workers had been employed continuously in excess of a period to be specified by the Board of Trade. The Board of Trade specified twelve hours in any one day, and required also a statement of instances in which men had been required to return to work after less than eight hours rest.

The Eight Hours Question received a full discussion at the International Trade Union Congress at Paris, July 15-20, 1889, or rather at the two simultaneous Congresses of the Possibilists (to which most of the English delegates adhered) and the Marxists. At both Congresses resolutions were carried to the effect that eight hours should be the maximum day's work, to be secured by international law. This was accepted by the English delegates, amongst whom was Mr. Fenwick, M.P., the present Secretary of the Parliamentary Committee of the Trade Union Congress.† The practical unanimity of the Congresses, and the moderation of their demands, created a favourable impression in England.

The Trade Union Congress met at Dundee in September 1889, and considerable public interest was taken in the proceedings relating to the Eight Hours Question. The great strike of the London dock labourers was just then in progress, and Mr. John Burns, who was leading the "Dockers," was accordingly unable to be present at Dundee. The Eight Hours Movement was, moreover, seriously weakened in the Congress by an injudicious attack by some of its chief supporters upon Mr. Henry Broadhurst, M.P., then the Secretary to the Parliamentary Committee of the Congress. The President of the Congress (Mr. R. D. B. Ritchie, Dundee Trades Council) dealt with the question in the following significant terms :—

* See H.L. 33 of 1889, price 6d.
† Report of the Congress published by the Trade Unionist members of the English Delegation. (London: Co-operative Printing Society.)

"On few questions has public opinion made such rapid advance as that of Parliamentary interference with the working hours of adult males. Within two years our unions have almost entirely changed front upon this point, and the general body of the members are in advance of their leaders. Toward the decision now arrived at three important facts have contributed, namely, the success of the Ten Hours Factory Act; the comparative failure of the organised trades to maintain a nine hours system; and the hopelessness of the task of consolidating within reasonable time the enormous mass of disorganised labour. The great bogie which is raised against the adoption of an eight hours system is foreign competition; but the same outcry was made against the Ten Hours Factory Act, yet it only resulted in the introduction of improved machinery by which production was increased, so that at the present time more work is produced than when factories were run for seventy hours a week. But whilst improved machinery has facilitated the development of industry, it has not assisted in the equal distribution of the wealth thereby created, and in mills and factories women are being over-wrought, underpaid, and forced to work under most enervating conditions. . . . If the question was one affecting Trade Unionists alone, Parliamentary interference would not be necessary, and would most likely never have been suggested. But it is a question not only affecting Trade Unionists, but the whole working population, to fight whose battles on trade union lines the resources of the unions are entirely inadequate. Repugnant as the mention of Parliamentary interference is to many of us, myself included, it seems the only feasible means by which the unspeakable misery attending industrial warfare, where the contingencies of war have not been provided for, can be avoided." Mr. Ritchie then suggested that a wider adoption of the shift system would meet many of the alleged objections.

The Parliamentary Committee presented the report of the voting on the Eight Hours Question, there being 39,656 votes for an Eight Hours Day, and 28,511 for obtaining it by Act of Parliament. Twenty-eight unions, including the miners, compositors, carpenters, and railway voters voted for an Act. Against it were the coopers, Scotch ironmoulders, shipwrights, and four smaller unions, together with 56,541 votes cast on behalf of three Lancashire textile unions.

Votes upon the Eight Hours Question received by the Parliamentary Committee up to August 6, 1889.*

Name of Association.	No. of Members.	Are you in favour of Eight Hours?		Are you in favour of it being obtained by Act of Parliament?	
		For	Ag'st	For	Ag'st
Alliance Cabinetmakers' Association	1,700	436	31	391	75
Bakers of Scotland, Operative	3,214	1,271	..	1,181	90
Barge Builders	172	60	..	60	..
Bookbinders' and Machine Rulers' Consolidated Union	1,009	620	167	467	139
Bookbinding, Society of Women employed in	230	..	100	..	..
Boot and Shoe Makers, Amalgamated Society of	4,000	169	27	60	103
Boot and Shoe Rivetters and Finishers, National Union of	20,117	629	162	584	24
Cabinetmakers, Amalgamated Union of (Westminster Branch)	38	15	..	6	8
Carpenters and Joiners, Associated	3,966	680	60	427	119
Compositors, London Society of	7,400	2,201	1,411	1,578	561
Coopers, Mutual Association of	3,744	3,744	..	..	3,744
Cotton Spinners Amalgamated Association of Operatives	17,125	..	17,125	..	..
Do. (Oldham)	5,000	..	5,000	..	..
Cigarmakers, Mutual Association	850	324	155	229	101
Hosiery Union, Amalgamated	800	697	5	697	7
Iron Founders, Friendly Society of	5,664	3,608	1,350	1,843	1,410
Iron Moulders of Scotland, Associated	5,500	358	928	..	1,286
Miners' Union, Ayrshire	10,000	10,000	..	10,000	..
Do. Association, Cumberland	3,000	3,000	..	3,000	..
Do. Do., Derbyshire	4,000	2,253	15	1,851	60
Plasterers, Edinburgh District Operative	250	250	..	..	250
Do., Metropolitan Society of Operatives	95	41	..	41	..
Railway Servants, Amalgamated Society of	13,000	3,344	350	2,190	1,504
Razor Grinders' Protection Society, Sheffield	150	150	..	150	..
Rotary Power Frame Work Knitters, Nottingham	390	366	20	339	1
Scissor Grinders, Society of	200	200	..	200	..
Shipwrights' Society, Associated	5,000	854	134	339	564
Steam Engine Makers' Society	5,350	1,429	97	629	660
Stone Masons, Operative Society of	11,000	578	17	388	165
Typographical Association (H.R.S.)	7,590	1,505	1,191	1,269	1,141
Do. Society, Edinburgh	740	371	42	239	110
Northern Counties Amalgtd. Weavers' Association	33,750	..	33,750	..	..
Zinc Workers, London Operative	70	..	70	..	..
Associated Blacksmiths' Society, Scottish	1,900	476	10	331	162
Liverpool United Trades' Council	10,000	20	7	22	2
Wolverhampton Do.	..	..	7	..	7
Accrington & District Do.	4,500	..	4,500	..	..
	178,376	39,656	67,390	28,511	12,283

* *Report of Trade Union Congress, Dundee*, 1889, p. 52. Criticised in Mr. Maltman Barry's pamphlet, "The Labour Day." (Aberdeen: Avery & Co., 1d.)

When the discussion of the returns came on, Mr. Beveridge (Glasgow) pointed out the impropriety of the entry purporting to give the opinions of the cotton weavers, 33,756, and, sarcastically describing it as a case of "cumulative voting with a vengeance," moved its deletion. This proposal having been seconded, another was made, of the same nature and on the same grounds, in reference to the entries in the names of the Cotton Spinners' Societies (Amalgamated and Oldham), 17,125 and 5,660 respectively. No attempt had been made by the officers of the textile unions to ascertain the opinion of the general body of the operatives. The motion for these omissions, a distinct censure on the Parliamentary Committee, was adopted by Congress by 72 votes to 49. Even this, however, did not satisfy the delegates, for a further amendment being moved for the entire rejection of the return, was carried almost unanimously.

The Congress, however, soon made it manifest that it was by no means opposed to the legal limitation of adult male labour. It immediately passed, by a large majority, a resolution in favour of an Eight Hours Bill for miners.

In the following month, October 1889, this question came before the "National Conference of Miners," held at Birmingham. And the Conference, by a majority of 93 to 13,[*] declared itself in favour of a Parliamentary Eight Hours Day. The opposition to legislation came virtually only from the representatives of Northumberland and Durham. Here the coal-hewers have already, owing to circumstances explained elsewhere, a working day of eight hours or less.

In February 1890 the miners reaffirmed their support of Mr. Cunninghame Graham's bill, and in the following April they expressly censured the Parliamentary Committee of the Trade Union Congress for having failed to carry out the "mandate" of the Dundee meeting.

Towards the end of 1889 the Eight Hours Question was discussed by the Council of the London Liberal and Radical Union—a body representing all the London constituencies. On November 13th, after a long and heated discussion, a resolution in favour of the limitation of the hours of labour of Government and municipal servants to eight per day was carried by an overwhelming

* *Times*, October 12th, 1889.

majority. In the same year Lord Randolph Churchill unexpectedly declared himself favourable to an Eight Hours Bill on the principle of Trade Option.

This principle was first suggested in a draft Eight Hours Bill published by the Fabian Society. It was fully described in an article in the *Contemporary Review* for December 1889, by one of the present writers. By this time the Eight Hours Bill had become the subject of constant lectures and addresses by the Socialists and New Unionists. And it is largely due to their energy in lecturing and debating that the question has been forced into the region of practical politics.

On the 19th of May 1890 a public debate on the subject of a universal compulsory Eight Hours Law took place at St. James's Hall, London, between Mr. H. M. Hyndman, of the Social Democratic Federation, and the late Mr. Charles Bradlaugh, M.P. The latter had for some time been actively opposing any interference by law with the hours of labour of adult male workers. Mr. Bradlaugh's opposition was based mainly on grounds of principle, derived from the old "Individualist Radicalism," and the economics of the "Manchester School." The debate excited much public interest, and there was a large attendance, but no vote was taken.*

The International Trade Union Congress had appointed the 1st of May 1890 for a simultaneous international demonstration in favour of an Eight Hours Law. As the time approached, great curiosity was felt as to the attitude which the English working men would assume, and there was considerable discussion on the subject amongst the older Trade Union officials. The date fixed happened to be a week-day, and the grave difficulties in the way of any large week-day demonstration seemed, for some time, likely to prevent all English participation in the international movement. Ultimately it was decided to hold a London demonstration in Hyde Park on the first Sunday in May, and a similar decision was taken in other towns. A few irreconcilables, nevertheless, held meetings on the 1st of May. The arrangements for the London demonstration on the Sunday were at first undertaken by a committee specially formed by delegates from labour organisations. But, ultimately, the London Trades Council found itself

* Report of Debate. (Freethought Publishing Company.)

forced to take the matter up. Notwithstanding the original dissensions, the divided management, and the scarcely hidden hostility of the leading Trade Union officials, the demonstration proved an unparalleled success. No fewer than sixteen platforms had to be provided, and at least a quarter of a million persons were present. Experienced journalists agreed that no demonstration for twenty years had equalled it in magnitude. The resolutions proposed were significant. The Secretary of the London Trades Council (Mr. George Shipton) refused to have any express mention of a Bill or Act in the resolutions proposed at the platforms under his management. At those, seven in number, a general Eight Hours Day was demanded, but no means for attaining it were specified. At the other nine platforms an Eight Hours Law was explicitly demanded.

One result of this gigantic demonstration was the adoption, by the Metropolitan Radical Federation, after prolonged discussion, of an Eight Hours Bill on the lines of that drafted by the Fabian Society, as a part of the programme of the London Radical Clubs.

In May 1890 a Conference met at Berlin, by invitation from the German Emperor, to discuss what could be done by international legislation to improve the condition of the working classes. The Conference was attended by delegates from the English Government. But Lord Salisbury had refused to allow them even to discuss the question of limiting the hours of labour of adult males. The Liberal Party in the House of Commons had felt itself able to condemn this official caution of their opponents. The question was raised on a motion for the adjournment of the House on 25th June 1889, by Mr. Cunninghame Graham, which received the support of the Liberal leaders. The motion was rejected by 189 votes to 124, but it was generally felt that the question must now be considered as an open one.* The Conference, in the result, did not agree upon any important resolutions relating to male adult workers. It proposed, however, to limit the duration of work in unhealthy mines, and to establish a Sunday day of rest.

The international movement for an Eight Hours Day was further promoted during the summer of 1890 by the successful international Conference of Coal-miners held at Jolimont, in Belgium.

* *Hansard*, vol. 337, p. 753.

Even the Political Economists were forced to recognise the growing feeling in favour of a limitation of the hours of labour.

At the Leeds meeting of the British Association in September 1890, a paper was read by Professor J. E. Crawford Munro, of Owens College, Manchester, on "The Probable Effects of a General Reduction in the Hours of Labour." A guarded opinion was expressed that there would be a resulting economic loss, which would fall partly on interest and partly on wages.

On the very day that the Political Economists were coming to this conclusion at Leeds, the Trade Unionists were taking a much more decisive step at Liverpool, where the Trade Union Congress was meeting. This Congress, which was much more largely attended than any previously held, was watched with much interest, as it was known that the Eight Hours Question would at last be brought to a clear issue.

The President (Mr. William Matkin of Liverpool), in his address,* spoke strongly in favour of a general Eight Hours Bill, and suggested its application to each industry as soon as the workers concerned had made up their minds to ask for it.

The Parliamentary Committee had then to excuse itself for having neglected to act on the mandate of the previous Congresses relating to the Eight Hours Bill for miners.

Finally, the Congress came to the general question, on the following resolution moved by Mr. C. S. Marks (London Society of Compositors):—"That, in the opinion of this Congress, the time has arrived when steps should be taken to reduce the working hours in all trades to eight per day, or a maximum of forty-eight hours per week; and while recognising the power and influence of trade organisations, it is of opinion that the speediest and best method to obtain this reduction for the workers generally is by Parliamentary enactment. This Congress therefore instructs the Parliamentary Committee to take immediate steps for the furtherance of this object."

This somewhat impracticable resolution was hotly debated, and the following amendment was moved by Mr. Patterson (Durham Miners' Association):—"That, in the opinion of this Congress, it is of the utmost importance that an Eight Hours Day should be secured at once by such trades as may desire it, or for whom it

* *Report of the 23rd Trade Union Congress*, 1890.

may be made to apply, without injury to the workmen employed in such trades; further, it considers that to relegate this important question to the Imperial Parliament, which is necessarily, from its position, antagonistic to the rights of labour, will only indefinitely delay this much-needed reform."

This amendment was lost by 173 votes to 181. The resolution was then put and carried by 193 to 155. On the following day a resolution supporting the Eight Hours Bill for miners was carried by an overwhelming majority. The character of the majority has been questioned, but Mr. John Burns states that "Out of the 454 delegates at the Congress, 193 voted in favour of the eight hours by Act of Parliament, 155 voting against; 184 of the 193 who voted in favour represented 900,000 skilled and unskilled workers; while the 155 who voted against, and the 106 who were neutral, only represented 540,000."* The nature of the opposition is further analysed in a subsequent chapter.

The excitement caused by this vote had not passed away when an interesting Parliamentary by-election took place at Eccles, a populous suburb of Manchester, containing some important coal mines. The deceased member had been a Conservative, whose family was largely interested in these mines, and the new Conservative candidate was a member of the same family. The Liberal candidate was Dr. H. J. Roby, a distinguished scholar who had gone into business in Manchester.†

Dr. Roby had at first refused to promise support to the Eight Hours Bill for miners, but soon found himself compelled to give way, or else abandon the contest. This adhesion, in the very heart of the capitalist opposition to the Eight Hours Movement, caused a great stir in the Liberal party. Various prominent Liberals in Lancashire resigned their connection with their party. Nevertheless, Dr. Roby won the seat, in the face of great territorial influence on the Conservative side.

---

* "Speech on the Liverpool Congress," p. 16.

† It is an interesting fact that the firm of "Ermen and Roby" had previously been "Ermen and Engels," Dr. Roby's predecessor in the partnership having been Mr. F. W. Engels, the distinguished Socialist, author of *The Condition of the English Labouring Classes* (1845), and lifelong friend of Karl Marx. Mr. Engels still takes an active interest in the international Socialist movement.

Towards the end of the year a proposal was made that the subject should be discussed at a meeting of representatives of miners and coal-owners, with a view to the voluntary introduction of an Eight Hours Day. The Conference met on January 20th, 1891, and again on February 11th, but no agreement was arrived at, and there was no immediate practical result.

An enormous impetus to the movement for legal regulation of the hours of labour was given by the long continuance and ultimate failure of the Scotch Railway Strike, which broke out on the Caledonian and North British Railways on December 20th, 1890, on a demand by the men for a uniform Ten Hours Day. The directors absolutely refused to listen to the men's demands, and insisted upon their unconditional surrender.

During the autumn of 1890 it became usual for both the Liberal and the Conservative candidates for seats in Parliament to express themselves guardedly in favour of an Eight Hours Bill for miners, and of the legal limitation of the hours of work on railways. Immediately Parliament opened, on January 23rd, 1891, whilst the Scotch strike was still flickering, Mr. Channing proposed the following resolution in the House of Commons:—"That, in the opinion of this house, the excessive hours of labour imposed on railway servants by the existing arrangements of the railway companies of the United Kingdom constitute a grave social injustice, and are a constant source of danger both to the men themselves and to the travelling public; and that it is expedient that the Board of Trade should obtain powers by legislation to issue orders, where necessary, directing a railway company to limit the hours of special classes of their servants, or to make such reasonable increase in any class of their servants as will obviate the necessity for overtime work."

The debate which ensued was very significant. Mr. Channing's motion received the general support of the Liberal party, as well as of many Conservatives. Sir William Harcourt spoke in its favour, and the official Liberal whips "told" for it. The arguments on behalf of *laisser faire*, and the evil of limiting by law the hours of adult male labour, were tacitly abandoned by the Liberal party. In the end, the motion was only defeated by 17 votes, the usual Government majority being about 80. Nor did this vote represent a defeat for the principle of legislation; for the Government promised to propose the appointment of a select committee to consider whether, and in what way, the hours of labour of railway servants should be regulated by law. This committee was appointed a few days later.

The progress of opinion among Trade Unionists is typified by the following report of the proceedings of the Birmingham Trades Council, in January 1891 :—"At a special meeting held to consider the Eight Hours Question, Mr. Gilliver proposed, 'That this Council, while recognising the desirability of reducing the hours of labour in some of our national industries, and willing to render assistance to all sections of workmen in any proper effort to secure for themselves such a limitation of the hours as may be needful in their case, and agreed upon by those engaged in such trade or industry, records its opinion that such changes as may be found to be necessary will be soonest and safest wrought out by organisation and the legitimate agitation of the workers engaged therein. And this Council is further of opinion that any compulsory limitation of the hours of labour applied to the adult manhood of this country by Act of Parliament must prove subversive of all true freedom, extinguishing the rights and individual liberty of its citizens.'—Mr. Dobson proposed as an amendment, 'That this Council hereby records the opinion that an Eight Hours Day is desirable, and that such day can be best secured by Act of Parliament.'—The amendment was carried by 27 votes to 13."

The Trades Councils of London, Liverpool, Glasgow, Hull, and other large towns have also passed resolutions in favour of Parliamentary action.

It is not easy to summarise with any certainty the exact position of public opinion in Great Britain at the beginning of 1891 upon this hotly-debated question. It may be said that nearly all philanthropic opinion, and a vast preponderance of the wage-earners, are in favour of an Eight Hours Day. This is resisted with almost equal unanimity by the "business" world and capitalist opinion generally. Those who are in favour of an Eight Hours Day are, by a fair majority at any rate, in favour of securing it by legislative enactment, which for the moment chiefly finds expression in support of the Miners' Eight Hours Bill. Socialist influence, and much of the modern Radicalism, works strongly in the same direction. A majority of the wage-earners appear to be in favour of legislation ; a large majority of the middle class, the Political Economists, and professional men are against it. The members of the House of Commons are gradually being won over to it, but secretly dislike it. In certain industries—such as the railway and tramway service, and coal-mining—there is an enormous preponderance of feeling in favour of legislation, and this preponderance is having great effect as regards legislation for those industries only.

(c.) *The Movement in Australia.*

When the gold discoveries had given the first great impulse to the growth of mechanical industry in Australia, the usual working day for artisans seems to have been ten hours. This was then the general working day in England. During the leaps and bounds of the early prosperity of Victoria, artisans' wages rose to a fabulous height, and the Trade Unions, instituted on English models, were able practically to impose their own terms. The old ideal of an Eight Hours Day soon came to the front.

The record of the movement in Australia begins, as far as we have been able to ascertain, with a public meeting held by the stonemasons in Melbourne at the beginning of April 1856.* It will be remembered that, three years previously, in the abortive strike of the London building trades in 1853, the Eight Hours Day was commonly spoken of as the real goal of the struggle,† and it is not unlikely that some of the defeated men found their way to what was then specially the land of promise. The idea started by the Melbourne stone-masons rapidly spread to the other trades, and meetings were held in quick succession. An "Eight Hour League" was formed at a meeting of the united trades, and immediate notice was given by public announcement that, after the 21st of April 1856, no man belonging to the unions represented would work for more than eight hours a day. The strength of the artisans' position in the labour market at that time was such that no resistance was possible, and the Eight Hours Day, thus won by less than three weeks' agitation, has ever since been general among the artisans of Melbourne. The 22nd of April has annually been kept by them as a public holiday, and is now known as the Eight Hours Day.

* Sir Chas. Dilke, *Problems of Greater Britain*, vol. i. p. 249.　　† See p. 17.

GROWTH OF THE MOVEMENT. 39

From Melbourne the Eight Hours Movement quickly spread to the other parts of the Colony, then very sparsely inhabited, and also to New South Wales. An Eight Hours Day was generally established in various skilled trades in Sydney within a few years, but it is by no means universally adopted, especially in the smaller towns. Subsequently the movement spread to Brisbane, Adelaide, and most of the towns of New Zealand, and public opinion thoroughly supports eight hours as the normal day for artisans throughout the whole of Australasia.

At the time when the Melbourne workmen obtained their Eight Hours Day there was neither need nor possibility of securing it by legal enactment. Effective legal control over industry necessarily grows but slowly in a new State.

But it must not be imagined that the working men of Victoria have manifested any objection to use the influence of their collective political organisation to secure the protection of labour. It will be unnecessary to refer here to the drastic legislation interfering with labour contracts in such matters as truck, sanitation, prevention of accidents, etc. But the regulation of the hours of labour has not been forgotten. In 1874 a stringent Factory Act limited the hours of women in factories to eight per day, and applied most of the English factory law for their protection. This too sweeping limitation of the hours of labour of one sex only excited at first some discontent, but it gradually became accepted and enforced, and eleven years later, on the amendment of the Factory Acts, was re-enacted in an improved form, without opposition. Nor has there been any objection to legislation restricting the hours of adult male labour. In 1877 an Act was passed limiting the hours of work of all persons employed below ground in any mine to eight per day. The employment of women underground was at the same time absolutely forbidden.

This law was re-enacted in 1883, when its application was extended to all persons in charge of steam machinery in connection with mines.* It was again reaffirmed in more definite form when the mining law was amended in 1886.

---

* The law now in force is that of 1886, in which the previous provisions are embodied. Sec. 2 of Act No. 803 is as follows:—"No person shall be employed below ground in any mine for more than eight consecutive hours at any time, or for more than forty-eight hours in any week in cases of

In 1883 a clause was inserted in the bill regulating the Melbourne Harbour Works, absolutely limiting the hours of labour of persons employed by the contractor to eight per day, and making also a similar provision with regard to the employés of the Harbour Commissioners, but, in this case, with regulations for overtime.*

A similar clause was in the same year inserted in the Melbourne Tramway and Omnibus Act, and Sir Charles Dilke records that it has been inserted in various other Tramway Acts.†

During the years 1881 and 1882 the excessive hours of labour worked in some occupations in the Colony attracted considerable attention. Journeymen bakers were working 15 hours a day; drapers' assistants at work sometimes as much as 18 hours; bar attendants were on duty for 14 or 16 hours a day. A bill was introduced into the Legislative Assembly by the Hon. Alfred Deakin and Mr. Gardiner, peremptorily ordering the universal closing of all shops at 7 P.M. This was, however, felt to be too

emergency; and a person shall be deemed, and is hereby declared, to be employed below ground and in the service of the owner of a mine within the meaning of this Act and of the Regulation of Mines and Mining Machinery Act, 1883, from the time that he commences to descend a mine until he is relieved of his work and commences to return to the surface by the authority of the owner or his agent." The law relating to machine-men is as follows:—
"No person in charge of steam machinery used in connection with any mine, or for the treatment of the products of any mine, shall be employed for more than eight consecutive hours at any time, or for more than eight hours in any twenty-four hours. Such period of eight hours shall be exclusive of any time occupied in raising steam, and in drawing fires and exhausting steam in connection with the machinery in the charge of such person, and of any time in which such person is employed, in case of breakage or other emergency."—Sec. 6 of Act No. 783 of 1883.

* "Every contract, when for executing works of improvement in the port of Melbourne, shall contain a condition that the contractor for such works shall not employ any workman or labourer for a longer time than eight hours in each day. Provided also that no workman or labourer employed by the Commissioners shall be required to work more than eight hours each day, except in cases of accident or emergency, and in all such cases the overtime shall be paid as follows:—Time and a quarter for the first two hours; time and a half for any period in excess of two hours; double time for Sundays and holidays."—Harbour Trust (Further Amendment, 1883), 47 Vic., No. 763, sec. 54.

† Act No. 765 of 1883, sec. 10: *Problems of Greater Britain*, vol. ii. p. 286.

drastic, and a Royal Commission was appointed in 1882 to investigate the whole subject.*

The evidence taken by the Commission revealed that the supposed universal sentiment in favour of an Eight Hours Day had not sufficed to protect various large classes of workers, such as bakers, shop assistants, and attendants in restaurants, from being kept at work for excessive hours. Most of the witnesses were strongly in favour of further legislation, and but little hesitation was shown to restriction of the hours of labour of adults. Public opinion was indeed found to be much more advanced on the point than any one had suspected. The Report records, for instance, that the Secretary of the Melbourne Early Closing Association, who appeared to give evidence, "expressed himself as opposed to any innovation upon the tactics hitherto pursued, and more especially to legislative interference with what he termed 'the liberty of the subject.' Subsequently a poll of the members of the Association was taken as to the advisability or otherwise of regulating the hours of labour in shops by Act of Parliament, and resulted in 279 members voting in the affirmative and only 48 in the negative."†

The proceedings of the Commission, which extended over two years, excited much attention in the Colony, and the Commissioners report, "as a gratifying circumstance," that through their instrumentality "the Eight Hours Movement throughout the Colony has received a powerful impetus." The journeymen bakers got their hours reduced from 15 to 10 per day. Nevertheless, so complete had been the failure of over thirty years of voluntary agitation that the Commissioners unanimously reported that they were "convinced of the absolute necessity for legislative action.... In proposing any remedy for the relief of employés in shops, your Commissioners rely on the results of practical experience rather than on the theories of those political economists who hold that legislative interference is in violation of the law regulating supply and demand. Several witnesses consider that the pressure of educated public opinion will in time achieve all that is necessary; while others maintain that nothing more can be

---

* The Commissioners included the Premier of the present Ministry (Hon. James Munro) and the Colonial Secretary of the last (Hon. Alfred Deakin).

† Employés in Shops Commission: Second Progress Report, p. 5 (*Victorian Parliamentary Papers*), 1883.

effected by moral suasion. Your Commissioners believe that moral force is devoid of the necessary potentiality to bring about the reform desired, and that an Act of Parliament alone can impart solidity and permanence to the Eight Hours Movement in connection with shops and similar establishments."*

The Commission also reported in favour of the extension of the Factory Act of 1874, including its Eight Hours limit, to all employments of women,† and recommended various important amendments of that Act. Mr. Deakin, who had then become the Solicitor-General, introduced, in November 1884, a bill extending and re-enacting the provisions of the 1874 Factory Act. This measure, *The Factories and Shops Act*, 1885, became law at the end of 1885, and came into force on the 1st of March 1886. It represents the fruit of experience of the working of the Factory Acts both in England and in the Colony, and is, in many respects, an admirable model. It enacts an Eight Hours Day for all employments of women and boys,‡ and otherwise much strengthens the usual provisions of factory legislation. It will be remembered that the registration of work given out to be done in domestic workshops which the Act requires, obtained the strong praise of the House of Lords' Committee on the Sweating System.§ The Act, moreover, extends to shops and warehouses most of the provisions relating to factories, and pro-

---

* Employés in Shops Commission: Second Progress Report, p. 13 (*Victorian Parliamentary Papers*), 1883.

† "The Eight Hours System shall be one of the fundamental principles of the bill."—*Summary of Recommendations*, p. 13 of Final Report.

‡ *Working Hours for Females and Boys.*—"No person or persons shall employ in any factory or work-room any female or any male under the age of sixteen for more than forty-eight hours in any one week in preparing or manufacturing articles for trade or sale.

"If any occupier offend against the provisions of this section, he shall for each and every week in which he offends be liable to a fine not exceeding twenty pounds.

"Provided that, in order to meet the exigencies of trade, the Minister may, if he think fit, after due inquiry from time to time, by a notification under his hand published in the *Government Gazette*, suspend, subject to such conditions as may appear requisite, the operation of this section in any one or more factories or work-rooms, or in all factories or work-rooms of a particular description. Such suspension shall have no force or effect for more than three months from the date of such notification."—Sec. 29.

§ H. L., No. 207 of 1890.

vides, in a series of clauses of considerable legislative skill,* for the compulsory closing of all shops, with certain specified exemptions, not later than 7 P.M., with an extension for Saturdays until 10 P.M., *unless* a majority † of the shopkeepers in any one trade in any town petition the Town Council for exemption. This, it will be observed, is the converse of the "trade option" advocated by Sir John Lubbock for retail shops, and in the Eight Hours Bill of the Fabian Society, and the more stringent form actually adopted is in itself a significant comment upon the supposed reluctance of the Australian working man to Government interference. The execution of the law was left to the Town Councils, who were very lenient to the shopkeepers. By-laws were made which seemed intended to make the Act a dead-letter. The Melbourne Town Council, for instance, fixed the fines for contraventions at one shilling for the first offence, and three shillings for any subsequent one.

In many trades, in one town or another, the necessary majority of the employers petitioned for exemption, without, of course, consulting their assistants, but public opinion attached a proper weight to these petitions. In many places, by "mobbing" the shops of the recalcitrants and "rabbling" their customers, the public obtained a withdrawal of the petitions. In spite, however, of lax administration, the law has had an enormous effect in shortening the hours of shop assistants, and the seven o'clock limit on ordinary days bids fair to become universal.‡

In the other Australian Colonies neither legislation nor public opinion on the hours of labour is so advanced as in Victoria, but the tendency is in the same direction. An Eight Hours Day is enforced by the Trade Unions in the stronger trades, such as carpentering and building operations generally. The hours of women workers and of shop assistants are, however, often much longer. Sir Charles Dilke mentions a riotous mob parading the

---

* See Chap. ix.
† Sir C. Dilke erroneously says "a two-thirds majority" (*Problems of Greater Britain*, vol. i. p. 250).
‡ Mr. C. Fairfield, in a violent tirade entitled "State Socialism at the Antipodes" in *A Plea for Liberty*, states that the Act has proved a dead-letter. But he does not assert that the hours of closing of shops in Melbourne have not been much earlier since its enactment.

town of Rockhampton, in Queensland, forcing the recalcitrant shopkeepers to close their shops.*

The "class war" between capitalists and wage-earners is, as we have lately seen in the great Australian strike of 1890, often even more embittered than in England, and the capitalists do not hesitate to use their political influence for the protection of their interests. Both in Queensland* and New Zealand bills establishing a normal Eight Hours Day were passed by the Lower House of the Legislature, which is elected by manhood suffrage, but were rejected by the Upper House, representing the propertied class.

In conclusion, it may be said that public sentiment in Australia is universally in favour of an Eight Hours Day, but that this sentiment, backed up by very powerful Trade Unions, has by itself as yet succeeded in securing the Eight Hours Day only for skilled artisans and a small minority of labourers. We accordingly find this public opinion resulting in Victoria in a whole succession of legal enactments, from 1874 down to the present time. By these an Eight Hours Day is legally enforced for women in all manufactures whatsoever; for miners underground; for engineers in charge of mining machinery; for tramway workers; for men employed by the contractors on various public works; for the servants of public bodies. And attempts at similar legislation in the other Colonies are constantly being made, but have, as yet, been defeated by the capitalistic second chambers.

(d.) *The Movement in the United States and Canada.*

Karl Marx observes that, in the United States, all expression of independence on the part of the workers remained paralysed as long as slavery soiled a part of the territory of the Republic, but that the death of that institution immediately opened up a new life, and the first fruit of the war was an Eight Hours Movement.† The records of Trade Unions and strikes in the Northern States do not bear out the supposition that slavery in Virginia

---

* *Problems of Greater Britain*, vol. i. p. 371.

† *Le Capital*, chap. x., § vii., p. 129 of French edition of 1875.

exercised any restraining influence on the artisan of New York.*

The great impetus given to American manufacturing industry at the close of the war had probably more effect in stirring up the Eight Hours Movement than the transformation of the negro from a slave to a wage-labourer. And Dr. Ely points out that the length of the working day has formed a topic of absorbing interest to the wage-earners of the United States from the very beginning of its industrial history.†

As early as 1825 the building trades and the ship carpenters and caulkers of New York and other places along the Atlantic coast were striking for a Ten Hours Day.‡ This movement was thenceforth carried on continuously by them and other trades with frequent strikes.

The hours of labour at that time seem to have been about twelve per day for artisans. The textile workers were less fortunate. The working day, even for women and children, often began at 4.30 A.M., and went on for fifteen hours. Most of the New England mills ran thirteen hours a day all the year round.§ It is not generally remembered that the factory girls of Lowell, in the classic days of the "Lowell Offering" (1832-1840), worked seventy-eight hours per week.|| In 1831 an organisation of working men was formed at Boston to secure, among other objects, a Ten Hours Day.¶ A widespread agitation seems then to have been set on foot, with innumerable strikes, few of which were successful. The

---

* See the *Third Annual Report of the Federal Commissioner of Labour*, 1887 ("Strikes and Lock-outs"), pp. 1029-1050. In 1835 a New York newspaper observed that "strikes are all the fashion." Compare also the *Reports of the Massachusetts Bureau of Labour Statistics* for 1880 and 1888, and that of the *Pennsylvania Bureau of Industrial Statistics* for 1881, for records of strikes prior to those dates; also, Dr. Ely's *Labour Movement in America*, and McNeill's *Labour Movement the Problem of To-day*.

† Dr. Ely's *Labour Movement in America*, p. 55.

‡ *Third Report of Federal Bureau of Labour* (1887), p. 1032.

§ Seth Luther's "Address to the Working Men of New England" (1832), quoted in Dr. Ely's *Labour Movement in America*, p. 49.

|| *Report of Massachusetts Bureau of Statistics of Labour*, 1883.

¶ "The New England Association of Farmers, Mechanics, and other Working Men." See the *Massachusetts Bureau of Statistics of Labour*, 1870, and Dr. Ely's *Labour Movement in America*, p. 50.

Ten Hours Day became, however, general in Baltimore between 1835 and 1840, as the result of a strike among the labourers.* Shortly afterwards the influence of the Federal Government was thrown in the same direction by means of its powerful example. The President, Martin Van Buren, gave orders that the working day in the Navy Yard at Washington and all other public establishments should be reduced to ten hours.† This important adhesion led to the general adoption of the Ten Hours Day in shipbuilding establishments along the coast, which has been ever since maintained. In 1847, however, the masters made a determined but unsuccessful attempt to revert to longer hours.‡

As early as 1845 we find the textile workers of Massachusetts petitioning the Legislature for a Ten Hours Bill, the petition being largely signed by male operatives. But no legislation was passed in that State until 1874, twenty-seven years after the English operatives had obtained a similar boon. The first legislation on the subject that we have been able to trace is a law of 1849 of the State of Pennsylvania, providing that ten hours shall be a day's work in cotton, woollen, silk, paper, bagging, and flax factories.§

This was much in advance of other State Legislatures. Four years later Georgia was enacting, for the benefit of persons under twenty-one, that their working day should be from sunrise to sunset! ||

In 1855 Pennsylvania reinforced its previous Act, as regards operatives under twenty-one, by expressly prohibiting their employment in textile factories for more than ten hours a day, or sixty hours a week.¶

By 1851 carpenters and masons had generally won the Ten

---

* Dr. Ely's *Labour Movement in America*, p. 57.

† 10th April, 1840. See *Report of Massachusetts Bureau of Statistics of Labour*, 1880, and Dr. Ely's *Labour Movement in America*, p. 55. Two attempts were subsequently made to increase the hours in the Navy yards, in 1852 and 1863, but they caused so much resistance that they were abandoned.

‡ *Third Report of Federal Bureau of Labour*, p. 1039; McNeill's *Labour Movement*, p. 113.

§ Brightley Purdon's *Digest of the Laws of Pennsylvania*, p. 771; p. 672 of Public Laws of 1849, quoted in *First Annual Report of Federal Commissioner of Labour*, 1886, p. 481.

|| Act of 1853-54; now see. 1885 of *Georgia Code of 1882*.

¶ *Public Laws of 1885*, p. 472.

Hours Day. The textile operatives were less fortunate. Some of the mills at Lowell adopted the new hours in 1853, but as late as 1865 the mills at Southbridge were still running thirteen hours a day.* Indeed, the Ten Hours Day did not become universal in the textile industries of Massachusetts until the Legislature tardily came to the aid of the workers in 1874.†

This interference of the Legislature was largely due to pressure from the then powerful Federated Trade Society, known as the "Knights of St. Crispin."‡ Before, however, the Ten Hours Day had become by any means universal, a demand for an Eight Hours Day seems to have been widely formulated. This was probably suggested by the success of the Australian workers. Marx records that a General Workman's Congress at Baltimore (16th August 1866) declared that the foremost and greatest need of the present time was the promulgation of a law fixing the working day, in all the States of the Union, at eight hours. A similar resolution was agreed to by a meeting of workmen at Dunkirk, New York State, in the same year.§ These and many other meetings were organised by the National Labour Union,|| a widespread organisation formed mainly to secure an Eight Hours Day.

It was this body which gave the first great impulse to the movement. The ship-carpenters at Greenpoint, Rhode Island, and many other traders in New England and New York, struck for the Eight Hours Day in April 1866, but the strike failed at the end of six weeks.¶

The agitation thus set on foot received legislative recognition in Connecticut in 1867, when it was decreed that eight hours' work should be a day's lawful labour *unless otherwise agreed.*** A

---

* *Report of Massachusetts Bureau of Statistics of Labour*, 1880, p. 21; *Third Report of Federal Bureau of Labour*, 1887, p. 1049.

† In 1880 the textile operatives in other States, who were unprotected by law, still worked longer hours—viz., Maine, 66 per week; New Hampshire, 64½ to 66; Rhode Island, 66; Connecticut, 69; New York, 66 to 72.—(*Report of Massachusetts Bureau of Statistics of Labour*, 1881.)

‡ Dr. Ely's *Labour Movement in America*, p. 68.

§ Karl Marx, *Le Capital*, ch. viii., § vii., p. 129 of French edition of 1875.

|| Dr. Ely's *Labour Movement in America*, p. 69.

¶ *Third Report of Federal Bureau of Labour*, p. 1050; McNeill's *Labour Movement*, p. 350.

** Now Title 14, ch. vi., sections 9 and 10 of *General Statutes of 1875*, p. 194.

similar law was passed in Illinois, on 5th March 1867.* In the same year Vermont was moved to begin the protection of children under fifteen by forbidding their employment for more than ten hours a day.† Laws similar to those of Connecticut and Illinois were passed by Pennsylvania in 1868, and New York in 1870.‡

Another result is thus described by Dr. Ely:—

"On the 24th of June 1869 a bill for an Eight Hour Day was introduced into Congress by General Banks, whose wife, by the way, was once a factory girl at Lowell. This passed the House and Senate, promptly received the signature of the President of the United States, General Grant, and was enforced in the Navy Yard at Charlestown, Mass., July 6th of the same year. But the politicians who at the time of the elections are so fond of the labourers, usually care little for the enforcement of the laws in behalf of labour, and in violation of the spirit of the law the employees of the United States were notified that our wealthy and powerful Government would reduce wages one-fifth; but that those who so desired could work ten hours at the old rates. The working men showed their indignation in such manner as apparently to make the politicians think of votes at future elections, or to fear trouble, and the order was reversed by the President. But success was again illusory. The Eight Hour Law is still on our statute books, and a like law exists in several States, but it is a dead letter."§

These laws are significant rather as showing the growth of public feeling than as precedents for the legal limitation of the maximum hours of labour. Indeed, the refusal of even the Ten Hours Day remained a frequent cause of strikes, especially among the textile workers, by whom a powerful "Ten Hour League" had been formed. The coal-miners of the Mahanoy Valley, Pennsylvania, went on strike for an Eight Hours Day in 1868, another premature attempt which was unsuccessful.

After the suppression of the Paris Commune in 1871, a number

---

* Hurd's *Revised Statutes of Illinois*, ch. 48, p. 592.
† See 4320, *Revised Laws of Vermont*, Acts of 1867, No. 36.
‡ *Public Laws of Pennsylvania of 1868*, p. 99 (Brightley Purdon's *Digest*, p. 1009); *Revised Statutes of New York*, p. 2354; *Laws of 1870*, ch. 386.
§ *Labour Movement in America*, p. 70.—The question of the alleged failure of these laws is discussed in Chapter ix.

of refugees found their way to the United States; and after the meeting at the Hague in 1872, the "General Council" of the rapidly-dying "International" was transferred to New York. This brought a wave of French and German Socialism into America,* and from that date a more aggressive tone is discernible in the labour movement.

In 1872 "Eight Hours Leagues" were formed in several cities; and in Connecticut, New York, a whole series of strikes for an Eight Hours Day broke out among the building trades, the furniture makers, the pianoforte makers, and others. An imposing demonstration of 20,000 workmen paraded the streets of New York, demanding the Eight Hours Day, and among the banners was one of the "International," whose members were in the procession of the strikers. After an embittered struggle the men were successful in some of the building trades; and for a time Eight Hours became the usual working day in these trades in New York State.†

The industrial depression which set in after 1873 throughout the United States caused the question of any further reduction of the hours of labour to fall temporarily into abeyance. The great railway strikes of 1877, and other labour disputes during this period, related mainly to proposed reductions in wages. This condition of the labour market is probably the reason why the Knights of Labour‡ did not make the Eight Hours Day an express demand, but referred in the "Instructions" merely in general terms to the necessity for shorter hours of labour.§ Even at the General Assembly in 1878, when a full "Declaration of Principles" was adopted, the Eight Hours Day was not expressly mentioned. The Eight Hours clause, now No. xxi., "To shorten the hours of labour by a general refusal to work for more than eight hours," was apparently added about 1883.

* Dr. Ely's *Labour Movement in America*, p. 227.
† McNeill's *Labour Movement*, p. 142; *Tenth U.S. Census*, vol. xx. p. 474; *Third Report of Federal Bureau of Labour*, p. 1059; Ely's *Labour Movement in America*, pp. 71, 228.
‡ This body was started in 1869, but was not effectively organised until 1873.
§ "Historical Sketch of the Knights of Labour," by Carroll D. Wright, *Quarterly Journal of Economics*, January 1887.

Similar reasons no doubt made the years between 1873 and 1880 comparatively barren of labour legislation. But the limitation of women's labour in textile factories by the Massachusetts law of 1874 marks an epoch. This Act by itself has done much to make a Ten Hours Day almost universal, for men as well as for women.*

In 1876 also Maryland secured a Ten Hours Day for persons under sixteen. And in the same year California and New Mexico (miners only) enacted that the normal day should, in the absence of special contract, be eight hours. In the case of California such special contract is forbidden in work done for the State. †

During these years of depression the Socialist spirit was more and more entering the labour movement. The Trade Unions which then became active, such as the cigar-makers, show marked traces of this influence.‡ Among the laws called for by this Trade Union, the first two are as follows :—

"(a) Prohibition of industrial labour for boys under fourteen and for girls under sixteen years of age.

"(b) Limiting the hours of labour to not more than eight per day, and enforcing such a law by the executive powers of the State."

The organisation called the "Socialistic Labour Party" includes, amongst its "social demands," " Reduction of the hours of labour in proportion to the progress of production ; establishment by Act of Congress of a legal work-day of not more than eight hours for all industrial workers, and corresponding provisions for all agricultural labourers."§

Since the year 1880 both labour legislation and strikes for reductions of hours have been abundant in all the industrial States. But no new principle has been established. The "normal" day, in the absence of special contract, is now legally fixed at eight hours in Indiana‖ and Wisconsin,¶ in addition to the six

---

* *Report of Massachusetts Bureau of Statistics of Labour for 1889*, p. 516.

† *Maryland Acts of 1876*, ch. 125 (Revised Code of 1878), p. 820 ; *New Mexico Laws of 1876*, ch. 38 (Compiled Laws of 1884, sec. 1568); *California Code of 1876*, tit. 7, ch. 10, sec. 3244.

‡ See their "Constitution," given in the Appendix to Dr. Ely's *Labour Movement in America*, p. 312.

§ Dr. Ely's *Labour Movement in America*, p. 369.

‖ See *Foreign Office Report*, C—5866.

¶ *Revised Statutes of Wisconsin*, sec. 1729, p. 504.

GROWTH OF THE MOVEMENT. 51

States already mentioned. In most of the other industrial States it is similarly fixed at ten hours. The example of California in fixing the hours of work done for the State at a maximum of eight per day has been followed in New York. Maryland also, for its State tobacco warehouses, adopts the Eight Hours Day.* In most of the Eastern States the employment of adult women in factories for more than ten hours a day is absolutely prohibited.† Wisconsin, a State which contains the large manufacturing city of Milwaukee (200,000 inhabitants), goes a step further, and prohibits the employment of women in any manufacturing establishment for more than eight hours a day.‡ In the case of tramways, American legislation is even more emphatic. In New York the law limits the working day of tramway servants to ten hours; in New Jersey to twelve hours, "with reasonable time for meals;" and in Maryland to twelve hours.§ Further, we have pleasure in chronicling that the State of Minnesota has got so far as to enact that the labour of locomotive engineers and firemen shall not exceed eighteen hours in one day.‖

During these years the Eight Hours agitation went on smouldering. Despairing of genuine help from the Federal or State legislatures, which are virtually controlled by the large companies and wealthy capitalists, the American workman turned again to the more costly methods of the Labour War; and numerous isolated strikes for an Eight Hours Day broke out in the different industrial States. In New York an attempt to secure a universal Nine Hours Day failed. This failure discouraged further strikes.¶ In Chicago, as elsewhere, the movement had gathered new strength from the growth of Marxian Socialism among the foreign immigrants, and what had before been an incidental demand of the Labour War became practically the main issue. A vigorous effort to institute an Eight Hours Day was made in many parts of the United States in the spring of 1886. *Bradstreet's* (the well-known

* *Foreign Office Report*, C—5866.
† For example, in Massachusetts, Rhode Island, Maine, New Hampshire, and also in Minnesota, Michigan, etc.
‡ *Wisconsin Revised Statutes*, Acts of 1883, ch. 135, p. 375 of Supplement.
§ *Foreign Office Report*, C—5866.
‖ *Minnesota Acts of 1885*, ch. 206, p. 277.—Even this limitation would be a boon to some of our British railway workers. See Chapter iii.
¶ *Report of New York Bureau of Statistics of Labour for 1887*, p. 28.

commercial journal) estimated the number of strikers for shorter hours in May 1886 at 200,000, of whom 50,000 were granted their demands, while 150,000 secured shorter hours generally with full pay without a strike. But on June 12th, 1886, the same paper estimated that one-third of these had lost what had been conceded to them, and predicted that a still larger number would lose the advantage gained. The great meetings held at Chicago in May 1886, in support of the movement, led to savage police repression. It was there that the fatal dynamite bomb was thrown, and the folly and brutality of this outrage, by whomsoever it was committed, did much to discourage the Eight Hours Movement.

In the same year an important article in the *Forum*, by Mr. George Gunton, brought the subject to the notice of economists.*

During the years 1888 to 1890 numerous attempts were made to secure an Eight Hours Day in particular trades and particular localities. But the project now most generally growing in favour seems to be that of a simultaneous strike, to extend to all organised labour throughout the United States. This is the plan now advocated by the American Federation of Labour, the rival of the Knights of Labour. The spirit in which the question is now treated in the United States is shown in the following extract from the speech of Mr. Samuel Gompers, President of the American Federation of Labour, delivered at the Annual Convention of the Federation held at St. Louis in December 1888 :—

" In my last report I called your attention to the fact of the immense number of our fellow-toilers who, through the invention and development of machinery as applied to the industries, are being continually thrown out of employment. When thousands and hundreds of thousands of our fellow working men and women, through no fault of their own, are consigned to be paupers, tramps, or worse, while all become competitors for the labour of those who are fortunate enough to find employment, I then, as now, laid particular emphasis upon the question that strikes deeper into the evils of society than all others combined—that question which raises man out of the sloughs of poverty and despair—that question which reaches the farthest ramifications of society—that question which creates the greatest revolution in the conditions of the people with the slightest friction upon any—that question of all questions, THE REDUCTION OF THE HOURS OF LABOUR." †

* *Forum*, vol. for 1886, p. 136.
† Quoted in *The Eight Hours Movement*, by Tom Mann.

At this convention it was decided "to issue printed circulars to all manufacturing firms in the country, requesting them to meet representatives of this organisation in conference" upon the question ; it was also decided to hold mass meetings in every city on the Eight Hours Question on four days in the year, including July 4th, 1889 ; Labour Day, September 2nd, 1889 ; and Washington's birthday, February 22nd, 1890 ; and the movement was to culminate in enforcing the Eight Hours Work-day, on May 1st, 1890.

The general strike thus announced for 1890 only partially came off, owing largely to the lukewarmness of Mr. Powderley and his organisation, the Knights of Labour. But several hundred thousand men, in different parts of the United States, struck work, and a large proportion of employers yielded. For a time it seemed as if the Eight Hours Day had nearly been won. But very shortly afterwards most masters increased the hours again, and the battle is still to be fought. Another struggle is announced for May 1st, 1891.

To sum up, we find it difficult to gauge with accuracy the strength and results of the Eight Hours Movement in the United States. For fifty years past there has been a continuous progress towards shorter hours of labour ; but America still compares unfavourably with England. American textile operatives and coal-miners, in particular, work considerably longer than do Englishmen engaged in the same trades. In New England,* New York State, and Pennsylvania, the working day is still ten hours, but very few labour for more than that time. In only a few States are the hours of male adults limited by law, and then only in special industries. On the other hand, various legislatures have attempted to lead public opinion by declaring eight hours to be the normal working day. In spite of this encouragement very few trades have succeeded in actually securing an Eight Hours Day. In one State, Wisconsin, eight hours is a compulsory measure for women in manufacturing establishments. In New York, the stone-masons, cigar-makers, painters, and some of the glass-workers,† maintain more or less

---

* In Massachusetts only 6.16 per cent. of the male adults, and 0.80 per cent. of the women and miners, normally exceeded ten hours a day in 1889 ; these were chiefly in the manufacture of food preparations and drugs. (*Report of Bureau of Statistics of Labour for 1889*, pp. 447-517.)

† *Report of New York Bureau of Statistics of Labour*, 1887, pp. 89-104.

precariously an Eight Hours Day. The same is true of about three per cent. of the manufacturing establishments in Massachusetts. Such is the result of over twenty years' agitation for an Eight Hours Day, in a country where the power of the working man to control his own destiny is often supposed to be almost unlimited. We can therefore scarcely wonder that the "Federation of Trades and Labour Unions" now no longer relies on Trade Union action, but urges "the enactment of eight hour laws by State Legislatures and Municipal Corporations."*

Still less has been effected in Canada. In the eastern and central provinces of the Canadian dominion the usual day's work for artisans consists of ten hours, as in the neighbouring States of the Union.† Labour organisations are strong in Toronto, Hamilton, and Montreal, and are often in federal union with those of the United States. They are weak in the rural districts. In Toronto and some other cities of Ontario, a few strong trades have, as in the United States, won a Nine Hours Day, which prevails amongst the builders and cigar-makers. In Toronto the paper-box makers work 49 hours a week, and the carpenters average 45 hours. At St. Catherines, in Ontario, the cigar-makers have an Eight Hours Day. At Quebec the ice-cutters have the same. But the Quebec cotton-mills work 66 to 78 hours per week, with continuous stretches of seven hours without a meal, and the tramway servants, shop assistants, and tailors' workmen have, as usual, excessive hours of labour.‡ In the town of Quebec the system of giving out work to be done at home in the ready-made clothing trade has introduced many of the horrors of the London sweating system.§

In 1889 a Royal Commission upon the conditions of labour in the Canadian Dominion made a long and important report in favour of the promotion of shorter hours of labour. The Commission recommended that the Factory Acts of Ontario and

---

* Dr. Ely's *Labour Movement in America*, p. 305.

† *Report of Royal Commission on the Relations between Labour and Capital*, 1889, Appendix F.—Also *Report of Ontario Bureau of Industries*, 1887 and 1888.

‡ Tramway servants often work 16 hours a day; women and children at millinery and dressmaking 15 hours a day.—*Ibid.*

§ *Ibid.*, Appendix O

Quebec, regulating the employment of women and children, should be strengthened, so as to absolutely forbid their work in stores and factories for longer than 54 hours in a week, or ten* hours on any one day. The Commission further reported "that the working day for men might be reduced with advantage to workmen, and without injury or injustice to employers." But they did not agree upon any recommendation for direct legal prohibition of the excessive hours in the case of adult males. They recommended, however, that the Canadian Government should use its influence by way of example, and that all contracts for Government work should contain a stipulation that the hours of labour of those employed should not exceed nine per day.†

The largest manufacturer of cigars in Hamilton, Ontario, reduced the hours of labour from ten to nine and a half, and then to nine, a few years ago, without reduction of wages, and with, as he informed one of the present writers in 1888, extremely satisfactory results. The day's production, as the Canadian Royal Commission expressly records, suffered no diminution at all, and the gain from cessation of friction was marked.‡

A few Eight Hours demonstrations have been held in Canada in conjunction with demonstrations across the border. But the Eight Hours Movement has made, as yet, but little progress in Canada.

(*e.*) *The Movement in other Countries.*

1. FRANCE.

The Eight Hours Movement on the Continent seems to have arisen first in Paris. One of the foremost demands of the working men, whose rising in 1848 overthrew the government of Louis Philippe, was the legal limitation of the hours of labour. This may be ascribed partly to the influence of Karl Marx, but

---

* Sir Charles Dilke erroneously says 51 and 8 respectively. (*Problems of Greater Britain*, vol. i. p. 117.)

† *Report of the Royal Commission on the Relations of Labour and Capital in Canada* (Ottawa, 1889), p. 9.

‡ Sir Charles Dilke refers to what is apparently the same case, to a similar effect. (*Problems of Greater Britain*, vol. i. p. 117.)—See *Report of Royal Commission*, p. 38.

much more to the inspiration of Louis Blanc. Older influences, however, had been at work.

In 1841 an Alsatian manufacturer, Daniel Légrand, a disciple of Oberlin, petitioned the French Government for a Factory Act which should at least limit the hours of labour, male as well as female, to twelve per day.*

Similar petitions had been presented by other philanthropists, but without avail. They showed, however, the current of men's thoughts. And one of the first results of the popular victory of February 1848 was a decree limiting the hours of labour.

This decree (dated March 1848) enacted that the hours of labour should not exceed ten per diem in Paris, and eleven per diem elsewhere in France. It was modified by the law of the 9th September 1848, which established Twelve Hours nett as the maximum working day.†

It is hardly necessary to observe that this hasty legislation was completely ineffective. No inspectors were appointed or other means taken to secure the enforcement of the law.

To the plutocratic Cæsarism which followed the Republic the law itself was altogether repugnant. It was not, indeed, explicitly

---

* "La Legislation Internationale de Travail," by Benoit Malon, *La Revue Socialiste*, December 1890.

† *Article Premier.*—La journée de l'ouvrier dans les manufactures et usines ne pourra pas excéder douze heures de travail effectif.

Art. 2.—Des règlements d'administration publique détermineront les exceptions qu'il sera nécessaire d'apporter à cette disposition générale, à raison de la nature des industries ou des causes de force majeure.

Art. 3.—Il n'est porté aucune atteinte aux usages et aux conventions qui, antérieurement au 2 mars fixaient pour certaines industries la journée de travail à un nombre d'heures inférieur à douze.

Art. 4.—Tout chef de manufacture ou usine qui contreviendra au présent décret et aux règlements d'administration publique promulgués en exécution de l'article 2 sera puni d'une amende de cinq francs à cents francs.

Les contraventions donneront lieu à autant d'amendes qu'il y aura d'ouvriers indûment employés, sans que ces amendes réunies puissent s'élever audessus de mille francs.

Le présent article ne s'applique pas aux usages locaux et conventions indiqués dans la présente loi.

Art. 5.—L'article 463 du Code pénal pourra toujours être appliqué.

Art. 6.—Le décret du 2 mars, en ce qui concerne la limitation des heures de travail, est abrogé.

repealed; but it was ingeniously eaten away by a series of decrees.

A decree issued on the 17th May 1851 exempted certain occupations and trades from the law of 1848. It declared that the limit of twelve hours established for the working day of men and women in factories should not apply to stokers, firemen, or watchmen in factories, to men in charge of furnaces, drying-stoves, or boilers, to persons employed in sponging ("décatissage"), or in the manufacture of glue, or in soap-boiling, milling, printing, and lithographing, or in casting, refining, tinning, and galvanising metals, or making projectiles of war. Similar exceptions were extended to the cleaning of machinery after working hours, or to any action required to be taken in case of accidents to motors, boilers, machinery, or buildings, or, in general, in case of any accidents whatsoever.

In respect of certain occupations, an additional hour was conceded to persons paid to wash and stretch stuffs in dyeing and bleaching works, or in manufactures of Indienne (gauze). Two additional hours were granted in sugar-mills and refineries and chemical works. A similar privilege to men in dyeing, or printing, or sizing, or pressing works was conceded, on the express understanding that the hours in excess of twelve should only be allowed during 120 days a year, and only if application had been previously made and granted, on the intercession of a mayor, by the departmental prefect.

A decree of the 31st January 1866 gave an additional hour to workmen in silk spinneries, but only during 60 days within the four months of May, June, July, and August.

With the advent of the Third Republic a change came over the attitude of the Government. In May 1874 fifteen inspectors were appointed to control the operation of the law of 1848 and its amendments. In the same year, and again in 1883, more stringent Factory Laws were enacted for women and children. On the other hand, in November 1885 an administrative circular was issued, excluding from the operation of these laws all workshops where only human labour force was used, and where fewer than twenty workers were employed in one building.

The law of 1848 is, however, still nominally in operation, and is so far effective that it was thought necessary, by a decree of the

3rd April 1889, to exempt from its observance labourers employed on any works executed by order of the Government in the interest of the national safety and defence. Nevertheless, so numerous are the exceptions, that very few of the workers now benefit by the law. In the Department of the Seine, which comprises Paris, we find for the year 1887 a population of working people of 83,012 adult males, 28,373 women, and 37,650 male and female children, subject to inspection, and employed in 30,201 establishments. Not more than 3336 of these were subject to the legal limitation of the hours of labour established by the decree of 1848. It is stated, on official authority, that the average time of adult labour in the Department of the Seine in 1887 was between ten and eleven, and invariably under twelve hours.

This statement does not, however, refer to factory labour, for the British Consul reports that Frenchmen are present in the factories at least fourteen hours out of every twenty-four.*

From 1864 to 1871 the old *International* did much to promote the Eight Hours Movement in France. But all agitation for labour reforms was for a long time checked by the "White Terror" which succeeded the suppression of the Paris Commune in 1871. In 1880 the agitation was definitely resumed by the "*Parti ouvrier*," and since that date the Legal Eight Hours Day has formed a plank in the platform of every labour party in Paris and the large towns.†

At the International Trade Union Congress held in London in 1886, the French delegates were in favour of an Eight Hours Law. At Paris, in 1889, two International Labour Congresses met; one under "Possibilist," the other under Marxist auspices. At both a solid vote was given for a Legal Eight Hours Day.

In order to maintain the international character given to the Eight Hours Movement at the Paris Congress of 1889, a journal printed in three languages was started at Zurich towards the end of the year. It is an unpretentious little sheet, entitled, *The Eight Hours Working Day*.

In 1890 a deputation presented to the Chamber of Deputies several hundred petitions from Trade Unions and Socialist groups

* *Report of H.B.M. Consul-General for France*, 1889, in C—5866.

† See especially the article on " La Legislation Internationale de Travail," by Benoit Malon, in *La Revue Socialiste* for December 1890.

in all parts of France in favour of an Eight Hours Day, and of the other resolutions of the International Congress.

The British Consul-General thus summarises these petitions :—*
"The greatest importance was attached to the limitation of time on the following grounds :

"That eight hours' work means employment and bread for a number of people who are now unemployed and hungry. It means putting an effectual stop to the enforced idleness of men deprived of work by the progress of machinery. It means a certain increase of wages, inasmuch as it stops competition between the employed and the unemployed, because eight hours' work plus eight hours' sleep, leaves eight hours of leisure to working men ; and a day of eight hours is a clear profit to small traders by increasing the consuming and purchasing power of the working classes."

Strikes for shorter hours broke out among the Paris gasmen and glass-blowers, who asked for three shifts a day instead of two. The chief centre of disturbance was, however, Roubaix, where upwards of 30,000 workmen spent May 1st in the streets clamouring for an Eight Hours Day. The day at Roubaix had hitherto been divided in most of the factories of the place as follows :—Beginning work at 6 A.M., half-an-hour for breakfast at 8, an hour for dinner between noon and 1 P.M., half-an-hour's rest at five o'clock, close of work at 8 P.M. This means 14 hours in the works, of which two hours are devoted to food and rest. The strikers did not, however, insist on an immediate reduction to eight hours, but contented themselves with asking that work should begin at 7, that two hours should be given for dinner and rest at noon, and that work should cease at 7 P.M. In some cases the same wages were asked for 10 hours as for 12. In other cases more was demanded for 10 hours than had hitherto been paid for 12. The masters merely declared themselves unable to make any concessions as to shorter time until the Government procured an international agreement to that effect.†

Over 70,000 men went on strike, and considerable disturbance ensued. The strike failed. During the last fortnight in April the delegates of the French coal-miners met in congress at St. Etienne, and passed resolutions in favour of an Eight Hours Day. On May 1st many of the miners in various parts of France struck for this demand, but had to submit without gaining anything.

* *Foreign Office Report*, No. 109, C—5896-27.   † *Ibid.*

During the session of 1890, largely in consequence of these strikes for an Eight Hours Day, a committee of the Chamber of Deputies was appointed to inquire into the conditions of labour. This committee, in order to ascertain whether the working classes were in favour of a law to limit their hours of labour, issued a voting-paper to a large number of Paris workmen. The result was as follows :—*

For a law fixing a limit of —

Eight hours, without overtime	5,419
Eight hours, with overtime	1,513
Nine hours	1,247
Ten hours	7,010
Eleven hours	166
Twelve hours or upwards	263
Total in favour of legislative restriction	15,618
Against legislative restriction	6,776
Spoilt papers	868
Total votes	23,262

The principal trades represented in this ballot were as follows :—

Building	4,788
Metals	4,379
Wood and Furniture	2,157
Clothing	1,675
Printing and Stationery	1,467
Alimentation	891

It will be seen that in this test ballot 72½ per cent. voted for legislative regulation of the hours of labour, and that a little over a third of these desired that such legislation should fix the time at eight hours, without overtime. In view of the constant assertion that workmen who are in favour of an Eight Hours Day merely desire to begin overtime pay a little earlier, it is worth attention that over five-sevenths of those who asked for an Eight Hours

---

* *The Economist* (London), 31st January 1891, p. 143. Incomplete returns (to the same effect) were given in the *Economiste Français* in November, and the *Board of Trade Journal*, December 1890, p. 687.

Law at all, asked also for the prohibition of overtime. Only 27½ per cent. of the voters were found to be opposed to legislative interference at all. The Trade Unions were also consulted in their corporate capacity. Out of the 171 unions which have replied, 154 are in favour of limitation, 15 against, and 2 not pronounced. The 154 unions in favour of limitation are classed as follows:—Day of eight hours, without overtime, 82 ; with overtime, 22. Day of nine hours, without overtime, 3 ; with overtime, 3. Day of ten hours, without overtime, 21 ; with overtime, 17. Six give no opinion on this point.* The preponderance of feeling in favour of a legal limitation of the hours of labour is therefore very marked, although only 60 per cent. desired an eight hours limit.

2. GERMAN EMPIRE.

In Germany the demand for a law limiting the hours of labour has formed a part of the agitation of the Social Democratic Party, but it was not expressly named in the manifesto of 1875,† which merely referred in general terms to the shortening of the working day. It will, however, certainly find a place in the revised programme of the party now under consideration. Meanwhile, factory legislation, both Imperial and State, has to some extent regulated the labour of women and children, and this has, as usual, tended to reduce the hours for men. The law of 1st June 1877, with the amendments of the 17th of June 1887, prescribes a maximum day of ten hours for persons under sixteen.‡ But the laws are very imperfectly enforced, and mills employing young persons often run eighty-four hours a week. Artisans work eleven and twelve hours a day, and are strongly in favour of shorter hours. In Leipzig the masons had, in 1889, recently carried a Ten Hours Day ; but this was a local arrangement, which has not been generally followed.

The movement for an Eight Hours Day exists chiefly among the Social Democrats,§ whatever their trade, and among the coal-miners. In 1888 the coal-miners in Westphalia struck for an Eight Hours Day, and secured the intervention of the young Emperor in their favour. Accordingly, in Westphalia, Silesia, and Saxony,

* *Board of Trade Journal*, December 1890, p. 688.
† *Encyclopædia Britannica*, ninth edition, article "Socialism."
‡ See Report in *Board of Trade Journal*, July 1890, p. 84.
§ The Social Democrats polled over 1,500,000 votes at the elections in 1889.

the miners work only an eight-hour shift wherever a high temperature prevails; elsewhere a ten-hour shift is still worked.* This limitation of the hours in unhealthy mines was adopted by the Berlin Labour Conference in May 1890. Many of the workers in the mines and other industrial establishments of the Prussian Government have since received the boon of an Eight Hours Day. Other trades are moving in the same direction. The printers of Leipzig, for instance, held a meeting on September 23rd, 1890, and declared themselves in favour of a working day of eight hours. One speaker declared that in the year 1889 alone the printers had spent 123,776 marks (nearly £6189) in assisting the unemployed. Finally, a resolution was adopted declaring it a matter of the greatest urgency that the working day be of eight hours duration only.†

3. SWITZERLAND.

This Republic enjoys the distinction of having been the first country to declare in its very constitution the legislative right of the nation, in its political organisation, to limit the working day even for male adults.‡ Nor has this power been allowed to sleep. The Federal Factory Labour Law of 1877 limits the maximum hours of labour for all adult labour in factories or workshops to eleven per day, and to ten on Saturdays or public holidays.§ Provision is made for a reduction, by order of the Federal Council, of these maximum hours in unhealthy trades, and for the general interpretation of the law. Cantonal legislatures may institute not more than eight holidays during the year, in addition to Sundays, and on these all work is prohibited. Other stringent provisions of this remarkable law will be found in the Appendix. It is significant

---

* See p. 44 of C—5866, of 1889.

† *Deutscher Reichs Anzeiger*, 25th September 1890; *Board of Trade Journal*, November 1890, p. 569.

‡ The Federal Constitution of 29th May 1874 contains the following clause:
Art. 34. La Confédération a le droit de statuer des prescriptions uniformes sur le travail des enfants dans les fabriques, sur la durée du travail qui pourra être imposée aux adultes, ainsi que sur la protection à accorder aux ouvriers contre l'exercice des industries insalubres et dangereuses.—" La Legislation Internationale de Travail," *La Revue Socialiste*, December 1890.

§ *Foreign Office Report*, C—5866.

that the constitutional right of "Referendum," or appeal to the people, was exercised with respect to it, and that it was upheld by the direct vote of a considerable majority of the electors. The congresses of the Swiss Labour Federation in 1887 and 1890 were loud in testimony to the advantages of the law.

During 1890 a law was passed, in consequence of the Berlin Labour Conference, limiting the hours of labour of railway workers to a maximum of ten per day.

The workmen of Geneva, Zurich, and other industrial centres have at various times agitated for a reduction of the eleven hours to eight, but hitherto without success. *L'Union Ouvrière* of the Canton of Vaud, and other important co-operative establishments, so far put to shame those of the United Kingdom as to have adopted an Eight Hours Day for all their employés.

At an important meeting of the Swiss Labour Federation at Olten, in April 1890, the chief of the "Catholic" party, M. Decurtius, demanded a drastic extension of the Factory Laws, and the legal reduction of the maximum Eleven Hour Day to ten hours.*

4. BELGIUM.

Belgium has hitherto been the country where capitalistic exploitation has been most unrestrained. Attempts to enact Factory Acts were made in 1849, in 1859, and 1879, but failed in each case, owing to the opposition of the employers. The excessive hours of labour, even of young children, remained accordingly entirely unrestricted until 1884. In this year a Royal decree prohibited child labour in mines; but adult women still work underground.

The great miners' strikes of 1886 led to further consideration of the question. A Royal Commission was appointed in April 1886 to inquire into the matter. Many of the witnesses before the Commission urged the adoption of an Eight Hours Law, and testified to the growing opinion of the workers in its favour. The Belgian delegates, at the International Trade Union Congress in 1886, were unanimous in this view. But the Commissioners, in their report of October 1886, refused to recommend interference with the existing "freedom" of adult male workers. The bill prepared upon the report of the Commission related only to the

* *Board of Trade Journal*, June 1890, p. 710.

labour of women and children. It was further weakened in its passage through Parliament.*

5. SUMMARY.

In Holland, Denmark, Austria, Italy, and Spain, a large number of the labour organisations adopt an Eight Hours Law as a part of their programme, and such a measure is frequently pressed upon the legislatures of some of these countries by the members representing the working classes. The international demonstration of the 1st May 1890 was largely participated in, not only in all these countries, but also by Poland, and even by the workers in Havanna, and the chief cities of Chili and Peru. It may, indeed, be said generally, as regards the continental nations, that wherever the wage-earners are organised at all, their organisations demand an Eight Hours Law. But labour organisations do not exist, for effective purposes, among any but a minority of the workers on the Continent.

Meanwhile, as if to stave off the demand for an Eight Hours Law, factory legislation of the ordinary type is being everywhere adopted or rendered more stringent. Belgium and Holland, long the fields of the most unrestrained exploitation of labour, are both enacting lengthy codes of labour regulations;† in France, Germany, Spain, Italy,‡ and Austria,§ the law is being strengthened; Russia

---

* The bill became law 13th December 1889. An abstract of it is given in the *Board of Trade Journal*, February 1890, pp. 212, 213.

† See Belgian Law of 1889; Netherlands Law of 5th May 1889 (an eleven hours day for women).—Report in *Board of Trade Journal*, July 1890, p. 87.

‡ Italian Law of 11th February 1886, see *ibid.*, p. 87; Austrian Law of 1889; Spanish Law of 24th July 1873.

§ "In regard to the enforced reduction of the hours of work from twelve to eleven, it was asserted that it would cripple Austrian industry in its struggle with foreign competition; but evil prophecies have not been fulfilled, and the system of factory inspection has by this time become popular even with the employers of labour."—Report in the *Board of Trade Journal*, November 1889, pp. 583-85.

In most of the metal mines of Hungary there are three shifts of eight hours each. In some there is an arrangement by which forty-eight hours per week are worked by each man, in alternate periods of six hours. In the coal mines of the Hungarian State Railway the underground shift is eight hours.—*Foreign Office Report*, No. 710, 1890; *Board of Trade Journal*, July 1890, pp. 46-48.

GROWTH OF THE MOVEMENT. 65

and Denmark have entered the same path,* and even Sweden had a new Factory Bill under discussion in 1889. The Indian manufacturer, whose inhumanity in copying the early example of Lancashire is so fiercely denounced by the Lancashire of to-day, is now further restrained by the Factory Law of 1891. The gap between the restrictions on English and those on continental manufacturers is certainly not widening, and, as regards most countries, it is indeed rapidly growing narrower. In some respects, indeed, such as the minimum age for children's work, the provisions relating to the employment of mothers at the time of childbirth,† and the prevention of excessive overtime, England has already lost its honourable lead in factory legislation.

* Danish Law of 23rd May 1890; Swedish Law of 1st January 1882, amended by Law of 10th May 1889; Russian Law of 1st June 1882, amended by Law of 3rd June 1885.—See Report in *Board of Trade Journal* for July 1890, pp. 88, 89.

† German law prohibits the employment of women for three weeks after confinement; Swiss law for six weeks after, and eight weeks altogether. The Belgian Government Bill of 1887 proposed to forbid work during the monthly period, but this was struck out in the Legislature. (See Report in *Board of Trade Journal*, July 1890, pp. 85-89; and for February 1890, pp. 212, 213.) A provision prohibiting employment for four weeks after childbirth was inserted in the Factory Bill of the English Government in February 1891.

CHAPTER III.

FACTS OF TO-DAY RELATING TO THE HOURS OF LABOUR.

THE object of the present chapter is to show what are the actual facts with regard to the hours of labour at the present day in some of the various trades and occupations in the United Kingdom. In carrying out this object we have dealt most fully with those occupations where State interference is most needed and is immediately applicable. But to make our examination complete we have also touched lightly upon those trades in which the conditions of work are already more tolerable.

Shop Assistants.

One occupation in which the evil of long hours is very seriously felt is that of the shop-keeper and shop assistant. On this subject an immense amount of valuable information has been collected by Mr. Thomas Sutherst, president of the Shop Hours Labour League. With his permission we quote freely from the little volume* in which he has embodied the results of his investigations. Mr. Sutherst, it may be explained, has voluntarily taken up the cause of shop assistants, and has for years past devoted both time and money to their service. As the general summary of his wide experience he writes :—

"I believe I am within the mark in stating that the majority of shop assistants in this country work from 75 to 90 hours in every week. Of that

---

* *Death and Disease Behind the Counter.* (Thomas Sutherst, 2 Harcourt Buildings, Temple, E.C., London.)

majority one-fourth work the full 90 hours per week, two-fourths 80 hours, and the remaining fourth 75 hours. . . . I do not wish to make it appear that shopkeeping is an unpleasant occupation, but that which is healthy and agreeable for a reasonable time becomes irksome and injurious if continued for a too long period. . . . Stuffs, calicos, and silk cannot be continually torn, cut, or moved without throwing off clouds of minute particles which necessarily impregnate the air of the whole shop. In the evening long rows of gas-burners help to use up what little freshness is left in the air."

This was written in 1884. But Mr. Sutherst informs the writers of this book that there has since been no improvement. And yet for years past various philanthropic and self-help agencies have been hard at work.

To confirm his general summary, Mr. Sutherst prints numbers of letters which he has received from shop assistants in all parts of London. Here are some specimens :—

"'William H., aged 22, grocer's assistant: Have been in three places since I was 15 years of age. My hours have been and are from 7.30 A.M. to 9.30 P.M., Fridays 10 P.M., Saturdays 12 P.M. At the end of the day my feet burn and my limbs ache. On Saturday it is something cruel. We have no holidays. I have known one death through the long hours, and many a one I have known broken down and be obliged to leave. It's very hard to have one's health ruined at the very beginning of life, and then having to go through the world with half a constitution.'

"'Charles T., aged 20, draper, at King's Cross: Been in business since 16. I was at Falmouth four years, and the hours there were reasonable. Here hours are from 7 A.M. to 9.30 P.M., Saturdays, 10.30 P.M. At meal times the food is simply bolted as quickly as possible. I am frequently called forward from my meals. There are twenty females and twenty males here. About half are under 20 years of age. There are busy and slack periods during the day, and the business now spread over so many hours could be done in half the time.'

"'Polly W., draper's assistant, aged 23: Went into business at 16. Average hours from 8.30 A.M. to 9.30 P.M. or 10 P.M., Saturdays 11.30 P.M. or 12 P.M. I have an early closing one day a week, but we are the only people who close now in the neighbourhood, as the others have broken through the voluntary arrangement. We feel that we could not blame our employer if he were again to open, for why should those selfish tradesmen have his trade? . . . We must always have a smile ready, however weary and ill we are.'

"'Agnes B., aged 17, draper's assistant: Hours 8.30 A.M. to 9.30 P.M., Saturdays to 12 P.M. No specified times for meals. We have to eat as quickly as possible, and then leave the table and go back to work. My feet and legs ache terribly towards the end of the day.'"

These specimens, out of an immense number of similar letters, are quite sufficient testimony to evils of which the British public is, or ought to be, fully aware. The importance of the question may be gauged by the fact that the shopkeeping population for the United Kingdom is estimated at about one and a quarter millions, of whom probably at least one million are in the position of hired assistants. Happily, within the last few years there has grown up a class of giant emporiums where the hours of opening are considerably less than in the smaller and medium-sized shops. But it must be borne in mind that in many of these establishments work does not cease when the shutters are up. Assistants are often kept for an hour or more after closing to put away goods and tidy up the shop.

The great evil of a shop assistant's work is the necessity, supposed or real, for constant standing. This is sufficiently wearisome and exhausting in the case of men; in the case of women it is even more serious. Mr. Lawson Tait, the famous specialist in women's diseases, writes to Mr. Sutherst:—

"I can speak of women only, and from a large hospital experience can say that the prolonged hours of labour to which young women are subjected, in such operations as millinery and shop work generally, are extremely detrimental to their health. . . . A great many cases have come under my observation of women suffering from uterine displacements, chronic inflammatory diseases of the ovaries and tubes."

Dr. Richardson, elsewhere quoted in the present volume, writes:—

"The effects of shop labour of the kind named on females under twenty-one, or on males under twenty-one, is of necessity injurious, as impeding their growth and the natural development of the organs of the body. To the female the mischief is of a kind calculated to extend to the offspring she may bear. . . . In my opinion eight hours daily is the maximum time during which labour ought to be carried on in shops."

Without for the present laying stress on this final dictum, it may be pointed out that the case of shop assistants is a peculiarly favourable one for the interference of the Legislature; for in their case there is no fundamental divergence of interest between the employers and the employed. Both shopkeepers and shop assistants are in favour of early closing. But in spite of this concord, shops are still kept open for a period which is universally admitted to be needlessly long. The reason is that no one shopkeeper dares to put up his shutters while his neighbour's shop is still open.

At first sight it would appear that this difficulty could easily be met by a voluntary agreement among shopkeepers to close at a fixed hour. That plan has been tried over and over again, and over and over again it has failed. With infinite trouble, shopkeepers, aided by their assistants, have canvassed particular districts. Finally, by means of argument, cajolery, and threats, they have persuaded all the tradesmen concerned to agree to close at a particular hour on a particular day. The agreement is put into force, and everybody is delighted. But scarcely have the beneficial effects of the early closing begun to be felt before some mean-spirited person snatches at the opportunity of a profitable trade afforded him by the closed establishments of his neighbours. He surreptitiously opens his shop and entices away their customers. Soon another follows his example. In self-defence the others must do the same. And in a short time the agreement obtained with so much difficulty is broken down.

It may be thought by persons not conversant with the inner facts of the early closing movement that this is an over-statement of the case against voluntary action, and many a reader will doubtless recall to his mind numerous instances where a voluntary agreement to close early has been, and still is, successfully maintained. Happily such cases do exist, but for one successful instance at least ten failures might be recorded. But it is not necessary to deal in generalities. Proof of the break-down of the voluntary system is to be found in the action of the London Early Closing Association, which has its headquarters at 100 Fleet Street. This association differs in many important particulars from the Shop Hours Labour League over which Mr. Thomas Sutherst presides. It is older, and it is more "respectable." Founded originally in 1842, it has gone on for nearly half a century trying to make a revolution with rose-water. It has preached that everything must be done by voluntary action, and that on no account must an appeal be made to the tyrant State. Its contributions have been furnished and its council manned for the most part by eminently wealthy and eminently religious tradesmen. And yet, in spite of this weight of conservatism, the Early Closing Association has been at length compelled by the force of hard facts to throw over its original programme and declare its conversion to the principle of parliamentary compulsion.*

This step was taken in 1887. In the previous year a Committee of the House of Commons had been appointed to consider a Bill promoted by Sir John Lubbock for restricting the hours of labour of children and young persons employed in shops. This committee reported as follows :—" Your committee, being satisfied that the hours of shop assistants range in many places as high as from eighty-four to eighty-five hours per week, are convinced that such long hours must be generally injurious and often ruinous to health, and that the same amount of business might be compressed into a shorter space of time."† In consequence of this report, Sir John Lubbock's Bill became law under the title of the Shop Hours Regulation Act 1886.

It is not too much to say that this Act has been a complete failure. In the first place, it only applies to persons under the age of eighteen ; secondly, the limit of hours imposed is the outrageously high one of seventy-four hours per week; thirdly, no machinery is provided for putting the law into force. Since the law came into operation a few prosecutions have been initiated by private persons, but it has been extremely difficult to procure evidence in support of them. Both Mr. Sutherst, of the Shop Hours League, and Mr. Stacey, of the Early Closing Association, state that the overwork in shops is at least as bad as before the passing of the Act, and possibly even worse, owing to the growing intensity of competition.

A more intelligent Bill has since been introduced providing that all shops shall be closed not later than eight o'clock on the first five nights in the week, and ten o'clock on Saturdays, except in

* Compare the similar experience of the Melbourne Society, described in the preceding chapter.
† *Report of Select Committee on Shop Hours Bill*, H.C. 155 of 1886.

FACTS OF TO-DAY.

cases where exemption has been granted by the local authorities. It was in connection with this Bill that the Early Closing Association declared its conversion to the principle of legislative interference. Other affiliated associations followed suit, and large congresses of shopkeepers petitioned in its favour. In the House of Commons the Bill came up for debate on a Wednesday afternoon in 1888, and was thrown out.

We have dwelt at some length on the case of the hours of labour in shops because it is a typical case for the interference of Parliament. As already stated, employers concur with employed in desiring shorter hours. But they are powerless to protect themselves against unscrupulous fellow-tradesmen.

Moreover, there is this characteristic about a shop assistant's position, that whenever he does disagree with his employer, he is less able to make a fight on his own behalf than almost any manual worker. For while an artisan who knows his trade can easily pass from one employer to another, a shop assistant is entirely dependent on the written character he carries with him. It is thus within the power of an unscrupulous employer absolutely to damn the prospects of any young fellow who exerts himself on behalf of his class.

Another most important reason for giving special prominence to the case of shop assistants is, that the young men and women belonging to this class are already well fitted to make good use of additional leisure. Not even the most unsympathetic of Tories would venture to suggest that it is necessary to keep shop assistants hard at work all the livelong day and far into the night in order to prevent them making beasts of themselves at the public-house. Whatever may be the case with the lower ranks of unskilled labour, shop assistants as a class do not get drunk. Their ambitions take a more intellectual turn. They already have a higher average of education than the majority of manual workers, and they are keenly desirous to still further improve themselves by hard study or rational amusement. They ask for leisure to enable them to go to evening classes and lectures; to join debating societies; to go to theatres and concerts, to gymnasiums, and volunteer drills. And consequently the cruelty of long hours is felt by shop assistants possibly more than by any other class, because they foresee and have already foretasted the numberless uses of leisure.

Public-houses and Restaurants.

Very similar to the case of shop assistants is that of bar-tenders in public-houses and waiters and waitresses in eating-houses. In London public-houses may be open from six in the morning till half-past twelve at night (except on Saturdays, when they close at midnight), and there is nothing to prevent a callous employer from keeping his barmaids and barmen at work the whole of this time. Moreover, public-houses, unlike the majority of shops, are open on Sundays as well as on week-days. In London the hours on Sunday are from one to three, and from six to eleven. Thus the total week's work which may be altogether required of men and women serving behind bars is 118½ hours. Of course this period is inclusive of meal times, and in some houses a special interval of an hour to two hours is granted for rest. But often no special rest time is given, and meal time is reduced to the barest minimum necessary for bolting the food. In London alone there are thousands of girls and young men who spend virtually the whole of the eighteen hour day behind the bar, in an atmosphere thick with the fumes of alcohol and stale tobacco, and robbed of its oxygen by flaring gas jets.

Clerks.

The case of clerks is also in many respects comparable to that of shop assistants. But on the whole, clerks, though their wages are low, are in London fairly well off as regards hours of labour. Bank clerks generally work about 45 hours, commercial clerks 48 to 50 hours a week. That all clerks, however, are not in this satisfactory position is proved by the fact that the recently formed Clerks' Union asks for "A general reduction of the hours of labour to a maximum of eight hours a day." The hours of labour in the large warehouses of the so-called "Manchester" trade are often excessive, especially during the busy season. The *Quill*, the organ of the union, in a leading article on November 8th, 1890, writes:—"For years the clerk has stood quietly by, enduring 'genteel' poverty, and submitting to semi-starvation. For years he has been willing to work 10, 12, and 14 hours a day, rather than run the risk of being cast adrift on a glutted market." And in the news columns of the same issue the following statements are made under the head "Doings in the City":—

"Of course there are some employers with a trifle more conscience than others, though they're few and far between. The majority have a partiality for a staff of say nine clerks where they ought to engage fifteen at least. They have repeated occasion for employing their clerks night after night, sometimes till eleven and twelve o'clock, ay, even to one o'clock in the morning, for three or four months at a stretch, without a fraction of remuneration."

Again, the *St. James's Gazette*, in an article on City Warehouses, on March 16th, 1891, writes:—

"The entering-clerks are the Cinderellas of the establishment. They are the juniors, and theirs the longest hours, the hardest work, and the least pay. The work is, indeed, excessive; they are writing their hardest from early morning till late at night. This branch of employment is open to criticism in the very best houses; in others it amounts to a scandal. The work consists in entering in the books all goods as they are sent down from the 'departments' on their way to be packed; and it has nothing to do with the counting-house, which forms a separate part of the establishment. The staff is completed by the packers—a fine lusty set of men well worth their 35s. a week."

These extracts are sufficient evidence that the black-coated, silk-hatted clerk is not invariably well off, even in the matter of hours of labour.

Railways.

But of all occupations, that in which the principle of State regulation of the hours of labour can be most easily applied, and is most urgently needed, is the railway service. A certain amount of information as to the length of employment of railway servants in the United Kingdom has been already collected by the Government, and the tabulated results have been published in returns issued by the Board of Trade in May 1888 and December 1890.*

These returns do not, unfortunately, state what are the actual working hours on railways, but only enumerate the cases where those hours have exceeded twelve per diem. In the earlier return there is, however, a letter from one company giving the information we here specially want in an intelligible form. The essential parts of the letter are as follows:—

---

* *Railway Servants*' (*Hours of Labour*) *Return*, H.L. 30 of 1888, and C—6158 of 1891.

"Particulars relating to the London, Brighton, and South Coast Railway Company's Staff :—

Passenger Guards.—Seven days per week men.
Working hours per day, 12 hours ; do. per week, 72 hours.
Overtime :—74½ hours. A quarter-day to be allowed extra.
77 hours. A half of a day to be allowed extra.
79½ hours. Three-quarters of a day to be allowed extra.
82 hours. One day's pay to be allowed extra.
A day's extra pay allowed for a full day's Sunday work.

Signalmen.

In three-men boxes each signalman works eight hours per day.
In two-men boxes each signalman works twelve hours per day.
All signalmen are seven day men.
Overtime, when made, is paid at the rate of wages earned per day.

Engine-Drivers and Firemen.

Ten hours work comprises a day's work, or 60 hours per week.
After 60 hours on the six week-days overtime is paid for at the rate of eight hours per day.
All Sunday work is paid for at the rate of eight hours per day.
Engine-drivers and firemen are allowed from 45 to 60 minutes before train time, and from 45 to 75 minutes after time of arrival of their trains at destination."

This letter appears in the 1888 return, but there is nothing in the later returns to show that any alteration has been made in the company's regulations. We may therefore assume that on the London and Brighton Company the nominal working day for guards, and some signalmen, is still twelve hours ; that drivers and firemen work nominally ten hours a day, and some signalmen only eight hours a day. It will be noticed, however, that in each case the secretary of the company mentions provision for overtime ; so that not only is the nominal working day in the majority of cases far too long, but the company evidently regard overtime as a regular incident. To what extent this incident occurs is shown in the figures relating to the London and Brighton Company in the later return to Parliament. To this general statement from the secretary of one of the southern lines we may add the following personal particulars collected from the men at the time

FACTS OF TO-DAY. 75

of the recent railway strike in Scotland. They are all taken, it is true, from men employed by one of the Scotch lines, but they are not on that account to be considered exceptional. With a small amount of personal investigation, any one will be able to parallel these instances on half at least of the railways in England.*

The following cases are taken haphazard from among employés of the North British Railway Company :—

"A. B., a fireman.—Hours worked each fortnight during the last eight months: 174, 174, 156, 186, 193, 188, 193, 254, 168, 193, 190, 192, 198, 155, 167, 194. Average per day, 15½.

"B. C., an engine-driver.—Hours worked for two months prior to the strike, per fortnight : 202, 186, 204, 172. Average per day, 15 hours 55 minutes.

"C. D., in Goods Department.—On duty in week (six days) ended Saturday, 20th December, 78 hours 50 minutes. Daily average, 13 hours 8 minutes.

"D. E. (grade not stated).—Hours worked in the three fortnights preceding the strike, 198, 191, 183; at work 24 hours on December 4 ; shortest day, 10 hours. Daily average, 15 hours 53 minutes.

"E. F. (grade not stated).—Hours worked between 3rd November and 20th December, with three week-days and five Sundays off, total 564 hours 47 minutes. Daily average, 14 hours 7 minutes ; longest day, 23 hours.

"F. G., a goods driver.—Hours worked during week ended 21st December, 99 only, 'as I was one of the very few who resolutely refused to work without getting sufficient rest.'"

Some fuller details are given in the Appendix.

And now to come to the Government return presented to Parliament in December 1890. Unfortunately, it is both incomplete and difficult to understand. This is not the fault of the officials of the Board of Trade, but of the House of Commons; for that body, on the motion of Mr. Provand, prescribed the form in which the statistics should be presented to itself and the public.

In order then to make the returns reasonably intelligible to the public, it is necessary to sift the figures and regroup them. What

---

* One of the writers of this volume not long ago had a conversation with a guard on the Manchester, Sheffield, and Lincolnshire Railway. This man stated that a few weeks previously he had been on duty 24 hours and 5 minutes. He was then asked to go on duty for another spell ! He had often been on duty 19 hours at a stretch !

we have done is to take each class of railway servants by itself, and set down the figures relating to the hours of work of that class. In doing this we have purposely omitted all the smaller companies, confining our attention to those great companies whose names are household words. We have also omitted many of the minor details published by the Board of Trade, which tend only to obscure the main facts.

With this general explanation we present the following tables :—

Particulars as to the Hours of Labour of Railway Servants.

PASSENGER GUARDS.

	A.	B.	C.	D.	E.
Great Eastern	310	5	...	...	...
Great Northern	280	88	44	...	...
Great Western	450	4	...	...	...
Lancashire and Yorkshire	264	88	27	7	7
London and North Western	449	3	...	...	...
London and South Western	304	...	...	...	...
London, Brighton, and South Coast	273	52	36	1	...
London, Chatham, and Dover	139	33	4	4	32
Manchester, Sheffield, and Lincolnshire	106	3	...	...	...
Midland	384	98	5	...	...
North Eastern	312	15	...	...	1
South Eastern	239	12	4	...	...
Caledonian	157	...	...	...	...
Glasgow and South Western	71	...	...	...	...
North British	193	16	36	...	...
	3931	417	156	12	40

Column A.—Number of men in the employ of each company. B.—Number of such men who were employed more than 12 hours at a time. C.—Number of instances of men being on duty for 15 hours at a time. D.—Number of instances of men being on duty 18 hours at a time. E.—Number of men who after being on duty more than 12 hours at a time resumed duty with less than 8 hours' rest.

Thus, to total up the returns for the fifteen largest railway companies, we find that in the month of March 1890 there were 3931 passenger guards employed. Of these, 417, or 10.6 per cent., were on duty more than 12 hours at a time. And of the 417, no fewer than 40 returned to work again after an interval of less than 8 hours for rest. In the same month 156 instances occurred of

FACTS OF TO-DAY. 77

passenger guards being on duty for 15 hours at a time. And 12 instances occurred of duty continued for 18 hours.

GOODS GUARDS.

	A.	B.	C.	D.	E.
Great Eastern	229	204	223	19	1
Great Northern	584	519	383	49	38
Great Western	1174	830	419	13	...
Lancashire and Yorkshire	486	393	448	63	77
London and North Western	1373	741	...	...	12
London and South Western	282	31	8	4	14
London, Brighton, and South Coast	163	56	73	...	...
London, Chatham, and Dover	51	25	6	26	...
Manchester, Sheffield, and Lincolnshire	329	288	429	64	118
Midland	1471	1368	1474	324	159
North Eastern	971	826	956	54	15
South Eastern	127	22	42	1	...
Caledonian	588	312	23	...	...
Glasgow and South Western	219	74	4	...	...
North British	645	455	1035	245	64
	8692	6146	5523	862	498

Column A.—Number of men in the employ of each company. B.—Number of such men who were employed more than 12 hours at a time. C.—Number of instances of men being on duty for 15 hours at a time. D.—Number of instances of men being on duty 18 hours at a time. E.—Number of men who after being on duty more than 12 hours at a time resumed duty with less than 8 hours' rest.

As might be expected, the figures for goods guards are much worse than for passenger guards. Out of a total of 8692 goods guards employed on the fifteen railways, 6146, or 70 per cent., were on duty more than 12 hours at a time in March 1890; and 498 of these returned to work after less than 8 hours' rest. Again, there were 5523 instances of goods guards being on duty for 15 hours at a stretch; and 862 instances where the period of continuous duty was 18 hours.

It will be noticed that the Midland Railway is in this case the worst offender, exceeding even the North British. The North Western Railway, which has the longest distances of all, and the greatest amount of goods traffic, manages to get along without calling upon any of its goods guards for excessive overtime. In the face of this fact it is impossible to contend that an Eighteen or a Fifteen Hours Day cannot be avoided on a busy line.

Engine-Drivers and Firemen.

	A.	B.	C.	D.	E.
Great Eastern	1,620	1,128	1,336	118	50
Great Northern	1,533	1,332	1,823	602	24
Great Western	3,114	2,608	2,169	66	104
Lancashire and Yorkshire	1,636	1,617	1,667	71	184
London and North Western	5,652	4,813	3,156	5	137
London and South Western	1,015	...	...	...	...
London, Brighton, and South Coast	731	685	1,229	183	265
London, Chatham, and Dover	368	311	442	78	43
Manchester, Sheffield, and Lincolnshire	945	644	1,112	102	43
Midland	3,930	3,705	5,408	991	45
North Eastern	2,893	2,370	4,721	542	67
South Eastern	707	675	1,807	137	123
Caledonian	1,426	1,216	828	34	3
Glasgow and South Western	578	518	398	26	12
North British	1,593	1,121	3,177	1016	213
	27,741	22,743	29,273	3971	1313

Column A.—Number of men in the employ of each company. B.—Number of such men who were employed more than 12 hours at a time. C.—Number of instances of men being on duty for 15 hours at a time. D.—Number of instances of men being on duty 18 hours at a time. E.—Number of men who after being on duty more than 12 hours at a time resumed duty with less than 8 hours' rest.

Both from their numbers and the responsibility of their work, engine-drivers and firemen constitute the most important class of railway servants. If any man ought to have all his faculties awake, it is the driver of a fast train. But instead of strictly limiting the day's work of each man, we find that the railway companies, with the single exception of the London and South Western, recklessly pile unlimited overtime upon an already protracted day.

Out of a total staff of 27,741 drivers and firemen, 22,743, or 82 per cent., were on duty more than 12 hours at a time in March 1890; and 1313 of these came back to work after less than 8 hours' rest. The number of instances of continuous duty lasting 15 hours was 29,273; and in 3971 cases the period was over 18 hours. If the South Western Railway can entirely avoid this excessive overtime, and the North Western nearly do so, it cannot be a necessity on other lines.

SIGNALMEN.

	A.	B.	C.	D.	E.
Great Eastern	1019	57	24	...	1
Great Northern...	1058	105	24	5	4
Great Western	1174	830	419	13	...
Lancashire and Yorkshire	1271	238	27	3	17
London and North Western	2293	92	6	...	1
London and South Western	874	...	...	...	...
London, Brighton, and South Coast...	592	1	...	...	...
London, Chatham, and Dover ...	269	16	2	3	16
Manchester, Sheffield, & Lincolnshire	709	115	22	20	6
Midland	2044	1809	272	25	609
North Eastern	1897	163	64	5	11
South Eastern	566	37	18	...	...
Caledonian	850	5	...	...	...
Glasgow and South Western... ...	385	13	...	...	...
North British	1028	61	62	5	7
	16,029	3542	940	79	672

Column A.—Number of men in the employ of each company. B.—Number of such men who were employed more than 12 hours at a time. C.—Number of instances of men being on duty for 15 hours at a time. D.—Number of instances of men being on duty 18 hours at a time. E.—Number of men who after being on duty more than 12 hours at a time resumed duty with less than 8 hours' rest.

Signalmen are, on the whole, better off as to hours than any class of railway servants. Many signal-boxes are now worked on the eight hours system, and the twelve hours system is generally confined to boxes where only a small amount of traffic passes. In such cases it often happens that the men on night duty prefer to work thirteen or fourteen hours, in order to get a corresponding reduction when in the succeeding week it is their turn for day duty. This fact accounts for many of the cases where the duty is returned as exceeding twelve hours. But though this is an explanation, it is not an excuse. Even if the actual labour involved in working a twelve hours signal-box is slight, the fact of imprisonment remains. To be shut up in a small cabin for twelve long hours with nothing to do but to watch for a couple of trains in each hour, is to most men quite as severe a strain as the concentrated bustle of a busy signal-box.

Nor is it a fact that all the cases of work extending beyond twelve hours are capable of the above explanation. This explanation, indeed, is only put forward by the Midland Company, and by them not for all instances. Other companies neither allege this excuse nor tolerate the system. The London and South Western shows not a single man on duty for more than twelve hours, the London and Brighton only one, and the Caledonian only five. But the other companies swell the tale. Altogether, as the above table shows, out of 16,029 signalmen, 3542 were in March 1890 on duty more than 12 hours at a time; and 672 of these resumed duty after less than 8 hours' rest. In no fewer than 940 instances was the term on duty continued for 15 hours; and in 79 instances for 18 hours. The fact is that thousands of signalmen are overworked, just as thousands of drivers, stokers, and guards are overworked, not because they choose long hours, but because the companies are too mean to employ a sufficient staff.

In commenting generally on the above statements, it is to be noted that the figures with regard to passenger guards are much more satisfactory than those relating to goods guards. And for an obvious reason—the safety of the public is concerned. A railway company, though it does not mind risking the lives of its employés, feels certain qualms in the case of its customers. It must, however, be confessed that these qualms are not very potent, for accidents repeatedly occur, the cause of which can only be traced to the exhaustion of overworked drivers or signalmen. On this account we find that many people who regard a general limitation of the hours of labour as rank socialism, are not unwilling to apply to Parliament for a special limitation of the working hours of responsible railway servants.

But why, it may be asked, is State interference justifiable when it is to be exercised on behalf of the general public, but totally unjustifiable when it is only the servants of the railway companies whose lives are in danger? Are not railway workers also members of the community? Are they not equally entitled with any other individuals to protection at the hands of the State? Or, turning the argument the other way, we may ask whether the principles of *laissez faire* are not equally applicable in the two cases? For if the servants of the companies are at liberty to resign an employment where the hours of labour are excessive, the travelling public is also at liberty to decline to use a railway which is made unsafe by the overwork of drivers and signalmen, and to go by coach.

Tramways and Omnibuses.

The arguments and facts which we have above brought forward with regard to railway servants apply, with only slight differences of detail, to the employés of tramway and omnibus companies. The conditions of labour of these most useful servants of the public are about as bad as is possible. The hours range from thirteen to seventeen a day on tramcars, and about the same on omnibuses. In order not to overstate the case, however, it may be admitted that anything beyond fourteen hours a day is exceptional in the case of omnibuses. On tramways it is to be feared that this limit is often overpassed, and we have been informed, on the best authority, of cases where a man is *regularly* kept at work seventeen hours a day.* Of course, too, it must be borne in mind that trams and omnibuses run on Sundays as well as week-days, and on many lines drivers and conductors only get an occasional Sunday off. In one case reported to us while collecting information on this subject, a tramcar conductor had not had a single Sunday off for two years.

It is impossible to speak too strongly about the barbarity of such a system as this. That the work of driving or conducting a tramcar is not in itself exhausting, is no defence for such cruel prolongation. For however light the work itself may be, it involves the loss of liberty during the whole period over which it is continued. A man who is tied fourteen or fifteen hours a day to a moving car or 'bus has no liberty left him for reasonable recreation, no liberty to see his wife and children and his friends; no liberty even for proper rest over his meals. He has only just enough spare time to get to his house at night, stow his supper inside him, and tumble into bed.

Moreover, the actual work involved in a driver's or conductor's occupation, though light enough for the first half-hour or hour, or two hours, becomes a serious strain towards the end of a long day. Let any one who doubts this try the experiment of riding for only

* One tramcar conductor in Bradford was found to be working regularly 115 hours a week, with no intervals for meals, for wages of three shillings per day. This was in March 1891.

five or six hours on the platform of a tramcar, with eye and mind alert all the while to look out for passengers behind or for obstacles ahead. After this the experimenter will probably not be very anxious to discuss the theoretical advantages and disadvantages of State action as compared with voluntary action. He will realise that men who are compelled by industrial competition to repeat this experiment daily for fourteen hours without intermission, will be glad to welcome any means of relief.

That it is perfectly possible to work tramways on the eight hours system with two shifts of men has been proved by the Corporation of Huddersfield. This body obtained from Parliament special powers to work the tramways of the town without the intervention of any contractor. After a trial of the old system of long hours, the Corporation decided to employ two shifts of men, each working eight hours, so as to keep the cars running sixteen hours a day. The experiment has been most successful. The men are extremely satisfied, even though their wages were slightly reduced. The public gets a better service of cars. And the Corporation, after paying all charges and allowing for depreciation, makes a profit on the undertaking. For further details of this experiment the reader is referred to the Appendix.

Mines.

The mining industry affords one of the strongest cases for the application of an eight hours maximum by force of law. Every one admits that eight hours underground is the maximum service that ought to be required of any man. The conditions of the work are of necessity unhealthy, while the dangers of this most dangerous occupation are aggravated by the carelessness which overwork invariably induces. Apart moreover from the actual detriment to health or the danger to life of the miner's occupation, due allowance ought to be made for the mere unpleasantness of the work. It is necessary that some one should go down into the bowels of the earth to dig coals for the community, and it is inevitable that the task should be a disagreeable one. Therefore if we are to make an effort to attain equity in our social arrangements, the men who are doomed to this work ought to have their daily task abbreviated as far as is economically possible.

FACTS OF TO-DAY.

That there is no economic objection to an Eight Hours Day in the case of miners' work is proved by the fact that many miners are to-day working less than eight hours. And this fact has been ingeniously taken hold of by the opponents of State interference, and used as an argument to prove that the men were perfectly capable of winning an Eight Hours Day for themselves by means of their unions, and want no help from the State. This argument is so apparently plausible that it is well to deal with it at once.

Nor are many words needed. The simple answer is that as a matter of fact the Eight Hours Day for colliers, in the district where it is most general, namely, Northumberland and Durham, has not been won by Trade Union organisation. It has, on the contrary, been voluntarily instituted by the employers in order to carry out a rather complicated system of shifts. In these counties two shifts of "hewers" are employed. The hewers are the men who actually win the coal, and constitute about 70 per cent. of the persons employed underground. They are assisted by auxiliary workers underground who draw away the hewn coal to the shaft, and by other workers above ground who deal with the coal when it reaches the pit brow. It is found that the hewers can profitably work for an hour to two hours before the men who remove the coal are required, and can in the same way go on working for some time after these men have gone above. Among these auxiliary workers a great many boys are employed. But by the Acts of Parliament regulating the mining industry boys may not be employed underground for more than 10 hours a day. Consequently to keep these boys at work their full time, two shifts of hewers will be required, each working 6 to 6½ hours. This and no other is the explanation of the fact that in Durham and Northumberland the full working day for hewers is about seven hours from the time of leaving the bank (the pit mouth) to the time of returning.

On this subject the following quotation from an article in the *Newcastle Daily Leader*, November 1890, opposing the Miners' Eight Hours Bill, is instructive :—

"According to the Government return, moved for by Mr. Provand, and dated July 8th of the present year, 27,714 persons are reported as being employed above and below ground about the

Northumberland mines. Of these, 11,840 only are engaged as hewers, working on an average about seven hours a day from bank to bank. These would not be personally affected except in so far as the interference with other labour necessary to their work would affect them, and the tendency which would be established to lengthen their hours to the maximum of the Act. There are other underground workers not engaged in getting coals, but in preparing and keeping the mines in order, to the number of 6,482. Those work an average of eight hours daily, and would not be affected except indirectly. That is, roughly speaking, 18,000 men and boys would only be affected through others. There are, however, 4,745 men and boys engaged in conveying minerals from the face to the shaft bottom, and these work on an average a little over ten hours. On the surface, working for the most part in conjunction with these, are 4,648 persons who labour about 9½ hours daily. At present there are two shifts of hewers for one shift of men and boys engaged in conveying the mineral from the face to the bottom of the shaft. The hewers work at the face a little over six hours, or, as we have explained, about seven hours from bank to bank. The single shift of men and boys who convey the coal work ten hours. Now, if it is made illegal for these to work ten hours, it will be necessary to find some other way of organising the pit."

The writer then goes on to state several alternative methods of organisation, but condemns them all because they would throw additional expense on the mine-owner "for the doubtful good of securing that no man or boy should work longer than eight hours a day." This final comment is amusing as coming from a man who at the time was probably seated in a cosy office, well lighted and well warmed, earning a comfortable living by the fluency of his pen. Possibly if the accidents of birth or brains had ordained that the same gentleman should earn only a meagre wage by working in a dim light and a foul atmosphere in moist galleries perhaps a mile away from the surface of the earth, he would not have said that it was a small matter whether his day's labour was eight or ten hours.

Durham and Northumberland, however, comprise only part of the mining area of Great Britain, and in other districts it is rare for the hewers to be so well off as in these two counties.

FACTS OF TO-DAY. 85

Information as to the hours of labour of miners at the different colliery districts in Great Britain has been collected by the Home Office, and was presented to Parliament in a return issued July 1890.* This return suffers from a defect, not usual in parliamentary publications, of being too much summarised ; that is to say, the hours worked at each colliery are not given separately, but are totalled for various districts, and an average struck—a process convenient for the statistician, but not consoling to the individuals who are on the wrong side of the average. However, the return even with this defect is very useful, and we extract from it the following essential facts relating to the principal colliery districts of Great Britain. Minor facts and minor districts are omitted for the sake of brevity and clearness.

DISTRICTS.	Persons engaged in getting coal (Hewers).		Persons conveying coal from face to pit.		Other underground workers.	
	No. of men and boys.	Hours from bank to bank.	No. of men and boys.	Hours from bank to bank.	No. of men and boys.	Hours from bank to bank.
East Lanark	11,662	9.28	3,668	9.51	1,644	9.35
West Lanark	8,011	9.4	2,331	9.42	1,802	9.71
Northumberland...............	11,840	7.08	4,745	10.13	6,481	8.2
Durham and Westmoreland	24,178	7.21	12,920	10.51	10,767	8.2
Yorkshire......................	34,742	8.8	13,442	8.9	8,190	8.7
North-East Lancashire	18,557	9.25	5,053	9.25	4,479	9.25
West Lancashire.............	15,744	9.32	5,730	9.81	6,330	9.49
Derbyshire	17,470	9.28	5,393	9.25	2,815	9.35
Nottinghamshire..............	10,159	9.6	2,569	9.63	2,189	9.6
South Stafford................	9,752	7.82	3,857	8.75	2,245	8.75
Brecon and Monmouth	13,453	9.22	2,634	9.34	3,541	9.23
Glamorganshire	29,888	9.13	8,253	9.03	14,086	9.05

In order to complete the information contained in the above table, it is necessary to add that in nearly all collieries the Saturday half-holiday is recognised to a greater or lesser extent. Thus in Northumberland, according to the return above quoted, the average week's work for hewers is 5½ days ; in Durham, 5.6 days ; and in Yorkshire only 5 full days. In West Lancashire and

* Mines (Hours of Labour) 1890, Parliamentary Paper 284.

Nottinghamshire the week's work is just under 5 days, while in South Wales it is as much as 5¾ days.

As already explained, these statements are summarised from averages taken over large districts.

The best information available as to the hours of labour worked in separate collieries throughout the country is given in a statistical report presented to the Miners' Federation of Great Britain, by Mr. Thomas Ashton, their secretary.* The report is based on returns supplied by check-weighers and district secretaries, and shows the hours worked at each colliery in the various mining districts of Great Britain, with the exception of Durham, Northumberland, and Cleveland.

Unfortunately, many of the persons making returns seem to have done their work very carelessly, and Mr. Ashton cannot pledge himself to the accuracy of all the figures. For this reason it is not worth while to attempt any general summary, but, by way of illustration, we may refer to the returns for the counties of Lancashire and Cheshire. The question, how many hours are worked at the coal face, is answered as follows :—At one colliery, 12 hours are worked; at two collieries, 11 hours; at 40, from 10 to 10½ hours; at 66, 9 to 9½ hours; at 54, 8 to 8½ hours; at 6, 7¼ to 7½ hours; at one colliery, 7 hours. The boys are returned as working at 63 collieries, 10 hours; at 65 collieries, 9 to 9¾ hours. The day men work from 9 to 10 hours; and, in some few instances, 11 hours.

These figures are typical of the rest, and, taken together with the government averages above quoted, prove the falsity of the assertion so frequently made that the colliers of England have already won an Eight Hours Day by their own exertions. Indeed, it is curious that the persons who make this assertion do not themselves perceive its inherent absurdity. For if the miners had already secured an Eight Hours Day, is it likely that they would agitate for an Act of Parliament to confer upon them that boon? And yet it is in answer to this very agitation that politicians, who get their facts out of their own inner consciousness, go about the country asserting that the miners already enjoy an Eight Hours Day.

* *Statistical Report of Hours worked at Collieries*, by Thomas Ashton, Bradford, Manchester, October 1890.

Happily the agitation has now become so strong that its meaning can no longer be mistaken, even by members of Parliament. And candidates for mining constituencies are now compelled reluctantly to declare themselves in favour of a Miners' Eight Hours Bill.

Hospital Nurses.

Another class of persons who are habitually and scandalously overworked are hospital nurses. Here are particulars as to the hours on duty of nurses in one of the large hospitals of London. The day nurses are expected to be out of their dormitories at 20 minutes past 7; they breakfast at half-past 7, and they enter the wards at 8 o'clock; they dine in two batches, half-an-hour being allowed for dinner, from half-past 11 to 12, and from 12 to half-past; they have tea from half-past 4 to 5, and from 5 to half-past; they have supper from half-past 8 to 9, and from 9 to half-past, and they leave the wards at a quarter to 10. The night nurses have breakfast at 10 minutes to 9 P.M.; they come on duty at half-past 9, and they leave the wards at half-past 10 the following morning.* That is to say, the day nurses are on duty for a gross period of $13\tfrac{3}{4}$ hours, out of which they are allowed $1\tfrac{1}{2}$ hours for meals. The night nurses are on duty 11 hours; time allowed for meals not stated. It is of course true that a nurse is not running about or actively at work the whole of the time she is on duty, but she is confined to the ward, and has to be continually alert. Moreover, the nature of her work involves very great mental strain. She has often to witness the most painful sights, but is nevertheless expected to be always bright and cheery. That hospitals are philanthropic institutions furnishes no excuse for imposing such inordinately heavy duty on the women who, by whatever motives inspired, have undertaken the work of sick nursing. If the hospitals cannot, with their present scale of income and expenditure, afford to increase their staff of nurses, they must either apply to the public for larger donations, or they must close some of their wards. Philanthropists have no right to inflict suffering on one section of the community in order to heal the ills of another.

* Evidence of the Treasurer of Guy's Hospital before the Royal Commission on Hospitals. (*Times*, 27th January 1891.)

Government Servants.

With regard to the hours of labour of government servants, some particulars are given in Chapters IV. and VI. It is there shown that the practice of overtime working in the government arsenal at Woolwich, and in the small arms factory at Enfield, is habitual, and by this practice the nominal Nine Hours Day is rendered nugatory.

The Post Office, on the whole, shows a better record in the matter of hours of labour. The working day for letter-carriers is nominally eight hours, spread generally over a period of twelve hours or more. During some seasons of the year, however, a good deal of overtime is worked, and is often not paid for. In the Savings Bank Department, an answer by the Postmaster General to a question in Parliament on March 2nd, 1891, discloses a scandalous system of overtime work. The average day's work of a male sorter in the Savings Bank in January 1890 was 11 hours 40 minutes. In the corresponding month of 1891 the average was 12 hours 36 minutes. The average day's work for boy messengers in January 1890 was 11 hours 18 minutes. In the corresponding month of 1891 it was 11 hours 20 minutes. Some of the elder boys have averaged 12¾ hours work a day during the month of January.

Trades under the Factory Act.

To pass to the "trades" of the country as distinguished from the "services" and occupations with which we have been so far dealing, we come first of all to the great staple textile industries. In all of these, cotton, wool, and silk, the hours of labour are fixed by law at a rigid maximum of 56½ hours a week. This maximum nominally applies only to women and young persons under 18, and children. But, as elsewhere explained, it effectually controls the hours of labour of male operatives also. The consequence is that practically all the workers in textile trades of England, some 800,000 in number, have a fixed working week of 56½ hours.

In non-textile factories and workshops the provisions of the law are less rigid. A normal week of 60 hours is prescribed, and provision is made for a liberal allowance of overtime. Here again the law only applies explicitly to women, young persons, and children;

FACTS OF TO-DAY. 89

but in a very large number of cases the nature and organisation of the industry require that the men should begin and cease working at the same time as the women. There are, however, some non-textile factories and many workshops* where men alone are employed, and in such cases their hours of labour are unaffected by the law.

Various skilled Trades.

With these cases we now propose to deal, so far as the scanty means at our disposal enables us. A good deal of the information here given is summarised from letters which we have received from secretaries of trade unions. Some of the letters themselves are printed in the Appendix.

BLAST FURNACEMEN AND STEEL SMELTERS.—For full details with regard to the hours of labour in these important industries, the reader is referred to the detailed statement relating to the British Steel Smelters' Association printed in the Appendix. The work is carried on continuously day and night in two shifts. As a rule the day shift works 10 hours and the night shift 14 hours.

SEED CRUSHERS AND OIL MILLS.—Here too the work is carried on day and night, but there is a slight break made between the two shifts, so that each shift only works 11 hours.

BAKERS.—The work of bakers is largely done at night, and the hours are generally very long. In London there was a bakers' strike in 1889 for a Twelve Hours Day, which was partially successful. Elsewhere there has been little improvement. In Liverpool, at the end of 1890, the hours averaged 80 per week.

TAILORS.—This is the trade in which the special evil popularly known as sweating is most prevalent. In the inferior branches of the trade the hours are most irregular, often extending to 16 or even 18 out of the 24, and the general condition of the workpeople deplorable. Even in the better-class trade, long hours of overtime are worked.

MILL SAWYERS.—In mills where sawing is taken in and done for timber merchants and cabinetmakers, etc., the hours are

---

* A workshop is defined in the Factory and Workshop Act to be a place where work is carried on without the aid of steam or other mechanical motive power.

nominally 10 a day (59 a week), but by overtime work they are brought up to 67 and even 73 and 74 hours in the week. On the other hand, where the sawing is done as part of the process of a special industry—*e.g.*, box-packing, case-making—the hours are only 56 a week, and little overtime is worked. The difference is undoubtedly due to the presence of women workers in the factory in the second case, and their absence in the first.

MILLERS.—In this trade in Liverpool the hours have recently been reduced to 58 per week.

FILE CUTTERS.—A good deal of home work is done in these industries, and the hours are then virtually without limit.

BOOKBINDERS, COMPOSITORS, ENGINEERS, BOILER MAKERS, IRON SHIP BUILDERS, BRASS FITTERS, STEAM ENGINE MAKERS, IRON FOUNDERS, SHIP WRIGHTS, RIGGERS, and COOPERS have all secured a nominal nine hours day, or 54 hours a week.* In every trade, however, overtime is a frequent incident, in some cases an habitual practice.

CARPENTERS and JOINERS, PLUMBERS, STONE-MASONS, and BRICKLAYERS work different hours in different towns, the nominal working week varying from 50 to 60 hours. In all cases overtime is a more or less serious incident, though in some towns vigorous efforts are made by the union to suppress it.

Fuller particulars as to the hours of labour of bricklayers, carpenters, and stone-masons are furnished by the following table, which has been carefully condensed out of many folio pages of figures in a Government Blue Book.† Each of the societies quoted has branches in most of the towns in the United Kingdom, and each branch fixes the normal day and the normal weekly wage for its own town. Both of these elements vary. Thus several towns may be working 54 hours a week, but the wages in one will

---

* With regard to ironfounders, the following table is instructive as showing how a decrease in the hours of labour is accompanied with an increase in wages. It is taken from the Board of Trade Report on Trade Unions above referred to.

FRIENDLY SOCIETY OF IRON FOUNDERS —11,710 Members.

Years.	Hours of Labour.	Average Wages.
1845-54	59½ to 63	£1 3 1
1855-64	57½ to 60	1 4 6
1865-74	56½ to 60	1 6 3
1875-81	54 to 58½	1 6 6

† *Second Report on Trade Unions*, 1838, C—5505.

be 39s., in another only 24s. 9d. As will be seen in the following tables, we give the highest and lowest wages fixed for different towns, and also the average of all the towns. The figures refer only to England and Wales, and do not include London. In the London district each of the three societies works 52½ hours a week for a wage fixed at £1, 19s. 4½d.

No. of towns.	Hours fixed.	Highest Wages.	Lowest Wages.	Average.
		£ s. d.	£ s. d.	£ s. d.
OPERATIVE BRICKLAYERS—6,693 members.				
14	57½ or more	1 16 10½	1 4 9½	1 9 6
59	56½	2 2 4½	1 5 10	1 13 9
12	54½–56	2 1 7½	1 5 0	1 14 0½
16	54	1 16 0	1 9 3	1 12 8
6	50 or less	1 15 0½	1 11 3	1 13 7½
CARPENTERS AND JOINERS—25,497 members.				
19	58½ or more	1 16 0	1 0 0	1 7 5½
94	56½	2 2 4½	1 6 0	1 13 7½
32	55 or 55½	2 1 7½	1 5 5	1 12 5
64	54	1 19 0	1 4 9	1 8 0½
16	51½–53	1 15 0	1 6 6	1 10 10
17	50	1 13 4	1 7 1	1 11 0½
12	49½	1 10 11½	1 8 0	1 9 5½
OPERATIVE STONE-MASONS—10,238 members.				
7	57–58½	1 16 6½	1 4 0	1 8 10½
38	56½	2 0 0	1 8 3	1 13 1½
29	54	1 18 3	1 9 3	1 13 4
16	51–53½	1 19 0	1 7 7½	1 12 7
12	50	1 16 0	1 9 2	1 12 2½
46	49½	1 17 1½	1 7 0	1 12 7
19	48½ or 49	1 16 4½	1 8 3½	1 13 5

Two interesting facts may be elicited from this table. First, that in towns where the normal week is under 50 hours, the average weekly wage is higher than in those where the normal week is over 57 hours. Secondly, that among all the various periods fixed, that of 56½ hours is adopted more frequently than any other. This, it will be remembered, is the period fixed by the Factory Act for all textile industries.

That there is good ground for believing that these two facts have a causal connection, is proved by the following extract from a circular issued by the Felt Hatter's Society of Denton in February 1890 :—

"The employers are requested to fix the regular working hours either from 6 in the morning to 5.30 in the evening for five days of the week, and from 6 in the morning to 12.30 noon on Saturdays; or from 6.30 in the morning to 6 in the evening for five days, and from 6.30 to 1 noon on Saturdays, less one and a half hours for meals—breakfast and dinner—thus making 56 hours per week, or practically the 'Factory Act' principle."

This quotation conclusively proves that the limit for the week's work fixed by law for women and children in textile factories has, by its example, had an influence in determining the hours of labour of male artisans, and operatives engaged in industries altogether independent of female labour.

This brief summary must be taken in connection with the fuller details given in the Appendix. The general conclusion to be drawn from it is that the average week's work for all the artisans and operatives of England, when overtime has been added, is not less than sixty hours.

AGRICULTURAL LABOURERS in England work from 54 up to 66 hours a week during the summer months, from dawn to dusk in winter. Oppressive conditions often abound. The following instance of a contract actually put into writing, at Slough (Buckinghamshire, England), may be taken as typical of much unrecorded tyranny:—

"I, WILLIAM BURTCHELL, agree to hire myself to Alfred William and Joseph Reffell for one year as carter at 7s. per week for the first half, 8s. per week for the second half-year, and £3 at Michaelmas, 11th October 1891, to make myself generally useful at all kinds of work, and to do anything I am asked to do at any time. In case of illness or accident I agree to support myself; to be in the stable at four o'clock every morning in order to get my horses ready for work by six o'clock; to rack up my horses every night at eight o'clock; to find my own whip, masters to keep it in repair; to get up in the morning when called by the carter; to be in every night by nine o'clock, except when required to be later by my masters; to clean boots and shoes on Sunday mornings."

CHAPTER IV.

THE PROBABLE ECONOMIC RESULTS OF AN EIGHT HOURS DAY.

1. *The Difficulty of the Problem.*

ECONOMIC prophecy has of recent years fallen into disfavour, and no political economist would to-day like to commit himself to a dogmatic assertion as to any inevitable results of a shortening of the working day. All that economists will feel assured in declaring is that the problem is not to be solved in the short and ready terms commonly used, either by the capitalist or the leader-writer on the one side, or the platform advocate of an Eight Hours Law on the other. The wonder which Lord Macaulay expressed in his great speech on the Ten Hours Bill still finds ample justification. "I am surprised," he said, "when I hear men of eminent ability and knowledge lay down the proposition that a diminution of the time of labour must be followed by a diminution of the wages of labour, as a proposition universally true, as a proposition capable of being strictly demonstrated, as a proposition about which there can be no more doubt than about a theorem in Euclid."* Nor can the question be summarily decided in terms of Marx's famous analysis of capitalism; an analysis which omits—no doubt only for clearness of argument—all reference to the variations in advantage between the different sites, soils, machinery, opportunities, and managerial abilities, between which, in actual practice, the industrial conflict is carried on. The probable economic effect, in actual life, of a further shortening

* *Speeches*, p. 448.

of the working day can be safely stated only in the most general hypothetic terms; and the exact results are likely to vary from trade to trade, from country to country, and even from mill to mill. The outcome will be different if the shortening of hours becomes quickly general in any one country, from that in the more probable event of a shortening only in particular industries at a time. An effective international movement would not have the same economic results as one virtually confined to a single country. It may however be observed with confidence that in the economic inquiry we may eliminate the means by which the assumed shortening of the working day is to be effected. The economic results of a diminution of the hours of labour will be precisely the same whether that diminution be caused by a law, or by an equally general ukase of a Trade Society. There is a common confusion of mind which leads opponents of an Eight Hours Law to profess themselves in favour of an Eight Hours Day, provided that it is secured by Trade Union action, and in the same breath to declare that any compulsory diminution of working time would ruin the nation's trade. This confusion finds no support in Political Economy, which needs therefore to deal only with the problem of a shorter working day, however obtained.

2. *The Result of Previous Reductions in the Hours of Labour.*

It will be convenient first to inquire what economic results have followed upon previous reductions of the hours of labour. It cannot, of course, be inferred without further investigation that a reduction from ten to eight hours per day would have precisely the same economic results as a previous reduction from twelve hours to ten. It will, however, be instructive, if only by way of removing some common misapprehensions, if we notice what has happened in the past experience of the community. There are on record three main classes of cases in which the hours of labour have been effectively reduced, under circumstances which permit of their examination from this point of view. The reduction in the hours of labour in the textile mills, which may be said to have begun in the United Kingdom from about 1817, has been continuous and considerable. Seventy-five years ago men commonly worked 90 and 100 hours per week. By successive stages these hours have been brought down to 56½. At every stage it has been conclusively "proved" by the manufacturers that the proposed new restriction of hours would deprive them of all margin of profit, would raise the price of the commodity, lower the wages of the workers, and destroy the export trade. Celebrated economists were found to demonstrate that the whole economic advantage of the running of the mill at all lay exclusively in the "last hour," and that its prohibition would involve, accordingly, the cessation of the industry. Yet the result has over and over again shown that manufacturers and theorists alike were wrong; the hours of work have been successively reduced, without diminution of production, fall of wages, rise of prices, or slackening of trade.

During the debates on the Ten Hours Bill it was usually taken for granted that wages would be diminished by it at least 16 per cent. Sir James Graham and Mr. Cardwell both assured the House of Commons that the fall would be 25 per cent.* Mr. John Bright (see Chapter VIII.) lent the weight of his practical experience to a similar assumption. And wages did occasionally fall off for a time. This question was hotly debated, for instance, in the great strike of the Preston cotton operatives in 1853. In the manifesto of the masters we find the following statements as to the course of wages since the passing of the Ten Hours Bill in 1847 :—" We at once admit that, owing to the depressed state of trade in 1847, *a general reduction of wages took place in the latter part of that year, or early in* 1848. . . . Being anxious to ascertain the difference (if any) between the earnings of the various classes of operatives in 1847, before the above-mentioned reduction took place, and those in the summer of 1853, before the ten per cent. was demanded, we find, from the returns furnished us from the wages books of several large and influential firms, that instead of any decrease, *there has been an actual increase*, varying from five to thirty per cent., after making due allowance for the difference in the hours of labour from sixty-nine to sixty hours per week." It is easy to imagine how this unintended demonstration of the

* *Annual Register*, 1844, p. 107, quoted in H. L. Smith's *Economics of State Socialism*, p. 109.

economic benefits of the Ten Hours Law was taken up by the operatives. In the reply of the Weavers' Association they say, with pardonable rhetoric, " Gentlemen, if your object had been to furnish statistical data of the benefit and blessings which have resulted from the passing of the Ten Hours Bill (that bill which you so long and so zealously opposed, and which you so often prophesied would be followed by ruinous and disastrous results—by-the-bye, we are told at the present time that if you cannot succeed in reducing our wages ten per cent. it will be followed by disastrous ruin), we could have understood your motive" for quoting these statistics of increased wages.* The experience of Preston was repeated in some other places, and any reduction in wages was quickly made up by a subsequent actual increase.

In 1859, Mr. Robert Baker, who had had a long experience as Factory Inspector, reported to the Social Science Association that "although the hours of work have been very much diminished, wages have increased in some cases forty per cent., and generally about twelve per cent.;" and that this reduction of hours and increase of wages had "not diminished any kind of textile production, and therefore it had not injured our national prosperity."† Nor has the gain been made at the expense of other industries. Political economists are emphatic in their conclusion that "the effect of the Factory Acts has been undoubtedly to raise the real wages of the working classes as a whole."‡

As regards the effect upon prices and the export trade, the following table is conclusive. During the successive reductions of working hours, the price of cotton yarn has fallen from 25.71 pence per pound in 1821, to 12.83 pence per pound in 1884. The average price of piece-goods during the same period fell from 11.73 pence to 2.81 pence per yard.§

---

* Manifesto of the Masters' Association, 27th Dec. 1853 ; Reply of the Weavers' Committee, 28th Dec. 1853 ; in *Soc. Sci. Assoc. Report on Trade Societies*, 1860, pp. 223-226.

† *Social Science Association Transactions*, vol. iii. p. 553 ; see also Gunton's *Wealth and Progress*, p. 306.

‡ Article on "Wages," by Prof. J. S. Nicholson, *Ency. Brit.*, vol. xxiv. p. 311 (1888).

§ *The Cotton Trade of Great Britain*, by Thomas Ellison (London, 1886: Effingham Wilson), Table 2.

EXPORT OF BRITISH COTTON GOODS.*

Average of Ten Years.	Quantities in Millions.		Value in Thousands	Per Inhabitant.		
	Yards of Cloth.	Lbs. of Yarn.		Yards of Cloth.	Lbs. of Yarn.	Value in Shillings
1821-30 - - -	340	39	£17,210	15	2	15
1831-40 - - -	589	90	21,390	23	4	16
Factory Acts 1831, 1833						
1841-50 - - -	965	137	24,215	35	5	17
Factory Acts 1844, 1847, 1850						
1851-60 - - -	1,988	171	38,030	70	6	27
Factory Acts 1852, 1856						
1861-70 - - -	2,444	136	59,620	81	4	40
Factory Acts 1861, 1863, 1864, 1867, 1870						
1871-80 - - -	3,693	222	71,930	110	7	43
Factory Acts 1874, 1878						

The continuing profitableness of the industry during this period is proved partly by its enormous extension, and partly by the gigantic fortunes left by the Hermons, Crosses, Ashtons, and other Lancashire mill-owners.

It would, of course, be unwarranted to deduce from the marvellous record of the cotton trade in England, that every reduction of the hours of labour necessarily produces these economic results. What the record does prove is that an enormous diminution of the hours of labour *may* be compatible with no increase in the cost of production, with a positive rise in wages, and a great advance in trade. It can no longer be inferred that a shortening of hours will necessarily reduce the week's wages, even if it temporarily reduces the day's production, and the workers are at piecework. The economic lesson to be learnt is that, in considering the effect of an Eight Hours Day, we must distrust all apparently obvious inferences on both sides. Similar results have followed reductions of the hours of labour in other countries, and equally to the surprise of the Political Economists. The State of Massachusetts passed a Ten Hours Law in 1874 although its textile industries were exposed to the competition not only of Lancashire, but also the immediately adjacent States, in

* See Mulhall, *Dictionary of Statistics*, Article "Cotton."

which the hours were at that time entirely unrestricted. It was almost as if the English Factory Acts applied to Lancashire, but not to Yorkshire or Cheshire. The manufacturers and the economists predicted ruin and starvation. Even after the event they persisted in the same prophecy, then simply converted into an assertion of manifest fact. Mr. Edward Atkinson, of Boston, the well-known advocate of unrestricted "Free Trade" even in labour, and (as it may be added) brother to the managing director of the largest cotton mills in Lowell, actually gave evidence before a Committee of the Massachusetts Legislature in 1880, as to the Ten Hours Law of 1874, that "its operation was injurious to working men, as they had to work for one-eleventh less than similar labourers in other States." The result was that the Legislature directed the Bureau of Statistics of Labour to inquire whether this was the case. Mr. Carroll D. Wright gives in the 1881 Report* the elaborate statistical outcome of this inquiry, and thus summarises the result: "It is apparent that Massachusetts with ten hours produces as much per man, or per loom, or per spindle, equal grades being considered, as other States with eleven and more hours; and also that *wages here rule as high, if not higher, than in the States where the mills run longer time.*" Wages in Massachusetts (though the operatives work by the piece) not only did not fall, but steadily rose from an average of $199.40 per annum in 1850, with about 70 hours work per week, to one of $258.19 in 1880, with 60 hours work per week. Nor was the industry destroyed, or even diminished, relatively to the other States where no limitation of hours existed. In 1831 Massachusetts had invested in the cotton industry $12,891,000, being slightly under one-half of the total for New England. In 1880 it had risen to $72,291,601, and still bore almost exactly the same proportion to the whole.† The result of this triumphant vindication of the economic advantages of a legal limitation of the hours of labour was that Rhode Island, New Hampshire, Maine, and Vermont, which had hitherto opposed the movement, now adopted the Ten Hours Law.

It is useless to multiply instances to the same effect. In Austria,

* *Twelfth Annual Report of Massachusetts Bureau of Statistics of Labour.*
† *Sixteenth Annual Report of the Massachusetts Bureau of Statistics of Labour,* 1885.

THE PROBABLE ECONOMIC RESULTS. 99

for instance, a new Factory Law came into operation during 1889, reducing the hours from twelve to eleven, even for adult male operatives, and in some cases the hours have been further reduced to ten per day. The following Consular report from the *Board of Trade Journal* (December 1889, pp. 715-16) gives the result:—

"*Results of Shorter Hours.*—In the woollen mills of Schmerler and Kretschmar, at Eger, the hours of labour have been reduced to ten with a highly satisfactory result. Not only has there been no falling off in the amount of production, but the output has even experienced a slight rise in regard to quantity as well as quality, and the average wages of the workmen have advanced forty kreutzers per week. Hence there is six hours per week less work, with an increased and improved production, and a slight rise in wages. The same experience was generally made, consequent upon the enforced reduction of the former twelve hours to eleven hours of work in the textile industry. We may therefore conclude that in Austria, the same as in England, a positive proof has been furnished that the shortening of the hours of labour in a certain reasonable degree is made up by the increased efficiency and intensity of the work and its results. There are exceptions to this rule, but they do not disprove its general correctness."

Another great class of instances is that of the artisans in the skilled handicrafts in England, whose hours, as we have seen, have been gradually reduced from about 75 to 54 per week. During this period wages have, on the whole, uniformly risen. It is worth while to place on record a few cases. The Glasgow clothlappers in 1851 were working 64 hours per week for 14s. to 16s. They obtained a reduction of hours to 62, and then to 60. Meanwhile their wages rose two shillings per week.* The Glasgow masons had a similar experience. In 1853 they were working 60 hours a week; they successfully insisted on a reduction to 57, and at the same time obtained a rise in wages from 23s. to 25s. per week.†

If it be objected that these cases occurred during the first years of untaxed corn, similar instances may be quoted from the period before Free Trade and effective Factory Acts, during the very

---

* *Social Science Association Report on Trade Societies*, 1860, p. 276.
† *Ibid.*, p. 285.

period of industrial "white slavery" in England. Between 1800 and 1840 the skilled artisan had won for himself the Ten Hours Day, reducing his hours of labour by about twelve per week. The well-known records of wages paid at Greenwich Hospital show that during the forty years wages of artisans rose 12½ per cent. in money, and much more even than that if compared with the prices of food.* Since 1840 the Ten Hours Day has been reduced to a Nine Hours Day, and wages have risen still higher.

Other countries record similar experiences in connection with the steady reduction of the hours of artisans. New York State witnessed, in 1887, 256 strikes for shorter hours, and one-seventh of the reports received by the Commissioner of Labour testify to a reduction of the working day, notably among the brewers, carpenters, coppersmiths, furniture makers, horse-shoers, painters, roofers, and stone-cutters. *In every one of these trades a positive increase in wages is also reported.* The brass-workers and bricklayers suffered, by exception, an increase of their hours. The wages of the former underwent no change, but in three out of five cases bricklayers' wages actually diminished.†

The third class of instances to which reference may be made is that in which a reduction to eight hours per day has taken place. As this is still generally in the future, not many cases of actual experience can be given, but those of which we have been able to obtain particulars are very striking. The Eight Hours Day was established in some of the South Yorkshire coal-mines about 1859. In 1860 the General Secretary to the Masters' Association stated as "a fact that cannot be disputed, that the production under the eight hours system that has been introduced into the South Yorkshire district this last twelve months, at some of the largest collieries, is greatly in excess of what was ever produced by an equal number of men when the men worked twelve or thirteen hours." He went on to attribute this to the greater energy and steadiness with which the men worked on the shorter shift.‡

In the United Kingdom at the present time the coal-hewers work "from bank to bank" eight hours per day or less, only in

* See Leone Levi's figures, quoted by Thorold Rogers in ch. xviii. of *Six Centuries of Work and Wages* (p. 140 of abridged edition).
† *Report of New York Bureau of Statistics of Labour*, 1887, pp. 64-104.
‡ *Report of Social Science Association on Trade Societies*, 1860, pp. 45, 268.

Northumberland and Durham.* In Northumberland and Durham this shorter day is not accompanied by any disadvantage in the week's wages, in comparison with other parts of the country where nine and ten hours are worked. In Victoria the reduction in 1856 of the hours of labour of the skilled artisans to eight per day was not accompanied by any fall in wages. The continued prosperity of the capitalist interest in this wealthy colony indicates that the Eight Hours Day has not spelt ruin.†

In the United States those trades which have, in many cities, secured an Eight Hours Day, invariably gained this without any fall in wages, even for a time. The cigar-makers and the stone-masons are two of the American trades which have most generally secured an Eight Hours Day during recent years. The cigar-makers often work "by the piece," and the rate of wages has usually slightly risen during these years. In New York city their day wages have risen from about $1.75 to $2. Stone-cutters' wages are much higher than formerly. Another example comes from Germany. Herr Heye, the proprietor of the large glass works of Gerresheim, near Düsseldorf, Germany, reduced the working day from eleven, and in some cases twelve hours, to a normal eight hours. He reports that in a very short time there was produced, without increase of staff, as much as before the reduction.‡

Another instance of a reduction of the hours of labour to eight per day is that of the Huddersfield Tramways, which are owned and worked by the Town Council. Here the reduction was made in March 1888, partly at the request of the workers, and partly because the tramways were becoming too profitable.§

* There are also some exceptional mines elsewhere with an eight hours day.

† In *A Plea for Liberty*, Mr. C. Fairfield argues that, in consequence of its Socialistic legislation, Victoria is virtually insolvent. It is sufficient answer to point out that, on the London Stock Exchange, which knows no sentiment, Victorian loans stand almost at the top of colonial securities, and return to the investor scarcely 3½ per cent. interest.

‡ *Revue des Deux Mondes*, November 1887, p. 132.

§ The explanation of this paradox is as follows: The Tramways Act of 1870 (33 and 34 Vic. c. 78), passed whilst John Bright was President of the Board of Trade, expressly prohibited local authorities from working their own lines. But the Huddersfield Town Council, after much importunity, succeeded in 1882 in obtaining power to do so by a private Act (45 and 46 Vic. c. 236). So afraid was the Board of Trade of this mild extension of municipal activity, that they insisted on a clause being inserted in the bill requiring the Town

The 14 hours day was accordingly increased to 16, but divided into two shifts. Wages were at the same time reduced, from 31s. to 26s. per week for drivers, and from 23s. to 21s. per week for conductors. The men usually seemed to prefer the shorter hours, even at the cost of lower wages; but there has not yet been time to see whether the fall in wages will be less temporary than that at Preston, on the passing of the Ten Hours Bill. It may be added that fares were not raised, the accommodation to the public was increased, the number of men employed rose by over 50 per cent., and the undertaking continues to yield a small profit over and above the payment of interest and sinking fund on the capital invested.

An instructive example of the economic effect of the adoption of an Eight Hours Day is the case of Brunner, Mond, & Co., Limited, the large chemical manufacturers at Winnington, Cheshire, and elsewhere. In 1890 the shifts were, at the men's request, reduced from twelve to eight hours each, and the piecework rates were increased. The increase, however, was not sufficient to maintain the weekly wage at the former level. A large number of additional men had to be engaged, and within a few months an additional ten per cent. increase in wages took place, which enabled the men to earn as much in eight hours as they had previously done in twelve.* Particulars of other cases will be found in the Appendix. The general result of these may be summed up as follows. The reduction to eight hours has taken place without any fall in wages, and with great advantage to all employed. In some cases production has not diminished at all, nor cost of production increased. Prices have in no case been affected, or the volume of trade reduced. In some cases a reduction of profit has taken place, but this is attributed to the fact that business rivals are left free to work the longer hours. In no case does the adoption of the Eight Hours Day appear to have been followed by any economic disaster.†

Council to lease out the lines to any contractor who should thereafter offer to pay a rental amounting to what the Board might consider a fair percentage on the cost of construction. It therefore became necessary to avoid making a profit which should tempt a contractor to insist upon compliance with this idiotic provision.   * *Times*, 8th January 1891.

† The warning against the fallacy of *post hoc ergo propter hoc* may be here usefully repeated. But these instances can legitimately be quoted in disproof of the argument that a reduction of the hours of labour necessarily implies a reduction of wages, etc.

3. The Theoretic Results of a General Reduction of the Hours of Labour in all Trades.

We are now in a position to endeavour to explain, by economic theory, the ascertained facts in connection with a limitation of the hours of labour. The economic problem differs according to whether we assume a general and equal reduction of hours throughout the community—an almost impossible event—or whether we contemplate the more probable issue of reductions in particular industries only. We begin with the more general and hypothetical case. A general reduction of the hours of labour might be expected to affect the total product, wages, prices, demand, international trade, profits, and the rate of interest.

Product.—It is difficult to predict whether and to what extent the aggregate gross product of commodities and services would be lessened in quantity or quality by a general reduction of the hours of labour. So far as positive evidence goes, the presumption is against any such diminution. The successive reductions of the hours of labour which this century has witnessed have been attended, after a very short interval, by a positive general increase in individual productivity. In many cases it has been found that the workers did more in ten hours than their predecessors in twelve. The effort to get more than a certain amount of work out of a man defeats itself. Even if an increase in quantity can be dragged out of that terrible "last hour" immortalised by Senior and Marx, it is often at the expense of the quality of the whole. And the speed of work lessens as the day advances. The shunters of goods trucks in busy railway centres, working twelve-hour shifts, do, as a matter of fact, dispose of 50 per cent. more trucks in the first six hours than in the second. It is calculated that in one large station this fact implies that the substitution of three eight-hour for two twelve-hour shifts would enable two hundred more trucks to be disposed of daily by the same actually working staff, at an additional cost in wages per truck of only 25 per cent.

In other instances it has been found possible to increase the speed of the machinery as the working hours were lessened, and there can be little doubt that this would often follow a further reduction. Moreover, a reduction of hours to eight per day would enable one intermission for a meal to be dispensed with. An

Eight Hours Day needs, for adults, only one break, and every employer knows the loss of time, slackening of speed, and weakening of energy which every break produces. This is pointedly referred to as a gain resulting from the Eight Hours Day in the letter from Mr. Samuel Johnson, and in the account of the interview with Mr. Mark Beaufoy, printed in the Appendix.

The possibility of maintaining the total amount of the product, notwithstanding a reduction of working hours, however incredible it may seem, is proved by too much evidence to allow of doubt. Universal experience in the textile trades may be accounted for by the greater speed now given to the machinery, but similar testimony comes from hand-workers. The cigar manufacturer at Hamilton (Canada),* who found that his workers made as many cigars in nine hours as in ten, is no exceptional witness. According to the testimony of the President of the Corporation of Miners in Germany, the workmen in mines attained their maximum production with eight hours of effective work. A temporary prolongation in autumn, for example, increased the output for the first three or four weeks; but after this period the production gradually sank, until it was no more for ten than for eight hours per day.†

The "business men" whose evidence is given in the Appendix agree that the product has not fallen off on their adoption of the Eight Hours Day. In the face of the experience of the Factory Acts, and of the corroborative testimony from all parts of the world, it seems no longer possible to infer, on purely theoretic grounds, that the product must necessarily be diminished by a further shortening of the working day. It is usually admitted that a longer working day would not be likely to increase the present product. Why should we assume, without argument, that the existing hours of labour are exactly those which result in the greatest possible quantity and the best possible quality of commodities?‡ A resort to actual experiment appears desirable, and

---

* See Chapter II.

† See article by Charles Grad, a member of the German Reichstag, *Revue des Deux Mondes*, November 1877, p. 132.

‡ Thorold Rogers, speaking of the excellent masonry of the Middle Ages, produced, as he proves, in an Eight Hours Day, says, "I am persuaded that such perfect masonry would have been incompatible with a long hours' day."—*Work and Wages* (abridged edition), p. 175.

the results of such experiments as have been made point rather in the other direction. General F. A. Walker, the eminent American economist, sums up for us the whole argument by a forcible imaginary case :—

"The new plea for the Eight Hours Law bases itself upon the theory that, on the whole, and in the long run, labour continued through only eight hours will yield as great a product to be divided among the several classes of the community as labour continued through the present somewhat varying term, from ten hours to, say, eleven or twelve.

"Now this claim is not, on the face of it, absurd. The rule of three cannot be applied to human labour without respect to conditions and circumstances innumerable. There is little doubt that all the successive reductions in the working day which have thus far taken place among certain labouring populations have resulted in an immediate gain to production, while they have led to a still further increase of productive power in the generation following. It has probably never occurred that a reduction of working time has been all loss, since a somewhat increased activity, a somewhat enhanced energy, has characterised each part of the time remaining.

" Let us take successive cases. Let it first be supposed that a community exists under the sway of a greedy remorseless tyrant, who compels all the able-bodied members of the community to labour in his fields or shops twenty hours a day, leaving but four hours for sleep, rest, and domestic duties or enjoyments. Now let it be supposed that this ruler is succeeded by a son, to the full as selfish as himself, but more intelligent. Doubtless it would not be long before the new-comer discovered that it was for his own interest to reduce the hours of labour to eighteen; and it would require no protracted experience of the new system to demonstrate that more wealth was actually produced in eighteen than had been in twenty hours. We may next suppose that years later the grandson of the first ruler is brought, by petition or by threatened rebellion, to consider the question whether he should reduce the number of hours from eighteen to fifteen. He would at the outset take this as a proposition to surrender one-sixth of his product for the pleasure and comfort of his working men —a proposition to which he would not graciously incline. But if he were as much wiser than his father as his father was wiser than the grandfather, he would soon come to see that this would not be so; that, at the worst, something less than a one-sixth loss would be involved in the change, since, for the fifteen hours remaining, the labourers both could, and doubtless would, work with somewhat more, perhaps much more, spirit than they could possibly do when worn out in body and mind by the longer day of labour. Should this more enlightened ruler call to his counsels the best physiologists and physicians, his most sagacious ministers, superintendents, and foremen, he would without much difficulty be brought to believe that the proposed reduction of time would involve no loss whatever to production; and trial would soon demonstrate to him, and to the most sceptical of his advisers, that protracting the hours of labour beyond the capabilities of the human frame had not been a source of gain, but of waste, hideous, appalling waste.

"Now, fifteen hours not unfairly represent the average day of work in European factories and workshops at the time when the attention of legislators first began to be directed towards the condition of the less fortunate classes, and when those classes began first to stir in their own behalf. It is the general belief of intelligent and disinterested men, that every successive reduction of the hours of labour from that point until the limit of, say, eleven hours a day, in ordinary mechanical pursuits, was reached, effected not a proportional loss of product, not a loss at all, but a positive gain, especially if not only the present productive power of the body of labourers is considered, but also the keeping up of the supply of labour in full numbers and in unimpaired strength from generation to generation.

"Personally, I should not hesitate to express the opinion that the further reduction from eleven hours to ten has been accomplished in some communities, like Massachusetts, without any appreciable loss to production, and with a clear, social, and physiological advantage to the community; but here we enter upon disputed ground."*

What is, in Massachusetts, still disputed ground has, in the United Kingdom, long since been admitted. A similar change in opinion may be predicted with reference to the reduction from ten to eight hours. Nevertheless, it is probable that in many occupations a net falling off would occur in the quantity of product produced, or amount of service rendered per day per head, not adequately compensated for by any improvement in quality. This might be either a temporary result, presently to be counteracted by the influences already referred to, or a permanent loss of productivity.† The reports of nearly all the English railway companies

* "The Eight Hours Law Agitation," by Principal F. A. Walker, *Atlantic Monthly*, June 1890.

† Professor J. E. C. Munro instances the evidence given to the Royal Commission on Depression of Trade—"The reduction of hours in the flax-spinning trade reduced the output in proportion, no relief being obtained from improved machinery." (Q. 7012.) It is difficult to reconcile this statement with the results in other branches of textile industry.

for 1890 bear witness to the necessity for increasing the staff brought about by a reduction of working hours. At the beginning of 1891 the London and North Western Railway Company reduced the hours of its shunters, with the consequence that their numbers had to be increased by one-third. When the gas-workers obtained the Eight Hours Day in 1888, many thousands of additional men had to be engaged to supply the same quantity of gas.

These cases make it obvious that a universal reduction of hours might even cause a reduction in average productivity per worker throughout the whole community. But this would by no means imply any diminution of the aggregate product. The first effect of any reduction of hours in many industries would be an increase in the number of workers. If the reduction of hours resulted in a diminution of the number of the "unemployed," who are obviously now maintained at the expense, one way or another, of the "employed," the aggregate product of the community might even be increased. This argument has been made light of by economists, and it must be admitted that it is often used by advocates of an Eight Hours Day in an inconsistent and untenable manner. It is by no means necessary to assume, as Professor Marshall supposes, "a fixed Work Fund, a certain amount of work which has to be done, whatever the price of labour."* As Professor Marshall himself goes on to point out, "the demand for work comes from the National Dividend," and the contention is that the National Dividend would not be diminished; the same product would be made; the same amount of work would therefore need to be done; some of those now working excessive hours would do less; and some now working irregularly or not at all might find an opportunity for doing more. Assuming for the moment that the aggregate product of the community does not fall off, there seems no economic objection to the contention that a limitation of the hours of labour might redistribute work.†

---

* *Principles of Economics*, vol. i. p. 700-2.

† General Walker adopts this view :—"Of course if by this plea for a general eight hour law, it is merely intended to divide up a given amount of employment and a given sum of wages among a larger number of labourers, there is nothing to be said about it, except that it is a very good-natured proposal, and that its acceptance would indicate an unexpectedly large amount of

That a reduction in the hours of labour, when it results in a diminution in average productivity, does result in the employment of additional workers, is proved by innumerable instances. The English railways, the Huddersfield tramways, and the gasworkers all over the kingdom are instances already sufficiently referred to. In the last case it may however be mentioned that the Gas Light and Coke Company, which supplies two-thirds of London, inserted advertisements in rural newspapers calling for several hundreds of able-bodied men from the ranks of agricultural labourers, who were at that winter season much in want of work. Nor is the sharing of work in this manner a new idea. In 1844 Sir H. G. (then Mr.) Ward, M.P. for Sheffield, who had voted against the Ten Hours Bill, was called to account by his constituents, and on the 28th January 1845 met in public debate certain representatives of the wage-earners. Sir H. G. Ward was an advocate for leaving the masters entirely uncontrolled, either by law or trade union rules. In the course of the debate his opponents produced several instances of the beneficial results of limiting the hours of labour in this very matter of providing for the unemployed.*

benevolence on the part of the more fortunate members of the working class." ("The Eight Hour Law Agitation," *Atlantic Monthly*, June 1890.) The English Trade Unionists, at any rate, always have in view this sharing of work with the unemployed in their respective trades. It forms the whole basis of their crusade against overtime.

* Among them were the following:—"In 1837 the combination of makers of joiners' tools broke up; the number of hands at that time in the trade was 80; in 1841 it had reached 109, besides apprentices; of this number two-thirds were receiving parish relief or working on the roads. By forming a union and limiting the hours of daily labour to eight they had succeeded in finding employment for all their men, of whom two-thirds were fully employed. The delegate of the saw-makers stated that in March 1844 his trade was in a very bad state. They had then in the union 210 men, of whom 186 were wholly or partially employed, and 24 were supported 'on the box'—*i.e.*, out of the funds of the society. By restricting the hours of labour they had made employment for 250 out of 265 members, at the expense of a payment of from 15 to 20 per cent. out of their wages. Two years ago the fork-makers and grinders were in great distress. By forming a union and restricting the hours of labour to six hours a day they were able to earn living wages." *

---

* *Social Science Association: Report of Committee on Trade Societies*, 1860, p. 645.

It has, however, been contended by critics* that a reduction in the hours of labour would not find work for the unemployed, because there are none such competent to take the work. It is, however, difficult to see how this view can seriously be held by persons acquainted with the facts of modern industry. It is certainly not shared by the Trade Unionists themselves. Professor Munro himself prints a table showing that, between 1872 and 1889, the Amalgamated Society of Engineers, composed of the very "aristocrats of labour," had from 397 to 5879 of its members employed, a proportion varying from 1 in 100 to 13 in 100 of its total membership. It may be true, as Professor Munro contends, that the reduction of the hours of labour does not, of itself, suffice to prevent fluctuations in trade and consequent fluctuations in the amount of engineering work to be done; but it can hardly be denied that, given the amount of work required in any one week, this could have been distributed over a larger number of competent men had such a distribution been desired by the men and enforced upon the employers. In 1879, when one engineer in eight was out of work, and in 1886, when a similar lot fell on one in thirteen, most of the others were working 54 hours per week, and many of them five to ten hours overtime. If the engineers had been able to do as the Sheffield trades actually did between 1837 and 1846, it cannot be doubted that work could have been more evenly shared.

Trades less skilled than the engineers show an even larger percentage of men out of work, and, as a matter of fact, neither railway companies nor gasworks have experienced any difficulty in largely increasing their staff. Nor is this state of things confined to England. Mr. Carroll D. Wright, the experienced Commissioner of the United States Bureau of Labour, estimates† that during the year ended 1st July 1885, 998,839 persons were out of work at one time in the United States, or 7½ per cent. of the whole body of workers. At that date it will be remembered that the 92½ per cent. at work were working on an average ten or eleven hours a day. General Walker, at any rate, sees no economic reason why the work thus done (and the wages thus earned) could not have been better

---

* As for instance, by Professor J. E. C. Munro in his paper before the British Association, September 1890, and by Professor J. E. Symes, in his article in the *Economic Review*, January 1891.

† *First Annual Report of United States Bureau of Labour*, 1886, pp. 65, 66.

distributed if the workers really desired this. It may, indeed, be admitted that many of the so-called "residuum" are unfit for severe manual toil, and that few of "the unemployed" could pass at once into the more skilled trades. But it is in such industries as the railways and tramways that the new demand is mainly to be expected, and it is quite possible to recruit these, as is, in fact, constantly done, from the ranks of labourers who are in a condition of irregular and partial work. A general shortening of the hours of labour would, in fact, be likely to result in a large transfer of workers from declining or imperfectly organised industries, such as wheat growing or London dock work, where employment is intermittent, to the regularly drilled and disciplined armies of the well-organised industries, with their regularity of work and wage.

There remains, as an alternative to an increase in the number of the employed, the increased use of labour-saving machinery. In almost every industry there are inventions already made, but which have to wait before being generally adopted because human labour is so abundant and so cheap. Connecticut uses more machinery than England, England more than Germany, Germany more than India. Any increasing scarcity of labour would undoubtedly stimulate both the invention and adoption of new machinery. To the extent in which this operated, the boon of a shortening of the hours of labour would of course not bear with it the additional boon of a thinning of the ranks of the unemployed. In actual practice probably both results would ensue, in degrees, varying in different occupations and in different countries. The outcome of it all seems to be that, in agreement with past experience, a further reduction of the hours of labour is not at all likely to diminish the aggregate product of the community. In some occupations, such as the railway and tramway service, the average production per head will almost certainly fall off, but on the other hand an additional number of workers will find themselves transferred from irregular to regular employment. But whether by greater energy, increased number of workers, or additional machinery, it appears probable that the total amount of the product can, as heretofore, be kept up. This probability is the key to the whole position, and the whole economic argument depends upon it.

Wages—Nor can it be assumed, as it usually is by the average man, that wages must fall if the working day is shortened. We have already referred to Lord Macaulay's indignant protest against this ignorant assumption. A whole crowd of subsequent cases, some of which have been mentioned, now warn us from any such hasty generalisation. The notion of the inevitability of a fall in wages on a diminution of the working day derives its force partly from the surviving superstition of a determinate "wages fund," incapable of increase, however many additional workers are taken on. It may indeed be true that the total amount which the wage-earners can obtain, so long as land and capital remain in individual ownership, is subject to very real, although quite intangible, economic limits.* But no economist would venture to assert that these limits have yet been reached.† The frequent assumption that profits cannot possibly suffer any permanent diminution is one which receives no support either from experience or modern economic theory.

If employers generally are engaging additional hands, *and the aggregate product is maintained*—a state of things which we have endeavoured to show to be probable—there seems no reason to doubt that capitalists are right in expecting even a rise in wages. Two masters, to use the old phrase, will be running after one man. A general reduction in the hours of labour is precisely equivalent to a diminution of the supply of labour daily offered for sale to the employers, without, necessarily, any diminution of the work done. The demand remaining the same (as there is the same amount of product required), the value will inevitably rise. Every employer

---

* See, for instance, a paper read at the British Association meeting at Newcastle in September 1889, by one of the present writers, in which these limits are asserted. ("The Relation between Wages and the Remainder of the Economic Product," by Sidney Webb.)

† "The working classes could have had more already, under the conditions existing, had they understood their interests better, and followed them up more closely and actively. *There is no reason to suppose that the possibilities of gain in this direction have been exhausted.*" ("The Eight Hour Law Agitation," by Principal F. A. Walker, *Atlantic Monthly*, June 1890.)—"There is no law of nature making it inherently impossible for wages to rise to the point of absorbing not only the funds which the capitalist (? *entrepreneur*) has intended to devote to carrying on his business, but the whole of what he allows for private expenses beyond the necessaries of life." (John Stuart Mill, *Fortnightly Review*, May 1869.)

admittedly expects to have to pay more in wages, and hence the bitter and persistent opposition of the spokesmen of this class to each successive restriction upon the hours of labour. If wages were really expected to fall in proportion to the shortening of hours, the employer would have but little motive in resisting the shortening; and no motive at all if he works his labour in shifts. The results of previous reductions of the working day seem, however, to show that the hope of the workers and fear of the employers is well founded. Every English railway and gas company during 1890 could confirm this view.

It is, however, sometimes objected that this rise in wages would be counteracted by a diminution in demand for labour, due either to diminished production, or to a rise in price. We have seen that the assumption of an aggregate diminution of production is an illegitimate one, and that even an increase might conceivably be looked for. This fact of itself implies the maintenance of the aggregate "demand." As Cairnes points out, "The total demand of a community would, under such circumstances, be represented by all the commodities and services there offered in exchange for other commodities and services; and these would also constitute the total supply in that community."* And, as Cairnes expressly added with regard to a universal Nine Hours Movement, "Why should it affect the relations between commodities in general and money?" Even granting, however, that such commodities might rise in price, the rise would, *ex hypothesi*, merely equal the increased amount paid in wages, so that, in the worst possible case, the "real wages" of the whole wage-earning class could not be less than before, and would indeed be more, because two-thirds of their products are not purchased by them. It is, however, almost certain that the necessary absorption of a portion of the "reserve army of industry," the unemployed and the partially employed, would so strengthen the power of labour in its negotiations with the employer, as to enable it to obtain even a rise in real wages by an Eight Hours Bill. That this has been the result of previous Factory Acts is undoubted. If the wage-earners press for such a measure, and are willing to risk its effect on wages, it is, at any rate, not for any other class to resist them on this ground.

* *Some Leading Principles of Political Economy*, p. 27. (Macmillan, 1874.)

A difficulty is sometimes felt in connection with the apparently obvious results of "piece-work." Where workers are paid by the hour or by the piece, a diminution of hours must, it seems at first sight, diminish their earnings. But wages by the hour or by the piece really follow the same course as wages by the day. The daily earnings of an average piece-worker tend to be identical with those of an equivalent worker for day wages, in accordance with which they are in reality arranged. What a workman considers is not the rate per piece, but the total that he earns in a week. Whether wages are depressed down to the very level of subsistence, or maintained above that rate by any "standard of comfort" to which the workers cling, it is the weekly total of the average worker which is economically first determined, and the piece-work rates do but fit this sum. This, indeed, is the actual process which is followed when a new job is introduced. The foreman puts a quick worker upon it at time wages, and sees how much is done in a week. The rate per piece is then fixed so as to fit the normal weekly wage.* But whereas in the case of time wages the onus of any reduction would be on the employer, in the case of piece-work wages it would be for the wage-earner to obtain an increase in the rates adequate to compensate for any falling-off in the product which the reduction of hours might cause. There is accordingly some risk of a reduction of the earnings of piece-workers if their productivity falls off with a reduction of hours. This is what happened to the Preston cotton operatives when the Ten Hours Bill became law, and to the chemical workers at Brunner, Mond, & Company's, when the Eight Hours Day was adopted. But in both these cases the play of economic forces soon caused a rise in the piece-work rates. The cigar-makers in New York have had a similar experience. Where no falling-off in production takes place (as is reported in the case of the Canadian cigar manufactory mentioned at page 104), there would, of course, be no fall in the weekly wages. To sum up: a general

* Professor J. E. C. Munro argued before the British Association that "if day wages governed piece wages we would expect to find the wages in skilled industries to approximate to the low wages of farm servants, but this has not been the case." This, surely, is the *reductio ad absurdum* of economic argument. No one contends that either day wages or piece-work rates can ride rough-shod over all the barriers between "non-competing groups."

reduction of the hours of labour may possibly lower the weekly earnings of some classes of workers, whose average production falls off, and especially such of them as are paid by the piece. But previous examples bear out what might be expected on theoretic grounds—viz., that the economic conditions which enable day wages to be maintained with shorter hours will quickly cause a rise in piece rates. On the whole, therefore, both experience and theory indicate that, so long as the aggregate amount of product be maintained, a reduction of hours can be made without any permanent fall in wages.

Prices.—The effect upon prices of a general shortening of hours might be complex. If, indeed, the wages of labour entered equally for all commodities into the manufacturers' expenses of production, the result would be, as we shall see, in the nature of a "general tax on profits," and would not affect relative exchange-values or prices at all. This has been thoroughly dealt with by the economists, and the reader may be referred to any manual on taxation* for a further elucidation of the results of such a tax. But as labour enters differently into the cost of different commodities, a universal reduction of the hours of labour, so far as it resulted in increasing the expense of manufacturing at all, would be analogous to a tax, not on profits, but on all commodities equal to the increased expense in each case, or to a general rise in the cost of labour to that extent. McCulloch worked out this problem for us† in a manner which still holds good. To equalise the expectation of profit as Mill sums it up, the value of the commodity, into which the cost of labour enters more than it does in others, must rise, and the corresponding alteration in relative demand probably implies a relative fall in the values of other commodities less affected by the change. There would be, as Mill points out, neither a general rise of values nor of prices, but a disturbance of both, some values rising and others falling.

But, in an enormous number of instances, prices, even in England or the United States, are so far fixed by custom that it would need a very great change to alter them. Penny newspapers or five-cent car fares could not be departed from without serious

---

* See, for instance, Mill's *Political Economy*, bk. v. ch. iii. § 3.

† *Principles of Political Economy*, pt. iii. sec. iii. § 2; see Mill, bk. v. ch. iv. § 1.

loss of custom. Retail prices are much more fixed by custom, and by the amount of the nearest current coin, than economists usually assume.

In the cases of such virtual monopolies as railways, tramways, gasworks, waterworks, docks, etc., prices are fixed with reference chiefly to the curve of demand. The aim in view is, of course, not the greatest gross return, but the greatest nett profit, and differences between much and little business in the expense of production cannot be left out of account. But in all these cases a large part of the expense of production is very slightly affected by moderate variations in demand or supply. Railway and tramway companies cannot reduce their working expenses in anything like exact correspondence with a falling traffic. Nor do they need to increase them in proportion to a rising one. Passenger fares and goods rates are therefore avowedly fixed mainly upon a view of "What the trade will bear"—that is to say, not at the cost of production, but at such amounts as will induce the greatest possible amount of traffic, consistently with covering the bare cost of the increased business. The price of gas, dock dues, and bridge and pier tolls are other instances of a similar nature. Uniform rates of postage and telegrams, and the recently adopted "zone tariffs" on the Hungarian railways, are other examples of the growing influence of this calculation. In all these cases prices could scarcely be moved by any moderate alteration of the hours of labour; and indeed price is probably the most rigid of all the possible economic variants likely to be affected by such a cause.*

International Trade.—It may be inferred with equal safety that a general alteration in the hours of labour would not necessarily affect the total amount of our exports. Any general appreciable rise of prices has been shown to be improbable. If some values were raised and exports checked, others would be lowered and exports encouraged. But even if the expenses of production of all

---

* Thorold Rogers appears to have held a similar view. "It is rarely the case, however, that the liberal reward of labour is followed by a material enhancement of price. *No one believes that if the London seamstresses, tailors, and matchbox-makers received double the wages which they do at present, there would be an appreciable difference in the price of the products sold, or any present risk that any of those industries would cease to be plied in this country.*"
—*Work and Wages* (abridged edition), p. 203.

commodities were raised, and with them their prices, it may be shown that the total exports would not thereby be reduced. This apparent paradox depends on the conditions determining international values, which, first elucidated by Torrens and Ricardo, have been accepted and developed by (to name only English authorities) Mill, Cairnes, Jevons, Professors Marshall and Bastable. Briefly summed up, the theory amounts to this—that international trade does not depend on the superiority of one country over another in relative expense of production, but upon the existence of differences between the relative advantage (or even disadvantage) possessed by either country in producing various classes of its own commodities. According to theory, "England might import corn from Poland and pay for it in cloth, even though England had a decided advantage over Poland in the production of both the one and the other."* This paradoxical result actually happens in fact, and we find ourselves profitably exporting cotton goods to America, woollens to Australia, knives to Sweden, and copper kettles to New South Wales, although these could all be produced with less labour on the spot. During the Australian gold fever Ireland actually sent butter to Victoria, and it would almost have paid for Melbourne to have got its washing done in London. They could produce all these things actually cheaper than we do, but as they can produce other commodities to even greater advantage, they prefer, in spite of hostile tariffs, to do so.

Hence the paradox, that our export trade does not depend on being able to produce more cheaply than our neighbours; and England to-day freely imports locomotives from Belgium, wooden frames from Germany, and "notions" from America, although these could all be produced, remembering the labour of carriage, with much less labour here. Bermuda supplies New York with the finest possible early potatoes, but actually imports from New York other potatoes for its own use rather than grow them. In each case these imports are paid for by the export of some commodity in which the advantage in production is greater. We weave our wheat on Rochdale looms, grind our meat on Sheffield stones, and hew our wool in Durham coal-pits, not necessarily because we can work these industries to greater advantage than our neighbours, or because we cannot produce the imported com-

* Mill, *Political Economy*, bk. iii. ch. xvii. § 1.

modities, but because we can weave, grind, and mine to greater advantage than we can produce food. It is the English farmer, not the American cotton-spinner, who is really competing with Lancashire.

If the cost of labour entered in equal proportion into the expense of production of all commodities, no shortening of hours or rise of wages would affect the relative advantage of one occupation over another, and, accordingly, this would also have no influence whatsoever on our international trade.

Any alteration in the export trade which the resulting disturbance of values would actually cause (owing merely to the varying extent to which different industries would be affected) would be merely an alteration in the proportion in which the aggregate of exports was made up.* The total export trade could not thereby be affected. This conclusion may be derided by the practical man, but it is, at any rate, the unanimous judgment of economists. What the practical man fears is a rise in general time wages, and, to use the words of Cairnes, "A rise or fall of wages in a country, so far forth as it is general, has no tendency to affect the course of foreign trade." †

Turning, however, to such considerations as the ordinary man prefers to any but his own economic reasoning, it may be contended that a gradual widespread shortening of the hours of labour would not be likely to affect our export trade—(1) because former similar reductions have not done so: the textile exports especially having enormously increased; (2) because, even now, the English cotton-spinner works fewer hours than his foreign competitors, and finds their competition keenest where their hours are shortest (as in Massachusetts), not where they are longest (as in Russia); (3) because it has been theoretically predicted and empirically proved that the reduction would not affect prices generally; and (4) because other countries are all rapidly increasing their factory legislation also. Even if some of them do not adopt an Eight Hours Law, they are all imposing new restrictions on their manu-

---

* This general conclusion does not therefore preclude the necessity for a very careful examination of the probable results of a shortening of hours of labour upon the export trade of any particular industry—a point which will be dealt with later.

† *Some Leading Principles of Political Economy*, p. 400.

factures. Moreover, in countless industries there can be no question of foreign competition. In the railway industry, and other internal means of transport; in the building and engineering trades; in baking, butchering, the supply of milk, and various other commodities; in the theatrical and newspaper industries; in all the forms of artistic or personal service, and in innumerable other departments of the industrial army, there need be no fear of foreign competitors.

Restriction of Demand.—Seeing that the cost of labour does not enter equally into the price of commodities, a general increase in that cost might, as we have seen, cause a "disturbance of values," raising some and lowering others. Grounds have been given for supposing that this alteration of values will not be great, but it would probably occur in some cases. Hence, there may arise, in the cases where prices are raised (*i.e.*, in trades using relatively little machinery and inexpensive raw material), a diminution in the demand for certain commodities, either for home consumption or for export. As the aggregate production or aggregate export trade need not fall off, this does not imply any nett reduction in demand for commodities or for labour, but it does imply a shifting of that demand. In some cases the commodities which have become dearer will cease to be consumed, and the amount formerly expended on them will be devoted to other purchases. Moreover, where wages benefit at the expense of profits, the increased demand of the workers will be substituted for any diminution in the personal expenditure of the capitalists. Some shifting of labour might therefore have to take place, but there is little reason to suppose that the diminution in any one occupation would at any time be considerable, or indeed more than the increased demand for labour due to the shortening of hours.

In some instances, however, the trade might be absolutely extinguished. It is possible that several of the minor industries of the East End are absolutely dependent upon the fact that a low type of "sweated" and overworked labour is employed at starvation wages. It is possible that the commodities so produced would not be worth having at all unless at the low price made possible by this "white slavery." In such a case, the extinction of the industry is the social price to be paid for the improvement of these workers' condition. The cheapness of their product is the price of blood, and the

Democracy may be trusted to want none of it. Our forefathers forewent slave-grown sugar, and the New Englanders gave up taxed tea, for ulterior social ends. We can at any rate do without farthing toys, or penny puzzles, if this is necessary to heal the spreading social ulcer of East End degradation.*

But what, it may be asked, is to become of the workers employed in these wretched industries : will they not be worse off than before? In no wise. The notion that labourers depend for their employment on work being "found" for them is a widespread but stupid fallacy. The money hitherto spent on these blood-stained commodities, the capital hitherto employed in their production, and the labour devoted to their manufacture, would alike be transferred—mediately, if not immediately—to other industries. The necessity for increasing the staff in all industries, which a reduction of hours would probably involve, would at once enable these workers to be absorbed, possibly at higher wages, and certainly under better conditions, than they had hitherto enjoyed.

Rate of Profit.—Where, then, it may be asked, will the pecuniary loss due to a shortening of the hours of labour really fall? It cannot be admitted that any general loss will necessarily take place, but if such a diminution in the nation's annual production should actually occur, it would fall mainly upon profits. The new Factory Act would have imposed a new restriction upon industry analogous to a general tax on profits, and such a tax cannot be shifted either upon the wage-earner or the consumer. Profits, in the ordinary sense, are made up of interest on capital, insurance against risk, and the wages of management. The two latter items would not be affected, and the whole result would be seen in a diminution of interest on capital.

Still more is this likely to be the result if no diminution in the aggregate product of the community takes place, as we have endeavoured to show to be the probable outcome. It is practically certain that a tendency to a reduction in the rate of interest on capital was one of the main economic results of the previous Factory Acts. The gradually increasing restrictions co-operated with the increased competition to reduce the "thousands per

---

* An experienced philanthropist said to one of the present writers, "I would pay a heavy price to extinguish these East End industries, at whatever temporary risk to the workers in them."

cent.," which made the fortune of Lancashire, to the normal rate of manufacturing profit now enjoyed. The nameless iniquities of the "white slavery" may be presumed to have been pecuniarily profitable to the factory slave masters, and every restriction of them was, at any rate, denounced as a confiscation of a part of the capital invested in the mills. Even as late as 1844, as we have seen, Sir James Graham and the capitalist press were raising the cry of "Jack Cade" against Lord Shaftesbury. The rate of loan interest, being the measure of the marginal effectiveness of capital, tends to fall with every limitation or restriction which is placed upon the employment of capital. As one profitable sphere of employment after another is forbidden, whether the slave trade, slave breeding, lotteries, the keeping of gambling hells, or gin-distilling, new openings must be found for the use of capital, or its effectiveness at the "margin of utilisation" inevitably falls, implying a corresponding fall in the normal rate of loan interest. If any general economic loss has followed the present restrictions, this is where it has fallen. If any pecuniary loss is involved to the community in a further shortening of the hours of labour, it is the recipients of interest and dividends who are likely to have to bear it. The distribution of the nation's income will have been altered so that (for less work) the wage-earners receive as much as before, and the capitalists a reduced amount. All interest will be affected. And it is conceivable that a future Chancellor of the Exchequer might even reduce the rate of interest upon "Goschens." A similar rise in the "margin of cultivation" of "land," especially mines, quarries, etc., may, at the same time, slightly diminish the aggregate "rent" of immovable capital, though this will almost certainly be masked by increasing urban developments.

Increase of Capital.—Such a fall in the rate of interest would formerly have been thought inevitably to lead to a slackening in the rate of accumulation of capital, and so to a renewed rise of interest. No effective encroachment, in the view of the older economists, could possibly be made on the tribute of interest, as any diminution thereof automatically brought about a subsequent increase, either through slackened savings or investment abroad. This obsolete theory is, as usual, still current in the minds of ordinary men and of leader writers, but the economist himself

THE PROBABLE ECONOMIC RESULTS.

knows it no more. Professor Marshall tells us* that many men would save as much if the rate of interest were lowered as they do now, and the uniform experience of the savings bank all over the world confirms this view. Professor Sidgwick, moreover, tells us that he is "aware of no adequate empirical reason for supposing, with Mill, Cairnes, and others, that the rate of interest in England at the present day is very near the minimum point,"† below which it could not fall without causing a diminution of capital.

The question of a possible emigration of capital is more intricate, but it may be observed—(1) that the rate of loan interest in England is uniformly lower than elsewhere, and yet the emigration of capital which has hitherto taken place has been a mere overflow of surplus annual savings ; (2) that quite three-fourths in value of what is called capital (including, that is, the land, mines, railways, harbours, buildings of all kinds) is absolutely incapable of emigration ; and (3) that other nations are increasing their factory legislation parallel with our own advance, so that the gap is not by any means widening. A revolution in Brazil or a panic in Argentina is, moreover, far more potent in discouraging foreign investments than any difference in the rate of interest. The notion of any important emigration of capital in consequence of an Eight Hours Bill appears, indeed, as chimerical as the same threat proved to be in the cases of the Ten Hours Bill and the general Nine Hours Movement.

To sum up the probable economic results, as far as they can be discerned :—

A general shortening of the hours of labour may slightly decrease the average productivity per worker, but will, by absorbing a part of the unemployed, probably increase the total production of the community.

Supply, and therefore demand, will, in the aggregate, not be diminished.

No effect will be produced upon prices generally, but some variations up and down may take place in the prices of some particular commodities.

Some industries may therefore be diminished, whilst others are

* *Economics of Industry.*
† *Principles of Political Economy*, p. 291.

increased; some few products may no longer be worth producing once the labour employed is properly treated.

Wages generally are more likely to be raised than lowered, though it is possible that they may remain stationary, or even temporarily droop, in a few industries.

The aggregate payment in wages will almost certainly be larger, and that for interest on capital smaller, than before.

The total export trade will almost certainly not be affected, though it may be somewhat varied in its composition.

And the main permanent results are likely to be a rise in "real time wages," and a fall in the normal rate of loan interest.

But even these economic consequences of a sudden and universal shortening of hours, whether by law or by trade union pressure, are not at all likely to ensue in any perceptible manner upon the gradual and partial shortening which is all that is likely to happen. In industrial organisation any sudden change, however good, produces a serious dislocation; but almost any gradual change, however important, can be endured without social injury. Time is of the essence of the matter.

4. *The Economic Results of an Eight Hours Day in particular Industries.*

We have hitherto been considering the probable economic results of a general shortening of the hours of labour in all industries throughout the country. Such a result might conceivably be brought about by a general law, or even by a widespread determination of public opinion. It is, however, much more probable that the shortening of hours will begin in one or two industries and spread gradually to others. Eight Hours Laws for miners, railway workers, and tramway men are likely to precede by some years any more general measure. This more gradual course has, it may be observed, the support of the precedent of the Factory Acts. The Act of 1802 applied only to parish apprentices, and those of 1819, 1825, and 1831 only to cotton mills; in 1833 legislative protection was extended to all textile industries, in 1842 to underground mines. The Acts of 1860, 1861, and 1863 applied to dyeworks, bakehouses, and lace factories. Then came the more general extension of 1864, which brought under inspection potteries, match factories, paper stainers, fustian cutters, cartridge and cap makers, and some other industries. By 1867 we had got to iron and copper works, the manufacture of hardware, cutlery, machinery, gutta percha, paper, glass, and tobacco, and the printing and bookbinding trades. The application of the 1878 Act to all factories and workshops was therefore reached only after seventy-six years of piecemeal legislation.

Assuming, therefore, that the shortening of hours occurs in one industry before another, it may be remarked that, although the results as regards productivity and the unemployed will not differ from those of a general shortening, those relating to wages, profits, prices, and the export trade need fresh consideration. A grant of the special advantage of shorter hours to any one industry involves an alteration of the "relative nett advantages" of that industry over others. The entrance of workers into that industry would therefore, so far as mobility of labour prevails, tend to be encouraged. This influence would tend to neutralise the forces making for a rise in wages in that industry, and would tend rather to raise wages in other industries where longer hours were still worked. The influx into the ranks of the gas stokers in 1888, when their hours were reduced from twelve to eight, prevented them from receiving at the same time anything more than a slight increase in wages, whilst it must have considerably strengthened the workers' position in those industries from which the new hands were drawn. In this way *every* wage-earner is interested in *any* Eight Hours Bill; and a shortening of hours in government factories, mines, and railways may benefit not only those whose leisure is increased thereby, but also the less fortunate workers outside, whose wages are thereby made to rise. This result may happen, too, either by the actual depletion of their ranks, or by the thinning of the horde of unemployed hanging on the outskirts of that portion of the industrial army.

In so far as the shortening of hours were to involve a loss of profits in the particular industry, the usual assumption is that this would be followed by a diversion of the flow of new capital from that industry to others relatively more profitable. This would, of course, not apply to government or municipal employments, where the increased cost of production caused by shorter hours would fall upon the public which had demanded it. Nor can it be said to apply in any real sense to such virtual monopolies as railways, which (in England in 1891) now absorb annually but little new capital.* Where this diversion of the flow of new capital does take place, either by a change in public demand, caused by alteration in prices, or by any other unsettling of the relative profitableness of industries, it must not be forgotten that it tends to raise wages in the trades to which the flow of capital is increased, just as much as it tends to depress them in trades momentarily less tempting to the investor or his banker. In this manner also other workers are likely to benefit in wages when any trade gets an Eight Hours Day for itself. The possible export of capital to other countries has already been dealt with and shown to be unlikely, even in the case of a general shortening of hours. Still less is it likely to happen merely because one or two industries in the community no longer offer the capitalist so large a profit as other industries in that same community.

It may indeed be suggested, in the light of past experience, that the check to the flow of new capital, even to any one industry, is hardly likely to occur to any appreciable extent. In many instances the shortening of hours would not diminish the production of the worker, and so no fall of profits would ensue. In others the shortening would be likely to give a fillip to the introduction of double shifts or of labour-saving machinery, and so actually increase the investment of capital and the margin of profit in that trade. In some other cases the persistence of the demand will permit a rise in price preventing any fall of profit. There might, nevertheless, remain a class of cases in which the industry, rendered less profitable to the capitalist, would become stationary, or even slowly dwindle, for want of new capital and new managerial ability. Industries producing for export might be unable to raise their prices consistently with retaining their foreign sales; and other producers might find that a rise in prices caused too great a check to demand to make the change a profitable one. We have already drawn attention to the fact, moreover, that some minor industries now exist, in all probability, only because of the very degradation of the labour employed in them. These might stop if the workman had to be treated as a human being, just as pyramid

* The increase of railway capital in the United Kingdom during the last ten years has been less than 2 per cent. per annum.

making died out when slaves could no longer be impressed by the tens of thousands. In all these cases the workers would run some risk of a reduction of wages if they insisted on any reduction of hours which really reduced their productivity, and if the resulting increase in cost of production could not in any other way be made up. This possible reduction would be more likely to occur at once in the case of workers by the piece than in that of workers by the day, and the risk is most obvious where profits are believed to have been already closely "shaved" by strong Trade Unions, and where the industry depends largely upon export sales.

(a.) *The Textile Trades.*

The considerations last referred to apply with special force to the spinning and weaving of cotton, and explain the natural hesitation of the Lancashire labour leaders to renew in 1890 their successful agitations for shorter hours, which ended with 1847 and 1874 respectively. Many towns in Lancashire produce almost entirely for export, and already feel keenly the competition of New England mills in the China market, and of the growing development of the Indian textile industry. It is contended that no rise in price is possible; that the acceleration of machinery has already reached its utmost limit, and that profits have been already cut so fine that "cotton pays no better than Consols." The fact that many of the operatives own shares in joint-stock mills makes them perhaps even more keenly alive to this point of view than the rank and file of other trades.

Many Lancashire operatives believe, however, that the actual experience of the past warrants them in disregarding the theoretical warnings of their leaders. They believe that no very great diminution of product would result from a shorter day; that this diminution could, on some articles, be made up by a slight increase in price; and that in other cases the margin of profit is sufficient to bear any nett loss that might be involved. The latter contention appears to be sustained by the very large number of new mills which were built during 1890, and by the fact that the average dividend on 85 cotton spinning companies reported in the *Economist* of 10th January 1891 was $7\frac{7}{8}$ per cent. Towards the end of 1890, indeed, the operatives so far proved this view by obtaining a rise in wages of 10 per cent., an amount which would certainly have allowed the alternative of a reduction of hours from 56½ to 48, had this been preferred. With regard, moreover, to the English export of cotton goods, it may be observed that this is growing at a very great rate per annum. The influence of American or Indian competition upon this increase has hitherto been comparatively small, and is not likely, in the near future, to be adequate to counteract the effect of new markets, diminished freights, and the growth of peace and prosperity in Africa. The competition which is really most felt by Lancashire mills producing for foreign markets is that of their rivals in the same county, and a general shortening of hours would, as it did in 1847 and 1874, leave the relative position of the competitors practically unaltered. The point is, however, essentially one for decision by the workers in the trade concerned, and the "Trade Option" clause of the Eight Hours Bill of the Fabian Society would preserve to this or any other industry the privilege of retaining their longer hours of labour as long as they felt disposed to do so. The general adoption of a shorter day in other industries would, in such a case, not injure the position of those who retained longer hours. It would, indeed, tend to raise their wages both by the discouragement of recruits to the ranks of the workers in a long hours trade, and by the encouragement of capitalists to invest in what would have become a relatively more than usually profitable industry.

(b.) The Coal Miners.

No such difficulties as those which beset the textile operatives are felt by the English, Scotch, and Welsh coal miners. These are practically unanimous in demanding an Eight Hours Day, although most of those in Northumberland and Durham withhold their support from the Eight Hours Bill backed by practically the whole of their colleagues. Nor does English public opinion generally resist this demand. It is commonly felt that the work of a miner is disagreeable, laborious, and dangerous. The industry is exceptional in its character, and a working day of eight hours or less already prevails in some mines, which are not reputed to be otherwise than profitable to their owners. Indeed, the fact that the 2104 coal mines in England and Wales are worth an estimated

THE PROBABLE ECONOMIC RESULTS. 127

rental of £3,601,836,* which is 7 per cent. of the value of the coal produced, and nearly 70 per cent. of the nett profit of working the mines, shows that this industry, at any rate, possesses a margin which could be considerably cut down without causing it to cease. The miners at present work, on an average, about nine hours per day, so that the reduction of output by a general adoption of the Eight Hours Day could not be very great. Any such reduction of output would moreover involve the advantage of economising our national stock of coal, in accordance with the suggestions of Jevons and Mill. What would be the result upon wages and prices?

It appears to be clear that the coal workers believe that an Eight Hours Day would, by checking the output, raise the price of coal. The owners and lessees of coal mines, as far as we have been able to learn, entertain a similar view. The demand for coal during 1890 has been very brisk, and prices have already risen considerably without appreciably checking it. As regards the home trade, indeed, coal has become so much of a prime necessity of life that a rise in price affects the demand even less than is the case with wheat. On the other hand, it must be remembered that the coal-fields of South Africa and Australia are rapidly coming into economic local use, with a possible check to our export trade. There seems, however, in this case no sufficient theoretic warrant for disputing the common judgment of those best acquainted with the industry, and it may therefore be accepted that the price of coal will rise when the Miners' Eight Hours Bill becomes law.

This anticipated rise in price, due entirely to intensity of demand, is independent of any expected increase in the cost of production. Whether any such increase would take place in all mines is not clear. We have already given instances which support the view that the miners would be likely to work with greater energy and steadiness if their day's toil were limited to eight hours from bank to bank. Some other mines might adopt the two-shift system now in force in the United Kingdom only in Northumberland and Durham. The rise in price might, too, stimulate production in mines not now worked to their full capacity, and the adoption of improved appliances for working. Nevertheless, it seems probable that a check might be given to

* House of Commons Return of 1890.

the rapidly increasing output of coal, and its production per ton thereby rendered more costly, in respect of the invariable part of the expense of working, than it would otherwise have been. This does not, however, necessarily involve any actual increase in the cost of production per ton. Since 1886 the total production in the United Kingdom has increased, on an average, by over six million tons annually, being about 4 per cent. on the output of the previous year.* A reduction of the output would therefore probably operate first in stopping what would otherwise have been an actual increase, and this would be consistent with no actual increase in the cost of production. The miners, however, expect to get with their reduction of hours a positive increase of wages, not only per ton, but also for the week's work, owing to the attempt of the managers to increase the staff. In this expectation they are probably correct, as coal miners are already very fully employed, and their numbers cannot be rapidly increased.† Nevertheless their numbers are liable to be gradually augmented as wages rise, and the miners, like other wage-earners, would find their higher wages endangered by new competitors for the work.

Higher wages would doubtless, as on former occasions, be considered by the public ample warrant for the increase in price of coal really caused by the limitation of the supply. No fall in rents or profits would therefore be likely to take place, and the shorter hours would have led merely to higher prices and higher wages. The public would have taxed itself for the benefit of the coal miners. This the public appears to be willing to do. There seems an almost universal feeling that the miners' hours should be shortened, and (as in the case of public employés) the acceptance of the measure proposed could only result from this public consent having been given.‡

* One mine as to which inquiry was made is employing in January 1891 10 per cent. more men than two years ago.

† Under the rules of the Mines Regulation Act a miner must have worked for two years in a pit before he can work at the face.

‡ It is interesting to note that those who advise the miners to shorten their hours by Trade Union action are advising them to tax the public for their own advantage, without seeking the public's consent. This appears to be as much open to ethical criticism as the action of landlords in maintaining the Corn Laws, or that of the capitalists who formed the Chicago " Wheat Corner " or Paris " Copper Ring."

It has been contended that a shortening of the hours in coal mines would be really an economical measure, as many accidents happen towards the end of the working day. This argument is fallacious, so far as it relates to explosions. Mr. Fenwick, the Northumbrian miners' representative in the House of Commons, has invariably disputed it; and, in order to remove all possibility of doubt on the subject, he made an analysis of the official returns for the ten years ended 1889. He found that during that period 146 explosions, involving the loss of 1439 lives, occurred in the first five hours of the shift; whereas only 57 explosions, involving the loss of 424 lives, occurred in the second five hours. Mr. Fenwick explains this preponderance during the earlier hours by the unnoticed accumulation of gas when no one is working in the mine. It would therefore seem to be a safer course to work the mine continuously, with three shifts at the face, and improved arrangements for haulage and drawing. This system, which would enable production to be confined only to the mines most easily worked, is probably impossible until all the coal mines in the country (like all the salt mines) are managed in one interest. It is possible that a shortening of the working day, with a rise of wages, might result in the closing of a few pits just on "the margin of cultivation," and so tend slowly to this advantageous concentration.

(c.) *Railway Workers.*

A unanimity almost as great as that of the coal miners prevails among the railway workers. Both the Unions and an enormous majority of the employés agree in demanding an Act of Parliament to limit the hours of labour. They do not, indeed, ask as yet for a universal Eight Hours Day, except for signalmen. For other railway workers they ask only for a Sixty Hours Week, with some limit on the number of hours to be worked at a stretch. The economic position, in the case of the railways, is comparatively simple. There is no question of the "capital leaving the country," or of the industry being destroyed by foreign competition. Each man's product falls, too, almost in proportion to his hours.* The economic inquiry is narrowed down to a question of wages, cost of

* See, however, the instance quoted at page 103, and the question of accidents referred to at page 80.

working, and profits. Nor can there be much doubt as to the effect upon wages. A reduction of the average working hours by at least 20 per cent. can hardly fail, in this case, to be followed by an almost proportionate increase in the staff employed. This would involve the engagement throughout the United Kingdom of at least 80,000 extra men as porters, shunters, guards, examiners, signalmen, drivers, and firemen. When every station-master in the kingdom was inquiring for additional men, it is hardly likely that wages would go down. A rise would, indeed, be almost inevitable, especially in the more highly skilled branches. Nor does this rest merely on theoretic grounds. During the year 1890 almost every English railway company was forced, by Board of Trade pressure and public opinion, to shorten the hours of some, at any rate, of its employés. With almost equal unanimity the Directors' Reports or the Chairmen's speeches allude also to increase of staff, rise of wages, and a corresponding rise in working expenses. The absorption into this one industry of 80,000 additional men could hardly fail, indeed, to raise wages in every trade in which men were previously getting less than railway wages.

The total cost of working would no doubt be increased by very nearly the amount of the growth in the wages bill. There can, however, be little doubt that the excessive hours now often worked conduce to railway accidents, and a systematic reduction might therefore probably lead to a diminution of the waste and loss caused thereby. To this extent the increase in the cost of working would be lessened. The nett increase in the cost of working could hardly be made up by higher prices. The percentage of working expenses to gross receipts has increased in the United Kingdom from 47 per cent. in 1860 to 52 per cent. in 1889, but goods rates and passenger fares have been greatly reduced. The public inquiry into railway rates, which has taken place both in the United States and in the United Kingdom, has made it abundantly clear that freights are fixed with almost exclusive reference to the demand, and with scarcely any regard for cost of working. "We charge," say the railway managers, "in each case what the trade will bear."*

* "The movement of a commodity by rail is determined by considerations wholly independent of, and not affected by, the cost of the service to be performed." (*Report of U.S. Senate Committee on Interstate Commerce*, 1886, p.

The rate is fixed, practically, so as to bring in the greatest possible amount of revenue, and railway business varies in profitableness with almost every item. Rates, moreover, are not easily changed, and an increase in the cost of working (such as occurred in the United Kingdom in 1890) does not, as a matter of fact, affect them in any appreciable degree.

The case is much the same with passenger fares, which have during the present generation been usually much reduced on the grounds already referred to. Uniform rates, such as the "zone tariff" of the Hungarian State Railways, indicate a still further disregard of cost of working in fixing the price of the service rendered. We may therefore assume that railway shareholders are warranted in believing that any increase in the cost of working will come out of their dividends. That there is ample margin for any such reduction is shown by the following statistics :—

United Kingdom, Year 1889 (to 31st December)—

Total Railway Receipts	£77,025,017
,, ,, Expenses	40,094,116
Surplus	£36,930,901

United States, Year 1888-89 (to 30th June)—

Total Railway Receipts	$1,089,985,831
,, ,, Expenses	768,627,345
Surplus	$321,358,345

The percentage which this surplus bears to the "total capital" is misleading, as this so-called capital includes, both in England and America, an enormous proportion of "watered" stock, and by no means corresponds with the amount of social capital really sunk in constructing the lines. It may, however, be said that the

184.)—"The cost of service principle is neither practised nor practicable. The attempt to base rates solely in cost is a pure chimera. Well-nigh every expert, whether scientist, official, or legislator, and every Parliamentary Commission from the early English to the late Italian and American, absolutely discards it as a principle." ("Railway Tariffs," by Dr. E. R. A. Seligman, *Political Science Quarterly*, vol. ii. No. 2.)—" En matière de tarification de transports il n'y a qu'une seule règle qui soit rationelle ; c'est de demander à la marchandise tout ce qu'elle peut payer." (Dictum of M. Solacroup, a leading French railway director. See Villey, *Traité d'Economie Politique*, 1885, p. 206, and article above quoted.)

average percentage on the swollen nominal capital is, in the United Kingdom, 4.21, and in the United States, 3.56.

A reduction of the hours of labour to 60 per week would probably involve an addition to the staff in the United Kingdom of about 80,000 men, whose wages, at an average of £50 per annum, would involve an increased charge of £4,000,000, or a reduction of the annual surplus from 37 to 33 millions sterling. The average rate of interest on the swollen nominal capital would fall from 4.21 to 3.75 per cent. It can therefore scarcely be contended that the introduction of a Sixty Hours Week for our railway workers would have ruinous economic results. If the community chose to take over the management of its own railways, it could safely reduce the hours of all the workers to forty-eight hours per week, and yet easily pay out of the annual surplus, without any rise in rates, the interest on the new "Railway Consols" which had been created to pay off the present shareholders.

(d.) Tramway Workers.

Closely analogous to the case of the railway worker is that of the tramway men. These now work usually from 14 to 16 hours, with very brief intermissions for meals, and are on duty usually for seven days in the week. A reduction of the hours of labour to forty-eight per week would involve therefore an average doubling of the staff. The "product," that is, the service to the public, would at the same time be slightly increased, as the working of two eight-hour shifts would enable all the lines to run cars during sixteen hours a day. Nor is it likely that the fares would be raised. The tramway managers, like the railway managers, fix the fares at the amount that will yield the greatest gross receipts, and the adoption of penny fares in London a few years ago shows that this was considered the most profitable rate. This calculation would not be affected by a rise in the wages bill, which is indeed the same whether the cars are full or empty.

Wages are not likely to fall at a time when the staff is being doubled,* especially as they are, in London and New York

* When the Huddersfield Town Council reduced, in 1888, the hours of its tramway workers from 14 to 8 per day, a reduction in wages was made, of 31s. to 26s. per week for drivers, and 23s. to 21s. per week for conductors. (See

particularly, among the lowest rates current for adult men. Probably the whole loss would fall on the shareholders. The statistics of tramways in the United Kingdom for 1889-90 are as follows :—

Total Receipts	£3,214,743
Total Expenses	2,402,800
Surplus	£811,943

This surplus amounts to six per cent. on the total capital. A Twelve Hours Day for all tramway workers, which is all that they yet demand, might perhaps involve the engagement of 4000 extra men, whose wages, at an average of £55 per annum, would come to £220,000, or about one-quarter of the present nett profits.

In the case of London, which contains one-eighth of the tramway mileage of the United Kingdom, the existing annual profits of £185,000 would enable the County Council, if it chose to work its own lines, to reduce the hours of labour from about 98 to 48 per week, and yet have surplus enough to meet, without any increase of fares, the annual interest on the cost of taking over the lines.*
It is, of course, quite possible that the increased cost of working tramways under an eight hours law would render unprofitable, and therefore prevent, the building of new lines in districts where, under present conditions, the margin of profit would be small. This is an obstacle which meets the social reformer at every turn. Public opinion has already emphatically declared that the advantages of cheap clothing and cheap furniture must be foregone, in so far as this is necessary to raise the condition of the underpaid workers in the sweating dens of the East End of London. In this case the public have to choose between a possible increase in cheap means of locomotion and the continued oppression of a large class of workers. Those who urge this objection to a general reduction of tramway hours will have to show that the gain to the

Appendix.) But in this exceptional case the men, who had previously been paid more than the current rate, had voluntarily agreed to take a lower wage, in consideration of their peculiarly favoured position compared with other tramway workers. Moreover, these men are employed by a public authority, in which case wages are fixed largely on non-competitive lines.

* The dividends of the two main metropolitan companies for 1890 were at the rate of 7 and 10 per cent. respectively.

public by extensions of the tramway system in a few districts will outweigh the social loss resulting from the overwork of the whole class of tramway men. The interests of the many would, in this case, be sacrificed for the benefit of the few.

(e.) *Shop Assistants.*

The economic consideration of a reduction in the hours of shop assistants is theoretically distinct from that of an early closing of shops, but for practical purposes it may be assumed that the latter alone is in question. It has been found absolutely impossible to protect shop assistants from having to work for as long as the shops are open, and a little longer. The system of relays, which is theoretically possible, has never, so far as we are aware, been put into practice in retail shops, and the utmost that has ever been granted in this direction by the most benevolent employer is the permission to go out for a walk for an hour or two in the dull part of the day. One class of retail shops, namely, public-houses, shares with textile factories the distinction of having the hour of ceasing work precisely prescribed by law. The hours of labour of the public-house manager, the barman, and the pot-boy, even if these are all adult males, are definitely regulated by an Act of Parliament which is rigidly enforced.

The chief economic problem in connection with the early closing of retail shops is the probable effect upon the volume of business. If this is maintained, the earlier closing involves an actual diminution in the cost of carrying on the business, even assuming that shop assistants' wages do not fall. The saving in gas, and in wear and tear of premises and plant, would amount to a considerable sum. But only in the most exceptional cases could any individual employer secure that saving by closing his own shop earlier than his rivals closed theirs. Although no diminution of business would ensue if all closed at an earlier hour, yet an enormous diversion of trade might take place to the advantage of those who refused to adopt this beneficent practice. In such a case the recalcitrant minority would probably not only continue to do during the later hours the business which they had hitherto done at that period of the day. They would also reap an added gain through their very want of public spirit, and pick up some of the business which would have continued to go to their rivals had these been as recalcitrant as themselves. Absolute freedom would, in this case, lead to the pecuniary discouragement of an admitted public advantage. The struggle for existence would promote the survival of the morally less fit.

This, indeed, is one of the cases referred to by Professor Sidgwick,* "where the coercion either of law or of the social sanction wielded by a deliberate and vigorous combination is *prima facie* indispensable, except in a perfectly ideal community of economic men." It is a case "in which a certain rule of conduct is recognised as expedient for all members of the community—or all of a certain class—if all adopt it, but not otherwise; while at the same time its adoption by a majority renders it decidedly the *immediate* interest of individuals to break through it. The observance of the Sunday holiday by traders may be taken as an example of this class, supposing it were not sustained by traditional custom and religious sentiment, but had to be introduced *de novo* from a mere conviction of its advantages. However firmly all were convinced that the gain, even economically speaking, of a weekly day of rest universally observed would outweigh the inconveniences of the weekly interruption of business, still these inconveniences would be so seriously felt that any individual could gain valuable custom by violating the rule; so that, except in a community where every one could rely completely on the intelligence and foresight of every one else, the general observance of this rule could hardly be introduced without the intervention of law, or of an express convention supported by strong social sanctions." It is obvious that the principle adduced by Professor Sidgwick with regard to the Sunday closing of shops applies also to their early closing on other days, and, indeed, also to a shortening of hours in any industry whatsoever.

Assuming, however, that all shopkeepers were brought to close earlier, it may confidently be suggested that no economic loss would thereby be caused to the community. It can hardly be doubted that the same amount of commodities would, in the aggregate, be desired and purchased, although the distributive business might be compressed into a shorter time during each

* *Principles of Political Economy*, book iii., ch. ii. p. 422.

twenty-four hours. If earlier closing in any particular industry diminished the temptations to the customer (as in the case of public-houses), the amount thus saved would almost certainly be spent in some other shops.* Retail distributors, as a class, would therefore lose nothing, and any trades specially affected (such as the dealers in alcoholic liquors) would find themselves able to recoup themselves at the expense of their landlords. It can hardly be doubted that the economic rent of public-houses in London would fall if the hours of sale were further restricted by law.

(*f.*) *Government Servants.*

The economic effects of the proposed limitation of the maximum working day of all public employés to eight hours would be comparatively simple. The total number of persons in the employment of the central government and local administrative bodies, excluding the Army and Navy, is perhaps 200,000. Those employed in clerical duties already work for only six to eight hours a day, and would therefore not be affected. The proposal applies, indeed, only to the manual workers engaged in the various industries which have already been, wholly or in part, nationalised or municipalised. Many of these have already had their hours reduced to eight per day. Most of the municipal gas workers enjoy this boon, which the Huddersfield Town Council has granted also to its tramway workers. The London County Council largely reduced the hours of labour of nearly all its manual workers during the first three years of its existence, and many of them now work only for eight hours out of the twenty-four. Policeman's duty has been, in many places, reduced to a similar limit, and the Post Office at any rate endeavours to observe its own rule of a normal Eight Hours Day. But the artisans employed by the State work usually from 54 to 60 hours per week, even when there is no overtime. The hours at the Royal Mint are from 8 A.M. to 7 P.M. At the National Workshops at Woolwich and Enfield the normal day of ten hours is largely increased by habitual overtime, which is dealt with in Chapter VI. It will be sufficient here to state that, in the four main government factories referred to in

* If, on the other hand, it were saved, this would hardly be considered as otherwise than advantageous to the community.

the House of Commons Return obtained by Mr. George Howell, M.P., the men worked on an average, during the four years 1886-90, no less than twenty-one hours per week overtime.

There is, in all these cases, no question of a possible falling off in the demand, and accordingly every reduction of the hours of labour is either pure gain all round, as when production does not fall off, or else an additional number of workers have employment found for them at the expense of public funds.* So long as such additional men are to be found offering their services—so long, that is, as the public business can be efficiently carried on with the shorter hours—it is difficult to resist the influence that the ranks of the unemployed, or the irregularly employed, are thereby thinned, either directly or indirectly. Work and wages would have been found for some among them in the manner least costly to the public, least demoralising to themselves, and most permanent in its beneficial action.

A reduction of the normal day in the public service would seldom be accompanied by any reduction in wages.† Some of the loss would probably be made up, in most cases, by increased intensity of work and diminution of meal times. But in nearly all cases the reduction of hours would, as regards public employés, involve an increased wages bill. The decision of the community to institute an Eight Hours Day for the workers whom it directly engages, would therefore be equivalent to a decision to tax itself for their benefit. But not for their benefit alone, or mainly with that intention. The public decision that eight hours should henceforth be considered as a fair day's work would have an incalculable effect on the action of private employers, and would probably do much to bring about a general voluntary shortening of hours. The Government must, by the nature of the case, set some example as an employer of labour, and if it sets a good, instead of a bad example, the advantage to its own employés will be reaped also

---

* As Mr. George Howell, M.P., remarks, in connection with the overtime at the government factories during the last four years, every five men displaced two others from full employment during the whole of this period. (*A Plea for Liberty*, page 290.)

† The case of the Huddersfield tramway workers is an exception. Even there, however, the reduction of wages was trifling compared to that of the hours.

by tens of thousands of those outside their ranks whose votes will have brought it about. The increase in the demand for labour will, in itself, co-operate in this beneficent result, and in this way many of the cases of excessive work, which it is difficult to prohibit directly by the blunt weapon of law, might be indirectly affected by a mere executive order altering the hours during which the Government will compel its own servants to work. It is unnecessary to pursue the effect of the increased cost in increased taxes. It may, however, be observed that any increase in the national expenditure is practically certain to be met out of taxes raised, not on consumption or otherwise from the great mass of the people, but by direct taxation falling specially upon rent and interest on the larger incomes, or else by death duties upon the accumulations of "unearned increment" and monopoly gains. An Eight Hours Day for public servants implies therefore, to a small extent, a better distribution of the products of industry.

CHAPTER V.

SANITARY AND SOCIAL RESULTS OF AN EIGHT HOURS DAY.

IN the preceding chapter we have shown that an Eight Hours Day is economically possible. We have shown that there is no reason to dread the loss of our foreign trade, or a decline in the wages of the working classes, or a rise in prices; that, in brief, we can safely embark upon an eight hours experiment without the slightest fear of national disaster. Having thus far made our ground secure, we now pass on to consider the special reasons which make an Eight Hours Day nationally desirable. To express them all in one word, an Eight Hours Day is needed for the sake of social health.

And since the nation is primarily an aggregation of individuals, and only secondarily a corporate entity, let us first of all consider the effect on the individual of the proposed reduction in the hours of labour. In an earlier chapter we have given particulars of the hours now prevailing in the principal trades and occupations in the United Kingdom. We see that railway men, and tramway men, and omnibus men have a working day of twelve to sixteen hours; that shop assistants and bar tenders are in much the same position; that iron smelters and other men engaged on continuous work are on duty twelve hours at a time; that thousands of men and boys are working underground nine to ten hours a day; that the immense body of mechanics in the country, though they have nominally secured a nine hours day, actually work much longer through the habitual practice of overtime; and, finally, that it is only in comparatively few occupations that the real working day is less than ten hours. Nor is this state of things peculiar to the United Kingdom. As we have shown in Chapter II., in the

United States only a small proportion of the workers labour for less than ten hours a day, whilst many still work for 72 hours a week. On the Continent of Europe the usual working time is at least as long. Even in Australia many classes of workers were lately found to have equally long hours. All over the industrial community the same tendency to a lengthy working day prevails, and only in a few occupations, and in a few exceptional localities, have the workers succeeded in reducing their hours to such an extent as really to retain for themselves an appreciable share of their waking life.

About the unhealthiness of such conditions of life it is hardly necessary to argue. All medical testimony points to the fact that whenever a monotonous occupation is prolonged beyond a very limited period, seven or eight hours at most, the physical completeness of the worker is impaired. He becomes a lop-sided animal. This is the case even when the work in itself is healthy enough, and when it is conducted amid healthy surroundings. Thus Dr. B. W. Richardson, in an address to the Sanitary Institute of Great Britain at the Brighton Congress of 1890, refers specially to the case of postmen. Here the work itself is sufficiently healthy, and efforts are made to keep down the hours, but the labour is monotonous and continuous, and there is often too much of it. " The result is "—to quote Dr. Richardson's words—"that the postman wears out too fast. The late medical officer to the General Post Office, Dr. Waller Lewis, was fully alive to this fact. He referred to it in his reports, and he several times spoke to me about it. There were some men, he told me, who sustained the tedious labour fairly, but none bore it well, and the weaker ones badly. The effect generally was to produce a premature old age; in other words, shortening of the life of the worker." But rarely in English industries are the conditions of labour even moderately healthy. The engine-driver and his fireman, whizzing through the cold air at forty miles an hour, and intermittently scorched by the heat of the furnace, can hardly be said to be working under healthy conditions.* The guard has a relatively

---

* We may here again quote Dr. Richardson :—"The engine-driver is taxed all round; he has much to do that calls the muscles of his body into active work; he is unable to rest; he is exposed to great dangers of heat and cold, wind and rain; he has to bear the rapid friction of the air over the surface of his body; and from minute to minute, for hour after hour, he is obliged to have his most active

SANITARY AND SOCIAL RESULTS.

better time, but he must turn out in all weathers; he has to endure the constant vibration of the train, and repeatedly to exchange the shelter of his van for the cold of the platform. As to the shop assistant, the larger part of his day, in London at any rate, is spent in an atmosphere vitiated by gas and loaded with minute particles from the goods sold and from the dust that each customer brings. Bar tenders are, if anything, worse off. Public-houses burn more gas than the retail shops, and the *habitué* of the bar is on the average a less cleanly person than the shopper. The rate of mortality among public-house attendants is well known to be far in excess of that in any other occupation, and although alcoholic intemperance has doubtless much to do with this result, part, at any rate, of that intemperance may not unfairly be attributed to the unhealthy condition of their lives. In the large iron industries, again, constant alternations between fierce heat and the cold of the outer air are trying even to the most robust constitution. Numberless industries also have specially noxious features, as, for example, the white lead industry, house painting, plumbing, fur pulling, etc., etc. And so we might go on through all the trades of the country showing the positive unhealthiness of the large majority of them. Doubtless in many cases a great deal of this unhealthiness might be removed by a little care on the part of the men, and a little expenditure on the part of the masters. But when all has been done in this direction that can be done, the great bulk of the manual work of the country must carry with it incidents of unhealthiness. Consequently the only way to diminish the ill effect on the human body is to diminish the period in each day during which the body is exposed to these noxious incidents.

By way of illustration of what we mean by the essential unhealthiness of some trades, let us take the plumbing trade. It is inconceivable that this occupation could ever be good for the health of the workman. Lead is one of the most poisonous of metals, and plumbers, in the course of their work, are often exposed

and labouring senses persistently on guard. . . . I am quite convinced that such kind of work ought never to exceed eight hours out of the twenty-four. . . . By argument based simply on the study of man himself as a working unit—the physician's argument, if you like—I venture to declare that eight hours is the extreme limit of labour compatible with healthy life for all callings of this character."

to the foulest smells. Neither of these conditions can be avoided. The work must be done by somebody. At present the people who do it are condemned to premature death. Few working plumbers reach the age of fifty. Of this fact eloquent proof is given by the published obituaries of the Society of Plumbers. Here is the complete death roll, so far as recorded, for the quarter ending September 30th, 1890:—

H. N.	Bradford	Aged	31
L. M.	Coatbridge	,,	42
E. S.	Gloucester	,,	43
M. C. W.	Grimsby	,,	34
J. S.	Jarrow	,,	39
G. S.	Kensington	,,	36
R. W.	West Central	,,	36
H. P.	Manchester	,,	39
J. H.	Shrewsbury	,,	32
	Average age at death		37

If this table may be taken as representative, and there is no reason for believing otherwise, plumbers die at an age when professional men have just reached the prime of life. A moment's reflection will show the false economy as well as the cruelty of such a state of things. Let us take an extreme view. Let us suppose that in order to enable the plumber to last as an efficient worker, to what we may with modesty call the normal age of 55, it is necessary to reduce his hours of labour to half the present figure. What matter? He now begins working at 20—before that age he will hardly be fully efficient—and he continues to 37. By prolonging his active life to 55, you therefore double his working period. Consequently the total work you get out of the man will be the same in either case. Probably indeed it will be more in the case of the short-day and long-life man. For a man will generally do more work in two days of five hours than in one of ten hours; and a long-life man will probably lose fewer hours through ill-health than a short-life man. Now add to these purely mercenary considerations the weight of human affection which centres round each human being, and then consider whether it is nationally wise to use up our people before they have barely reached the prime of life.*

As to the right length of the working day for full health we cannot turn to a better authority than Dr. Richardson. In the address from which we have already quoted, he says:—

"Taking it all in all, we may keep our minds on eight hours as a fair time for work. We may consider justly that a person who works hard and conscientiously for eight hours has little to be ashamed of, and that, for health's sake, he has done what is near to the right thing; if he take an hour to get to and from work, two hours for meals, three hours for reading or recreation, and one hour for rising and going to bed, including in this the daily bath which is so essential to health, he is in good form for good health. It matters little then what his occupation may be, since this laying-out of time is time well laid out for mind and body."

And again:—

"Muscular kinds of work demand, for the best reason, limitation of hours. Amongst those of us who have studied this subject most carefully, there is, I believe, little difference of opinion. We should, I think,

---

* This same line of argument has been worked out by Dr. Richardson with regard to a large number of trades. He says:—"Some years ago I made a study of the value of life according to occupation, and found a certain number of occupations which presented alarming figures, showing the shortening of life connected with them. I found, out of forty-two of the chief industrial occupations, no fewer than thirty showing a mortality above the average, and in some cases far above the average. For example, taking 100 as the average figure, I found that 138 potters died instead of 100; 129 bargemen instead of 100; 121 dock labourers instead of 100; and so on, with rather more favourable returns to other workers, who, though dying above the average, were more favoured, because, although overworked, they enjoyed somewhat better conditions of air, of food, and of clothing. I discovered also one particular fact showing how in the selfsame business hard overwork each day will reduce the value of life. I took the blacksmiths of the country and the blacksmiths of Marylebone, in London, from Dr. Dundas Thompson's tables, and found that while the deaths of the country blacksmiths were 19 per 1000, those of Marylebone were 31. In the country the blacksmith is a healthy man; he rises early and works moderate hours, say ten daily; in London he rises early and works twelve hours. In the course of his life he can strike, between the age of twenty and sixty, 36,000,000 blows on his anvil, 3000 each day of ten hours; but when two extra hours with 600 blows more are laid on him per day, there is added in the year sixty more working days, and in five years one whole year more of work—a full and sufficient reason, in combination with his unhealthier surroundings, for his shorter life."

be unanimous that the strongest man ought not to perform, day by day, work that should call forth more than 250 foot-tons of energy, or rather more than twice the natural work of the heart. But in some work this amount is increased over a third. In the work of the dock labourer it runs up to 315 foot-tons; in the pile-driver and pavior to 350; and in a few others to 370. Here the eight hours rule, at least, is absolute for health."*

We thus have in favour of the contention that eight hours is the best average limit for all kinds of work the authority of the man who more than any other has distinguished himself in the study of the science of preserving health. To this authoritative statement we may add the following practical consideration. To the majority of wage workers in the United Kingdom the difference between an eight hours day and a nine or ten hours day, means the difference between coming to work before breakfast, and coming to work after breakfast. In many skilled trades enjoying a nominal nine hours day, work begins at six o'clock in the morning. After two hours' work there is a break of half-an-hour or an hour for breakfast, which the men eat where they can.

Now it is all very well to preach the virtues of early rising, but even such a pre-eminently virtuous habit as early rising may degenerate into a vice. And we say without hesitation that the vicious point is passed when a man begins work at six o'clock in the morning on an empty stomach. Probably before he reaches his work he will have had a tramp of a mile or a couple of miles—possibly more—often in the rain, nearly always in the cold. Then after working half-heartedly for a couple of hours, he has to eat his breakfast in some dirty and probably draughty shed. It would be far better for the man, and far better for the work, if he had his breakfast comfortably before he started from home, even if this entailed his not

* *Report of Proceedings of Annual Congress of the Sanitary Institute of Great Britain*, at Brighton, 1890.—M. Charles Grad, a member of the German Reichstag, in an article in the *Revue des Deux Mondes* for November 1887, says:—"According to the evidence of the president of the corporation of miners in Germany, workers in mines reach their maximum efficiency with eight hours of effective work. A temporary extension of this period, in autumn for example, may increase the productivity during three or four weeks, but after this the output returns to its normal level, and remains the same for ten hours of work as for eight hours."

reaching work till eight o'clock. On the eight hours system either eight or nine o'clock would be a very convenient time for beginning work. The day would then be broken into two spells of four hours each—namely, from eight to twelve, and one to five; or from nine to one, and two to six. This is a point to which we have already called attention elsewhere in this volume, and we may again refer the reader to the Appendix for an account of the experience on the subject of Mr. Mark Beaufoy and Mr. Samuel Johnson. Our reason for laying so much stress on the point is that it is one that is practically felt by every working man. It was the chief demand of the Roubaix strikers of May 1890, referred to in Chapter II. In the present instance our special object is to insist upon its effect on the health of the worker. In the middle of the summer the six o'clock system is probably not unhealthy, and may be even pleasurable. But for ten months out of the twelve in this English climate of ours, to require a man to be at his work by six o'clock in the morning is to impose a severe strain upon his constitution. Still more is this the case during a Continental or American winter. There is no doubt that this incident in the life of an artisan is one of the causes for the relatively greater mortality in the artisan class as compared with the professional classes. And here it is worth while to point out that in the professional and commercial classes such early rising is, in London, almost unknown. A few phenomenally active lawyers or City men may be at work by nine o'clock, but at present ten is certainly the more usual hour, and quite a large proportion of business men do not reach their offices before eleven. Hours of business elsewhere are earlier than in London, but in all cases the artisan begins work an hour or two before the usual time for clerical or professional labour.

The case for an Eight Hours Day on account of physical health is thus extremely strong. Even stronger is the case for rest from work for the sake of mental health. If you treat people as slaves, they will remain slaves. If you compel men and women to work so long each day that they have not time to think, they will remain non-thinking animals. Under the present conditions of industry there are in all advanced industrial countries thousands of men and women who never have a moment's leisure until completely exhausted to sit down quietly and take stock of their position. All the time that is left to them between bed and work is spent in the pleasures that most immediately appeal to an overwrought body. The gin palace with its glaring lights and strong spirits, the music-hall with its silly songs and maudlin sentiments, are the direct results of a system of overwork that prohibits mental leisure. If the workers were actually chattel slaves these things would be of little consequence. Make your helots drunk and they will be less likely to rebel. But our helots are citizens and voters. On them, ultimately, if they choose to exert the power, rests the determination of the whole policy of the community. It is surely not wise that a large percentage of those potential despots should be incapable of forming an opinion on the questions committed to their decision.

Nor is it wise that a large proportion of the fathers and mothers in the country should not have leisure properly to discharge the responsibilities of fatherhood and motherhood. Anti-Socialists are for ever denouncing the growing interference of the State between child and parent. But that interference is necessitated because many parents literally have not time to look after their children with proper care. Many wage-earning fathers never see their children out of bed from Sunday to Sunday. Children, begotten in recklessness, are recklessly allowed to bring themselves up as best they can, picking up scraps of indigestible book-learning in the Public Elementary Schools, and assimilating full meals of riper knowledge in the gutter and the alley. It is not in this way that a nation obtains capable men and women, self-reliant citizens, able to take their places in the world as the self-governing members of a mighty empire. And, to touch on the still more intimate relationship between husband and wife, it is well to point out how cruelly the best features of this relationship are marred by long hours of labour. What chance has a tram conductor, on duty sixteen hours a day, of forming any real friendship with his wife? She becomes merely the mother of his children and the preparer of his food. In countless other cases the man is so tired when he comes in from his work, that he cannot stand the strain of the tiny worries of home life, and either goes out to enliven himself at the public-house, or, what is worse, stays in to vent his temper on wife and children. We are not here suggesting that it is the duty of the State to keep husbands in good temper. That indeed would be

SANITARY AND SOCIAL RESULTS. 147

a task beyond even the omnipotence of the British Parliament. But realising, as all people who stop to think must realise, how much of the happiness and well-being of the world depends simply on good temper, we wish to point out how closely the abbreviation of the day's work is connected with this quality.

To many cases, however, these arguments drawn from family life are inapplicable. An increasing number of men and women live their own lives independent, at any rate for a considerable period, of all family ties. But these no less than married men and women will appreciate the advantages of a law which for the first time gives them leisure. There are hundreds of things which working lads and young women would be glad to do if they had the time. The young workman of to-day aspires to belong to a volunteer corps, to join an athletic or football club; he has learnt to ride a bicycle and to pull a boat. That he should be able to enjoy these pleasures is obviously a gain to himself, and so far as they make him stronger and happier it is a gain to the whole community. About the pleasures and aspirations of young working women we speak with more diffidence. Apparently, however, walking exercise, theatres, and books are the principal attractions, and the absence of opportunity for these pleasures is keenly felt by thousands of girls earning their living as shop assistants, as milliners, or as waitresses. Moreover, there are plenty of attractions for the more seriously minded. In every large town in the United Kingdom there are evening classes where continuous study may be carried on. For the more advanced students a more elaborate fare is provided by enthusiastic lecturers from Oxford and Cambridge. Similar conditions exist in the large cities of America and the Continent. We need therefore have no fear that a working population set free will not know what to do with its freedom. The existing facilities for amusement, for study, and for physical recreation will be at once drawn upon, and a demand will arise for further facilities of the same nature. Already indeed we have evidence how a diminution of the hours of labour stimulates the desire for study, even in the most apparently unpromising quarters. Nowhere have University Extension lectures, even on abstruse scientific subjects, been so successful as among the miners of Durham and Northumberland. These men—as explained elsewhere—work on the average less than eight hours a day; and sometimes a miner, after his day's work is done, has been known to walk as much as eight miles every week to attend a course of lectures on astronomy.

The line of argument we have here been following disposes beforehand of an objection frequently brought against the proposal of an Eight Hours Day. Greater leisure, it is said, would only mean to many workers a greater temptation to drinking and general dissipation. We will at once admit that with some men for a time this might be so; that men unaccustomed to freedom would at first use their freedom badly. But all experience proves that with members of the Anglo-Saxon race, at any rate, this misuse of opportunities would be only temporary. The same argument was brought against the Saturday half-holiday, only to be most conclusively refuted by the result of experience. Each successive extension of liberty that Englishmen have gained has been accompanied by a step of the race upwards, not downwards. We are therefore perfectly entitled to assume that the new liberty given to the working classes by an Eight Hours Law would not induce any appreciable number of men permanently to degrade themselves.* The claim itself is evidence to the contrary. No class asks for leisure until it is conscious of wants which leisure alone can satisfy. The new leisure, we may confidently expect, would lead to an extension of wants in new directions. On one aspect of these we have already dwelt. We have pointed out that the younger generation of workpeople are eager to educate themselves, and would largely use their new opportunities for this purpose. But this is mainly a question of their individual enjoyment, and only affects the community gradually through its effect upon the race. The point to which we wish now to come is more directly social in its bearings.

The new wants thus arising cannot, as a rule, be satisfied without new expenditure. If people have more opportunities of going out, they will soon begin to want more new clothes.†

---

* Many witnesses before the Royal Commission on the Relations of Capital and Labour in Canada (1889) "were firmly persuaded that the over-wearied labourer is more inclined to seek renewal of energy in intoxicating liquor than the man who quits work before his energies are exhausted."*

† An apparently trivial instance may be given, which is not without relevance to the question of promoting the self-respect of the worker. When the

---

* Report, Appendix F, p. 37.

They will be obliged, too, to spend money on omnibus and railway fares. And being out, they must amuse themselves. There will be an increased demand for theatres, music halls, and other places of public entertainment. Popular lectures, too, will be in brisk request, and newspapers and magazines will find a wider range of readers. It is needless to extend the list. In every direction the wants of the labouring community will be widened; for men and women who are free to dispose of part of their day as pleases them best will no longer be content with the old narrow life. In this way the working classes will constitute themselves a better market for their own products. To some extent it is true this will be merely a transference from a wealthier market; for while the workman is buying more, the capitalist may be buying less. So far as this were to be the case, the industrial advantage of the change would be, that the new demand would be steadier than the old. The wants of the million can always be calculated upon with reasonable accuracy. It is the wants of the wealthy few that defy calculation beforehand. But it is possible, indeed probable, that an altogether new demand would be created. As we have seen elsewhere, the reduction of the hours of labour would in some industries necessitate the employment of more men, merely to get through the same amount of work as before. This aspect of the Eight Hours Question has especially attracted the attention of Mr. Gunton in his admirable little book entitled *Wealth and Progress.* He insists, with great force of argument and richness of illustration, that an Eight Hours Day will benefit the working classes not so much by effecting a redistribution of the wealth already existing, as by creating more wealth. The steady demand of the well-employed, well-paid masses will lead to economies in production, thence to the cheapening of products, and thence to increased consumption. This argument is rather wide of the beaten track of professional economists, who appear to despair of effectively raising the "standard of comfort," and for this reason we have not incorporated it in the chapters dealing with the technical economics of the Eight Hours Question. But the argument is largely justified

gas stokers at Beckton (East London) won the Eight Hours Day in 1889, it was noticed by their Trade Union secretary that several of them took out of pawn the black cloth coats in which they had been married, but which they had not, with a Twelve Hours Day, found much opportunity to wear.

by the experience of the Australian colonies. Both in Victoria and in New South Wales, according to Sir Charles Dilke, it is the general conviction that the relative prosperity of the masses, as compared with the wealthy few, brings an absolute prosperity to the colony.

The same general line of argument is also adopted in an interesting little volume on the *Physiology of Industry*, by Messrs. Hobson & Mummery. The contention of these gentlemen is that the possible consumption of commodities by the wealthy few is limited, but that the possible consumption of the million is practically unlimited. If therefore we can put the million into a position where they can spend more, they will spend more. The reduced incomes of the rich, if such reduction there be, will check that modern form of non-industrial hoarding, the heaping up of costly treasures in lordly palaces. The industrial organisation of the community will thus be more fully employed, more wealth for common enjoyment will be produced, and still further consumption will be stimulated. This theory is identical with the doctrine long since laid down by Mr. Ruskin in *Unto this Last*, that the "crown of production is consumption." In its broader aspect the doctrine is beyond dispute. The world only produces wealth in order to consume it, and if consumption ceases production will also cease. It is only because our industrial organisation is based on the system of payment of wages for work done that we have formed the notion that the essential thing is active production, in order to "make work." The essential thing, on the contrary, is active consumption, both for its own sake, and because it involves active production. A community that consumes little is *ipso facto* a poor community, even if it hoards much. The Indian coolie or the West Indian negro is content to live in a mud hut, to sit on the floor, and to eat his food with his fingers. His wages are 2¼d. a day. The English agricultural labourer, poor as he is, fortunately insists on boarded floors, papered walls, and plastered ceilings ; he insists on chairs and tables, knives and forks, and he covers the whole of his body with warm clothes. His wages are ten times 2¼d. a day. The Australian or American workman demands a higher standard than the English labourer, and gets accordingly several times his wages. No one can doubt that if the Indian coolie, the West Indian negro,

SANITARY AND SOCIAL RESULTS. 151

and the English labourer could be induced persistently to demand the requirements even of a Melbourne dock porter, the social and industrial wealth of India, the West Indies, and England would be greatly increased. It may thus legitimately be argued that anything which increases the wealth of the working classes will increase the social wealth of the community, even if it diminishes the riches of its individual proprietors. That an Eight Hours Day would tend to raise the wages of the working classes has already been shown. We contend, therefore, that the introduction of an Eight Hours Day, by leading to a rise in the "standard of comfort," would increase the total real wealth of the country.

Lastly we come to a point to which we briefly alluded above, namely, the relation of the worker to the State in his capacity as citizen. By the Reform Bills of 1867 and 1885 the suffrage has been extended in the United Kingdom to the greater number of the wage-earners. A good many working men, it is true, are still unable to exercise the suffrage owing to defective registration laws. But these defects will without doubt be shortly removed. Thus the governing influence in the nation has virtually asked every man in the kingdom to share in the work of government. Whether wise or foolish, the step has been taken, and cannot be recalled. But are the men who have thus been called upon to rule capable of understanding the task set before them? Undoubtedly a very large number are not capable, and under present industrial conditions cannot possibly become so. Their whole lives are spent in an unending round of work, broken only by a few intervals for feeding and sleeping, and an occasional outburst of drinking. Such men cannot be competent judges of any of the complicated questions that Parliament has to decide. And yet at an election the vote of a man who rolls from the beer-shop to ballot-box counts as much as that of the elector who has taken every pains to form a conscientious opinion on the point at issue. The remedy is not to restrict the suffrage, but to increase the intelligence of the electorate. That can only be done by giving more daily leisure to the bulk of the voters. An Eight Hours Day will for the first time put into the hands of thousands of working men an opportunity of becoming competent for the duties of citizenship. It will be the work of the rival political parties to see that the opportunity is not wasted. Similar considerations apply in varying degrees to all

Europe outside of Russia and Turkey. The United States has its own difficulties of a not unlike kind. Everywhere it is necessary to "educate our masters"; and to educate them not merely by teaching them to read and write, but by giving them in their lives opportunities of thinking and learning, instead of only working and eating.

CHAPTER VI.

THE QUESTION OF OVERTIME.

IN every argument that arises on the subject of the Eight Hours Day, the question is sure to be asked—" What are you going to do about overtime?" To answer this question is the object of the present chapter. And first of all, as to the facts! As has been stated more than once in this volume, the practice of overtime is extremely common in nearly all trades, skilled and unskilled. For proof of this statement we can only refer the reader to the annual reports of the secretaries of Trade Unions.* He

---

* Extract from a circular originally issued by the Manchester district of Amalgamated Engineers in 1871, and reprinted and re-issued in August 1890:—

"That, from the facts presented, this committee concludes that the system of overtime established in this district requires the utmost exertions to effect its entire abolition. The question is one of the utmost importance to our trade, and to allow its further progress to go unchecked would jeopardise the future well-being of the workmen. For it not only concentrates the labour in the hands of the few, but it acts prejudicially to the interests of the workmen by prostrating their health, and robbing them of privileges which it has been the object of the Nine Hours Movement to obtain—viz., the improvement of themselves and their families.

"That, with a view to remedy the evils of overtime, it is absolutely necessary to tax those employers who demand labour after the day's limit; and to effect this object the committee recommend the establishment of an uniform rate—viz., at least time and quarter for the first two hours worked each day; time and half for the next two hours; and double time for all time worked after four hours up to 6 A.M.; double time for Sunday, Christmas Day, and Good Friday. The calculation to be based on the fifty-four hours rate.

"That if night shifts require to be worked in this district, forty-five hours shall constitute the week's work at the usual rate of wages paid for fifty-four hours."

will here find constantly repeated protests against the practice of habitual overtime. For example, the secretary of the Iron Founders writes :—*

"We are quite aware how impracticable it would be to avoid overtime absolutely; but it is possible to abolish all overtime systematically worked. The evils resulting from too much time working are too numerous and too far-reaching for us to describe in a few lines. . . The question is one of the utmost importance to the whole nation, for every one must admit that overtime is one of the greatest social hoppers through which irregular employment is fed."

The letters we have received from Trade Union secretaries and delegates during the preparation of this book nearly all call attention to the prevalence of overtime. The practice is not confined to one trade or to one part of the country. Even in Newcastle—the home of the Nine Hours Movement—artisans may be seen—according to the *Workman's Times*, a north-country labour paper—streaming home from work at seven or eight o'clock in the evening, thirteen or fourteen hours after they began work. In London instances have come under the personal observation of the present writers, in which trade unionists have grumbled at their foremen for not giving them a greater amount of overtime. Mr. Mark Beaufoy states† that his first difficulty in the way of abolishing overtime work was the opposition of the men themselves.

But we need not elaborate the point. Every one at all conversant with labour questions knows that overtime is extremely common, and that the men themselves are the greatest supporters of the system. And yet the men, in their meetings and by their formal declarations, are constantly protesting against the practice. Nor is it difficult to reconcile these two facts. The men, acting in a body and thinking of their common interests, protest against overtime, because they know that it restricts the area of employment and lowers the rate of wages. But when each individual man comes to deal with his own case, these considerations are replaced by others of a very different character. To the individual workman, a request to work overtime presents itself mainly, if not entirely, as an offer of additional earnings. Of course he would be glad of more money,

---

* Vide *Second Report on Trade Unions*, 1888, C—5505, p. 174.
† See Appendix.

when it is offered to him. From his point of view he would be a fool to reject the offer. Moreover, if he reflects on the matter at all from a wider point of view, he will probably argue that his refusal will do no particular good to his comrades. One man who stands out against overtime will not abolish the practice. The system is there, and he may as well take advantage of it. If he doesn't, somebody else will. There is therefore nothing illogical, and nothing seriously discreditable, in the contradiction between the speech and action of the average trade unionist in the matter of overtime. He does the best he can for himself and family by working overtime, and he does the best he can for his society and his class by protesting against the practice. The double attitude is not ideal, but few human beings are uniformly consistent in their conduct. As to the actual amount of overtime worked, there is no reliable information except in special occupations. The figures relating to the railways have been fully given elsewhere, and we need not repeat them here. More useful for our present purpose are some valuable statistics collected through the exertions of Mr. George Howell, M.P.

In 1886 Mr. Howell* moved for and obtained a return of the number of men employed in Woolwich Arsenal, and in the Small Arms Factory at Enfield, and "the extent to which systematic overtime had been worked during the two years of 1884-85, and the two first months of 1886." The information obtained is published in Mr. Howell's book just referred to. It may be summarised and tabulated as follows. The departments included in the returns are :—

> The Royal Carriage Department.
> The Laboratory.
> The Gun Factory.
> The Small Arms Factory.

The full complement of men and boys allotted to the four departments was 12,390.

In 1884 only 7,446 men were, on the average, actually employed.

Of these 794 worked 548,568 hours overtime, or 13½ hours per man per week.

* See *Conflicts of Capital and Labour*, by George Howell, M.P. New edition, p. 287.

In 1885 only 10,254 men were, on the average, actually employed.

Of these 7,760 worked 4,832,950 hours overtime, or nearly 13 hours per man per week.

In January and February 1886 only 11,605 were, on the average, actually employed.

Of these 6,267 worked 601,139 hours overtime, or 27½ hours per man per week.

These figures give an aggregate total of 5,982,657 hours, or nearly 6,000,000 hours of overtime in two years and two months in these four departments. "During this period," says Mr. Howell, "thousands of skilled men were walking the streets of London seeking work and finding none. The hours worked overtime in these four Government departments would have given employment to about 1000 men at 54 hours per week for the entire period of two years and two months."

Mr. Howell subsequently moved for a return relating to the four years from 1886 to 1890.

During this period the average number of persons actually employed was 11,486. In no year was the number up to the full complement.

In the four years 1,758 men, on the average, worked overtime every week, and between them they made altogether 1,506,208 hours of overtime.

In 1886-7 the average overtime was 8½ hours per week per man.
In 1887-8 ,, ,, 20 ,, ,,
In 1888-9 ,, ,, 26¼ ,, ,,
In 1889-90 ,, ,, 29½ ,, ,,

Comparing the two returns with one another, we find that—

In the years 1884-86 every four men who worked overtime displaced by so doing one man from full employment.

In the years 1886-90 every five men displaced two men from full employment.

Mr. Howell thus sums up his conclusions:—"If an Eight Hours Day were ever enacted for grown men, stringent provisions would have to be added to prevent overtime, except in cases of absolute necessity."

It is, indeed, obvious that an Eight Hours Law which did not exclude habitual overtime would be simply delusive. At the same time it is equally obvious that there are some emergencies where most serious inconvenience would be caused to a large number of persons if occasional overtime were not permitted. Thus, for example, if the engine of a factory breaks down, and the man in charge could by a little extra work at night put it into running order again, it is far better that he should be allowed to do this extra work than that all the factory hands should be kept waiting next morning till the repairs are completed. Such cases as these are of common occurrence in mechanical trades, and it would be folly to pass an Act of Parliament which ignored them. Nor is there any difficulty in drafting a law which would fully meet such cases. In the existing Factory Acts in England the question of overtime in various industries is dealt with in the greatest detail. Probably some of this detail[*] is due rather to a desire to conciliate the opposition of interested parties than because any real need arose for it. But in any case the English Act of 1878 is instructive as showing the minuteness which is possible in legislation.

In the first place, however, it is worth while to lay stress on the fact that in the vast majority of textile factories overtime is absolutely prohibited. The working week is fixed at $56\frac{1}{2}$ hours, and no provision is made for any excess, except in the case of mills driven by water. In this case, now rare in England, the employer may recover time lost through drought or floods. But only one extra hour a day is permitted, and this must not interfere with the meal times fixed by law, or with the Saturday half-holiday. Further, the annual amount of overtime is limited to 96 hours in the case of drought, and 48 hours in the case of flood; and in neither case must the time recovered in one year exceed the time lost in the preceding year. Barring this complicated exception of rare application, no overtime at all is permitted in English textile factories. Yet the textile industries of England are perhaps commercially the most important in the country, and they are certainly the most sensitive to foreign competition. If then these trades can live and thrive under such rigid regulations, there is at least a presumption that the numerous exceptions for overtime allowed to other trades are not all of them necessary. This presumption is fully borne

[*] See Factory and Workshop Act, 1878, § 53, 54, 55, and the accompanying schedules.

out by an examination of the exceptions. In the principal overtime clause in the Act three main reasons for granting overtime are selected, and the particular cases which fall under each of these three heads are carefully enumerated. In every case the amount of overtime is limited to two hours a day, on not more than five days a week, and on not more than 48 days a year. Each instance of overtime must be promptly reported by the employer to the factory inspector of the district. These provisions apply to all women and young persons under eighteen in the factories and workshops specified in the schedule, as follows:—

(1) Those where the material of the manufacture is liable to be spoiled by weather, namely—

(*a*) Flax scutch mills.
(*b*) Brick and tile making.
(*c*) Open air rope works.
(*d*) Open air bleaching, or Turkey red dyeing.
(*e*) Glue making.

(2) Those where press of work arises at recurring seasons of the year, namely—

(*f*) Letterpress printing.
(*g*) Bookbinding.
(*h*) Lithographic printing.
(*i*) Machine ruling.
(*k*) Firewood cutting.
(*l*) Bon-bons and Christmas presents.
(*m*) Almanacs.
(*n*) Valentines.
(*o*) Envelopes.
(*p*) Aerated waters.
(*q*) Playing cards.

(3) Those where sudden press of orders arises from unforeseen events—

(*r*) Articles of wearing apparel.
(*s*) Furniture hangings.
(*t*) Artificial flowers.
(*u*) Fancy boxes.
(*v*) Biscuits.
(*w*) Job dyeing.

(*x*) Polishing, cleaning, wrapping, or packing up goods.

Further, the Home Secretary has power to extend this list for any of the three grounds specified.

Another overtime clause permits women, but not young persons, to be employed an extra two hours a day for 96 days a year in any of the following trades:—

Fruit preserving.   Fish curing.   Condensed milk making.

THE QUESTION OF OVERTIME.

By a third clause an additional half-hour is allowed in certain specified trades to a child, young person, or woman, where at the expiration of the day the process of manufacture is incomplete. But these extra half-hours must not increase the total week's work beyond the amount otherwise permitted. The trades specified are—

(*a*) Bleaching and dyeing works.
(*b*) Print works.
(*c*) Iron mills, in which young persons are not employed at night.
(*d*) Foundries   „   „   „
(*e*) Paper mills   „   „   „

Finally, Turkey red dyeing has an overtime clause all to itself. In this process unlimited extra work is permitted "so far as is necessary for the purpose only of preventing" any damage that may arise from spontaneous combustion or extraordinary atmospheric influence. After this it would be impertinence to say that the British Parliament cannot regulate the minutiæ of industry. These detailed provisions are accepted without demur by employers and workers alike.

Let us now take in order the three reasons assigned in the Factory and Workshops Act 1878 for permitting overtime. The first is obviously the most solid. The vagaries of the weather, especially in the English climate, cannot be provided against beforehand, and it would be straining at a gnat in order to swallow a camel, if by strictly prohibiting overtime we were to allow valuable products or materials to be wasted. In agriculture, for example, such strictness would be fatal. There are many agricultural operations which must be done promptly or not at all. Fruit must be picked when it is ready, or it will rot; the proverbial hay must be made while the sun shines; and the corn must be harvested before it begins to spoil. In such cases as these a rigid Eight Hours Day would be absolutely inapplicable. It would involve the nation in a heavy annual loss for which there is no sufficient justification. And here it may be pointed out that the nation already suffers unnecessarily a considerable loss owing to the rigidity of social custom and religious restraint. Every year an appreciable amount of fruit and hay and corn is spoilt because of the enforced interruption of work on Sundays. The best way of dealing with cases such as these occurring in agricultural and open air industries would be to adopt the rule that has been successfully established by several trade unions, that overtime work and Sunday work shall be paid at a higher rate than the work for the normal day. But about this we shall have more to say further on.

The next class of exceptions is less justifiable. "Press of work arising at recurring seasons of the year" does not necessarily involve the permission of overtime. Such press can also generally be met, either by taking more people into employment when the pressure comes, or by getting stock ready beforehand. Either of these ways is preferable to overtime working. Moreover, as a matter of fact, there is a great deal of superstition about the necessity for overtime working at certain seasons. No better illustration of this could be found than that of Mr. Beaufoy, related in the Appendix. An important part of Mr. Beaufoy's business is the manufacture of British wines, and, as every one knows, British wines are consumed more freely at Christmas than at any other time of the year. Consequently here appears a clear case for a season of overtime. And in fact when Mr. Beaufoy succeeded to the business there was no limit to the amount of overtime worked during the months of October and November. But Mr. Beaufoy on general grounds thought the system was bad, and determined to put it down. He has put it down absolutely and completely, and his business has benefited by the alteration.

However, it must be admitted that there are cases where such a simple solution of the overtime difficulty is not immediately practicable. From the above list of season trades where overtime is allowed we may select letterpress printing, bookbinding, and lithographic printing. The book trade, for some reason best known to publishers, is largely concentrated into the autumn and winter months. From September to March there is the greatest activity in book printing and bookbinding, and a corresponding slackness in the summer months. Such a general phenomenon cannot be ignored. Nor can the evils resulting from it easily be remedied. It is impossible to work for stock much in advance; for the materials for the work are not generally ready till late in the year, and the books must be sold before Christmas or early in the next year. Nor again is it easy in skilled trades to take on extra hands. The men are not always to be found in adequate numbers, and if they were there is often not enough shop room for them to work to advantage. Under such conditions as these the best solution is to allow a limited amount of overtime during the season of pressure, subject to an equivalent concession of holidays on full pay during the slack season. An arrangement of this nature made by the firm of Caslon & Co., type founders, is described in the Appendix. In Messrs. Caslon's establishment each man who works a full week of fifty hours has two hours placed to his credit, and can add them up and take a fortnight's holiday on full pay.

The above considerations and suggestions do not, however, apply to all the season trades in the Factory Act list quoted above. For example, we may take firewood cutting. In this case the prohibition of overtime should be absolute. Firewood cutting is work that any man or woman can do reasonably well after a few hours' experience. The pressure of work in this trade is annually recurrent, and at a time when there is a general slackness in unskilled labour. It is therefore highly desirable that this simple occupation should be reserved as a refuge for persons who are every year thrown out of work by the cold weather.

One more article may be selected from the list, namely, envelopes. It is difficult to understand why this trade was placed in the list of season trades at all. It may be true that more envelopes are used by the public at one season of the year than another. But obviously this circumstance can be arranged for by accumulating stock beforehand. Envelopes do not require frozen air chambers to keep them from spoiling or large warehouses to store them.

We have selected these three trades—printing, firewood cutting, envelope making—from the Factory Act list, to illustrate the three principles on which season trades may be dealt with. In some cases, as printing, overtime must be allowed, and should be compensated for by a full pay holiday during the slack season. In other cases, such as firewood cutting, overtime should be absolutely prohibited, in order to make room for persons out of employment. In the third set of cases, of which we take envelope making as the type, the necessity for overtime can be obviated by working for stock.

We now come to the trades "where sudden press of orders

arises from unforeseen events." Here our position is one of complete scepticism. The sudden press of orders only arises because overtime is permitted. If it were known beforehand that excessive hours of work were absolutely forbidden, then the general public and the shopkeepers would make their arrangements accordingly. If, for example, Jones knows that, owing to the operation of an Eight Hours Act, a pair of trousers cannot by any possible means be made in less than three days, he will take care to give three clear days' notice to his tailor. Or, to take a still more homely illustration, the housewife who knows that she cannot buy bread on Sunday will take care to order a double supply on Saturday. In the same way, if the biscuit trade, the fancy box trade, and the artificial flower trade were subject to the same rigid law as the cotton trade, every one would soon accommodate himself or herself to the necessities of the case. Orders would be given longer in advance, and the work would be spread more equably over the whole year, to the great advantage of the workers.*

In support of this contention we cannot do better than quote the opinion of Mr. Lakeman. This most energetic of factory inspectors has frequently stated, as the result of his long experience in watching almost every industry in the kingdom, that overtime is in most trades an utterly unnecessary evil. For a particular illustration we may further appeal to the opinion of the head of a large firm of tobacco manufacturers in Southwark. This gentleman informed one of the present writers in the course of conversation that he always refused to allow overtime. "Possibly," he said, "we lose a few orders in consequence, but we get a more regular and steady business, and we prefer it." Nor would even the few orders be lost if the rule applied to all competing firms. Thus we altogether reject the third ground on which overtime is permitted by the English Factory Act.

About the minor overtime clauses quoted above it is not

* It is often argued that dressmakers must be allowed to work overtime, in order to meet such cases as mourning orders. But this argument overlooks the fact that, if one dressmaker is too busy to execute the order within the allotted time, another firm could take part of it. The practice of passing on work is not unknown in other trades, and it will hardly be contended that all dressmaking firms will simultaneously be busy with mourning orders. There is no "season" in mortality.

necessary to say much. Fruit preserving, fish curing, etc., obviously come within the earlier category of industries, where the material of the industry or the process of manufacture may be spoilt by delay. The clause allowing an extra half-hour in certain cases to complete a necessary process is probably sometimes useful, and with the proviso that the total week's work shall not be exceeded, it is harmless. It might be extended, for good reason shown, to other industries.

To recapitulate then. We have shown that in mechanical industries overtime must be allowed in the case of unforeseen emergencies—as, for example, to repair a breakdown of machinery; that in agricultural and kindred industries overtime must be allowed to prevent the spoiling of materials; that in certain season trades overtime must be allowed to get through a pressure of work. The limit of overwork allowed need not necessarily be the same in all the various cases covered under these heads. But in all cases some limit should be imposed by Parliament. Further, in order to prevent the danger of overtime, even within these limitations, becoming habitual, we make two suggestions.

The first of these is that a spell of overtime during one part of the year should be compensated for by a definite holiday at the slack season. To this an objection might be raised that such an arrangement would involve elaborate records and calculations. The answer is, that the English law already enforces at least as complicated an arrangement in the case of mills driven by water power; and that every employer under the Factory Acts is bound to inform the Factory Inspector in writing of all cases of overtime occurring in his establishment. Moreover, the facts would necessarily be recorded in any well-kept wages book. The record thus already exists.

Our second suggestion is that where casual overtime, from whatever cause it arises, cannot be absolutely prohibited, it should be required by law that it should be paid for at an increased rate. This proposal has been specifically made by Mr. H. M. Hyndman in his draft Eight Hours Bill. He suggests that in cases of "special unforeseen emergency," "each person who shall, by reason of such emergency, work beyond the period of *eight working hours* in any one day, or *forty-eight working hours* in any one week, shall be entitled to receive, and shall receive, from the individual, firm, or company so employing such person, notwithstanding any stipulation or contract to the contrary, expressed or implied, double the rate of wages per hour which has been paid per hour during the normal working day of eight working hours, for each hour of overtime so worked."*

A similar provision was inserted by the Victorian Legislature in 1883 in the Melbourne Harbour Works Act, as regards employment under the Harbour Commissioners.† To these definite proposals we give our hearty assent. They rightly throw a considerable part of the pecuniary burden of overtime on the employer. He is the person who most immediately profits by the overtime work, and he ought to be willing to pay for it.

The objection—if it be an objection—that such proposals involve parliamentary determination of the rate of wages, will not for a moment hold water. The English Parliament is about to prescribe ‡ that the owner of land shall pay the tithe upon it, any agreement with his tenant to the contrary notwithstanding. This law will in many cases lead to the readjustment of rents. But it does not thereby follow that Parliament determines those rents. The enactment of some such clause as that suggested above would still leave employer and employed free to determine between themselves the normal rate of wages. The Legislature merely steps in to prescribe that whatever that rate may be, the double of it shall be paid for that amount of occasional overtime work which the nature of the industry makes necessary. This is a reform for which Trade Unions have long been struggling, and which in some trades they have practically obtained. Its general enactment would be of itself an excellent guarantee against overtime except in cases of real necessity. But, in order further to safeguard the normal working day, this provision as to wages should be accompanied with the system of compensation by means of holidays above suggested, and also with an absolute limitation—as in the English Factory Act—of the amount of overtime that may be worked in any one year.

* *Draft of an Eight Hours Bill.* (Social Democratic Federation, 337 Strand, London.)
† See Chapter II. ‡ Written February 1891.

CHAPTER VII.

HOW AN EIGHT HOURS DAY CAN BE OBTAINED.

UP to this point we have been considering only the question of the desirability and feasibility of an Eight Hours Day. We now have to consider the three possible means by which it can be obtained.

(a.) *Voluntary Action by Employers.*

It is possible that in many trades an Eight Hours Day might gradually be brought about through the action of individual employers who are far-seeing enough to realise that their interest lies in the reduction of hours of labour. That this suggestion is within the bounds of possibility is proved by a most interesting letter from the head of a large firm of engineers in the East of London. The letter is printed in full in the Appendix, but we may here briefly summarise it:—" We have reduced the working week from 54 to 48 hours, and we pay the same weekly wages as before. The men come to work at eight, after they have had their breakfast, instead of at six with empty bellies. They set to work at once, instead of shivering about in the cold and dusk. There is now only one break in the day, and each break means loss of time. The men are more comfortable, and consequently work better. Our opinion is that the change has been profitable to the firm as well as to the employé." This most interesting letter proves that an Eight Hours Day may under certain circumstances be as productive as a day of nine hours. On *à priori* grounds, this point has often been disputed. It may be true, it is said, that a man can do as much work in ten hours as he previously did in twelve, but it does not follow that he will do as much in eight as he previously did in nine. It does not follow in logic, but it may in practice, especially if the eight hours limit allows of a more convenient arrangement of the man's day. A man can work eight hours comfortably, with only one break for a meal, but for anything beyond that period two breaks are usually required. In order to secure these two breaks in many trades work begins before breakfast, and where this practice prevails the letter above referred to shows that a reduction to eight hours, enabling the men to start work after breakfast, may easily prove a net gain to employers.

The building trades form a good example of this system of working. In these trades it is the practice in London for the men to start work at six o'clock in the morning and leave off at five o'clock in the evening, with half-an-hour or an hour off for breakfast and an hour for dinner. Many workmen live several miles away from their work, and in order to be at their posts by six must be out of bed by four. Is it likely that they will be fit for much active work till they have had their breakfast? In such a case it might be thought that the employers would of their own accord introduce the Eight Hours system without any pressure from agitators, Trade Unions, or Acts of Parliament. Unfortunately, experience does not point that way. Custom counts for much in all our institutions, and there are few employers who would care to commit themselves on their own initiative to such a considerable change in the custom of the trade. Moreover, even if the employers in the building trade did of their own accord initiate the Eight Hours system by postponing the commencing of work till after breakfast, the question of overtime would still be left untouched. And here the interests of the individual employer and the interests of the individual workman are at variance with those of the general community. It is less trouble, and sometimes cheaper to the employer, to keep one set of men working overtime at a particular job rather than start another set. In this arrangement the individual workman will generally acquiesce, for the sake of earning more money. It may therefore easily happen that many firms will work overtime, not only to meet an occasional emergency, but as a general practice, and in this way the advantage of an Eight Hours Day may be rendered almost nugatory. Thus even in those trades in which it is to the employers' interest to begin work later in the morning, it would be desirable to have some external authority to prohibit *habitual* overtime in the afternoon. Moreover, the cases in which we can rely upon employers for the establishment of an Eight Hours Day are comparatively rare. It is obvious that the considerations so ably adduced in the letter above quoted do not apply to many trades and occupations. Even in such an apparently promising instance as the printing trade the experience of Messrs. Green, McAllan, & Fielden, related in the Appendix, goes far to prove that any individual employer would lose by the introduction of an Eight Hours Day unless all other employers adopt the same system. We have therefore to consider whether in such cases the men, aided only by their trade organisations, are capable of securing a general Eight Hours Day.

(*b.*) *By means of Trade Union Coercion.*

It may, in the first place, be observed that the numerical strength of the Trade Unions, as compared with the general body of wage-earners in the kingdom, is not large. At the last Trade Union Congress, held at Liverpool, September 1890, when the "New Unionists" were present in force, the number of unionists represented was estimated by the Standing Orders Committee at 1,470,191. This total is far in excess of any previous congress, and may be taken as an outside estimate of the strength of Trade Unionism in the United Kingdom. As to the numbers of non-unionists, there is no exact information. But the number of persons "employed" at wages in the industries of the kingdom is placed by the best statistical authorities at thirteen to fourteen millions, and this includes over four million women.* Accepting these figures, we may place the number of manual workers in the United Kingdom at over 13,000,000. The number of unionists to the total number of wage-workers is accordingly as 1 to 9.

In trying to estimate the effective strength of Trade Unions we must, however, make a marked distinction between the skilled and

* Mr. J. S. Jeans, *Statistical Society's Journal*, vol. xlvii. p. 631, places the number at about 14,000,000 ; Mr. Giffen, *Essays in Finance*, vol. ii. p. 461 (separate incomes of manual labour class), 13,200,000 ; Professor Leone Levi, *Times*, 13th January 1885, number of workers in manual labour class in 1881, 12,200,000 ; see Fabian Tract No. 5, *Facts for Socialists* (Fabian Society, 2 Hyde Park Mansions, London, N.W.)

the unskilled trades. In a highly skilled trade a small society may accomplish much; may indeed effectually leaven the whole lump. But in an occupation requiring little or no preliminary training the union is powerless unless it can control, not only the workers actually engaged in that occupation at any particular moment, but also the great mass of possible competitors from outside. It is, however, unnecessary to rely upon *à priori* speculations as to the power of Trade Unions. The past record of these bodies affords a much more valuable indication of their capabilities. It is often confidently asserted that the present comparatively short hours in many of the skilled trades have been won entirely by Trade Union effort. This statement by itself is misleading. It is true that the Trade Unions have been the immediate means of securing successive reductions in the hours of labour in such trades as the engineers and the ironfounders, and in many of the building trades. But it is also true that the societies were immensely helped both by the interference of the State and by the favourable economic conditions. It was the Factory Acts for the textile trades that set the example of a more general Ten Hours Day; and it was the immense prosperity of trade in 1872-73 that gave a small proportion of the working classes strength to obtain a further reduction of the normal day to nine hours.

It is, moreover, easy to attribute too much importance to the Nine Hours Day which has been gained in the skilled trades. To a large extent the change from ten to nine hours was a change in name only. In many industries overtime is so habitually worked that the average day is as long as before. For proof of this statement it is only necessary to turn to the annual reports of secretaries of different trade societies. In these will be found, yearly repeated, abundant protests against the prevailing habitual overtime. These protests are based upon declared policy of Trade Unions to abolish overtime except in cases of emergency. It would accordingly be misleading to credit Trade Unions with the establishment of a Nine Hours Day, without also recording that the same societies have been unable to put down the practice of habitual overtime.

Nor is this failure to be wondered at. In the matter of overtime the immediate interests of the individual workman and the interests of the workers as a whole are not the same. To the individual workman a request from his employers to work overtime appears

HOW IT CAN BE OBTAINED. 169

in the light of a welcome addition to his earnings. Men with families dependent upon them can hardly be blamed for their short-sighted willingness to accept such offers. But the harm done to the other workers is manifest and serious. In the first place the overtime of some men means the exclusion of others from employment. If, for example, the normal day is fixed at nine hours, then for every three men who accept three hours extra work, one man is kept out of the opportunity of a day's job. It rarely happens that trade is so prosperous that all the men trained for a particular industry are simultaneously employed. This is proved, if proof be needed, by the returns of the Trade Unions. The following list of seven societies includes the three largest Trade Unions in the kingdom; and the other four are all powerful societies. These seven are selected out of about seventy societies, simply because they alone make the returns in the form required for our present purpose. The year taken is 1887, which was rather better than the three or four preceding years, and about equal to the average of the last twenty years.

	Total number of members.	Average number of unemployed.
Amalgamated Engineers	51,869	3,292
„ Carpenters	25,497	1,497
Boiler Makers	25,100	4,164
Iron Founders	11,718	1,174
London Compositors	7,025	742
Steam Engine Makers	5,080	299
Glass Bottle Makers	1,484	92
	127,773	11,260

Here we are dealing with the pick of the artisans of England. All these six trades* represent important industries which are not less regular than the others. All the men who work in them are necessarily possessed of a large amount of technical skill. Moreover, these particular 127,000 men are Trade Unionists, and it is notorious that the best and steadiest men in each trade are nearly always to

* The Steam Engine Makers and the Amalgamated Engineers are two separate societies in the same trade. Similar statistics of the Amalgamated Engineers for a period of eighteen years are referred to at page 109

be found among the members of the union. And yet of these men, thus carefully selected at any time during the year, eighty-eight out of every thousand were *unable to find work*. Their inability is tested by the fact that they were in receipt of allowances—"unemployed benefit"—paid over to them by their own comrades, who would be perfectly conversant with their circumstances. In fact, it is probable that more than this number of unionists were really unemployed, for many men have too much pride to come on their society in case of a temporary loss of work.

These figures are taken from an average year, and thus constitute a statistical proof that there are generally plenty of spare men to be found in every trade. This is indeed admitted to be a constant feature of our industrial system. "The modern system of industry," says Mr. Charles Booth, "will not work without some unemployed margin—some reserve of labour."* Clearly it is more to the interest of the trade society and its members that work should be found for their spare men than that the more lucky individuals should be surfeited with overtime. This is instantly obvious if the spare men are themselves members of the trade society, for in that case the society must support them until they find work. Meanwhile the overtime workers will be pocketing their overtime pay and contributing no more than usual to the society's funds. Considerations of this nature led to the interesting action of the Sheffield trade societies referred to at page 108.

And if the spare men are not members of their Trade Union the harm done to the society by keeping them out of work is equally great. Every man out of work is a fierce competitor for any chance of employment. Day after day he continues his heartbreaking search for work, and as his hopes grow fainter and fainter, he grows gradually desperate, and offers to take work on almost any terms. Employers—themselves beset with the difficulty of conducting a business profitably in the face of modern competition —will be tempted to utilise such offers as an excuse for lowering wages, and will certainly use them as a conclusive argument against any rise in wages or shortening of hours that may be asked for. In brief, the competition of the unemployed is the most effectual instrument for keeping down the wages of the employed.

* *Life and Labour in East London*, p. 167.

We thus see that even those unions which were powerful enough under a happy conjunction of economic conditions to win a nominal Nine Hours Day are not powerful enough to make that nominal gain a reality. They cannot be relied upon to win an effective Eight Hours Day. In some cases possibly they might be successful in substituting the figure 8 for the figure 9, just as in 1873 they substituted 9 for 10. But this substitute, unless accompanied by strict provisions against habitual overtime, is hardly worth struggling for. It would merely amount in the majority of cases to a slight gain in money wages, and still leave untouched all the physical, intellectual, and social evils that flow from protracted hours of labour.

But even were Trade Unions powerful enough to secure a serious and effective reduction in the hours of labour, it may still be doubted whether it is to the interest of the community as a whole that the work should be left to them. The methods of Trade Unions are essentially the methods of war. A strike, with all its miserable accompaniments, is the only effective instrument which Trade Unions possess for enforcing their will.

Few people realise how much misery a strike of necessity entails. The long, anxious waiting, the insufficiency of food, the cessation of every luxury, and the spectacle daily growing sadder of the home bit by bit bereft of all its little ornaments and comforts, while its inmates, like its owner, are visibly suffering from downright starvation. These are the trials imposed upon the workman and upon his family when a Trade Union asserts its independence by striking.

Nor are the workmen actually engaged in a strike the only members of the community who suffer thereby. To many a little tradesman who has just with difficulty been able to keep his head above water, a strike in his neighbourhood will mean inevitable bankruptcy. And though it is upon the workmen and their dependents that the misery of a strike falls with the greatest severity, the employers also have their full share of trouble. Except in a few rare cases where a strike provides a convenient opportunity for alterations, the cessation of work necessarily involves loss to the employer. That loss may only be sufficient to slightly diminish his available cash balance; it may be sufficient to ruin him.

The expense and the misery involved by strikes is not the only reason against leaving to Trade Unions the work of securing an Eight Hours Day. Beyond the immediate effects there is the permanent result upon social peace. If the Eight Hours Question is left to be fought out between employers and employed by the methods of private war, the relations between the two parties must necessarily be embittered. Workmen cannot see their families starving and their homes dismantled without feeling hatred towards masters to whose obstinacy they will attribute the whole blame. In the same way employers, who see their chances of doing a profitable trade suddenly dashed to the ground by a cunningly timed strike, will find it difficult to repress feelings of bitter indignation.

Moreover, it must be remembered that the struggle for the Eight Hours Day, if it is left to the unions to fight out to the bitter end, will not cease with the first apparent victory. As soon as bad times come, the employer, to save himself from loss, will begin to cut down expenses. In 1879 the London building firms caused a serious conflict by their attempt to go back to the Ten Hours Day. In all cases where the Eight Hours Day has involved increased cost of production the first move will be to return to the old hours of labour. The Eight Hours Day won in the United States by the strikes of May 1886, was lost again in a few months in nearly every instance. As soon as one firm goes back to the long hours, the rest must follow suit. Consequently if the Eight Hours Day originally gained had no better protection than the power of the unions, it will probably be lost on the first breath of bad trade.

The unions, moreover, have hitherto seldom been able to fix the same hours all over the country, so as to put all employers upon the same footing. The Amalgamated Carpenters and Joiners is one of the most powerful of Trade Unions, having branches all over the world wherever the English race is found. Yet the hours of labour fixed by this society vary in almost every town in the kingdom. Again, the Amalgamated Engineers Society, which may rightly be called the premier trade society of Great Britain, has arrived at no absolute rule or regard to hours of labour. The nominal working week is indeed fixed at 54 hours for the greater part of England, and 53 hours for the North-East Coast; but the actual working week varies from place to place according to local customs. With regard to overtime, in some districts the overtime is barred as much as possible, in others it has to be freely allowed. In the printing trade, compositors' hours for the same class of work ("jobbing") vary from 51 per week at Southport and Aberdeen to 60 per week at Brighton and Limerick.* It is not contended that there is any special grounds for these differences, which result merely from the varying strength of the union in each locality.

In the case of the cotton industry and other textile trades, the hours are the same all over the country, and the operatives run no risk of having them lengthened locally because the union is weak, or generally because trade is bad. But in these industries the hours are virtually fixed by the Factory Acts. Apart from this and other instances where the law has interfered, the hours of labour in all occupations are still subject to local variation. We may therefore safely infer that Trade Union efforts to obtain an actual Eight Hours Day could at best only be successful in favoured localities, where it was least needed. These local successes would be relentlessly cancelled in times of depression.

There is still one point of view to be considered in this examination of the desirability of appealing to Trade Unions to secure an Eight Hours Day—namely, the point of view of the general public. Let us deal first with the particular trade in which the Eight Hours agitation is now the keenest—the mining industry. As shown in another chapter, the hours of labour of miners vary considerably from county to county. In some cases the actual hewers of coal have obtained a real Eight Hours Day below ground. But these are the exception. Still more rare is it to find the auxiliary workers, boys and men, in possession of the same limitation of their labour. Thus to make a universal limit of eight hours a day for all workers below ground would involve a series of strikes affecting nearly all the colliery districts of the kingdom. Can any one doubt that such a state of things would cause terrible suffering to the general public? The price of coal would rise to famine level. The gas companies would find their expenses enormously increased, and would put up the price of gas. Railway shareholders and steamship shareholders would feel a difference in their dividends. The great iron and steel industries would be brought to a standstill from the impossibility

* London Society of Compositors' Guide, 1889.

of carrying on work with coal at a ruinous figure. All this loss and suffering, extending and ramifying in every direction through the whole body politic, would necessarily be entailed by any attempt of the colliers to settle the Eight Hours question, as they are often recommended to do, by a combined effort among themselves.

Again, to turn to a still larger industry, where a reduction in the hours of labour is as sorely needed as anywhere—the railway service. About 400,000 persons are employed by the railway companies of the United Kingdom. Many of these, as shown elsewhere, are compelled to work for extravagantly long hours. Are they to be thrown back upon their own strength to secure a reduction of their working day? The lesson of the Scotch railway struggle in December 1890 shows us that it is the public that will suffer. As soon as the men on any line feel sufficiently well organised they will strike, the traffic will be interrupted or altogether suspended, according to the strength of the strikers, and infinite trouble and inconvenience caused to the whole community.* Moreover, it is not one strike or two that will settle the question. At first the men will only move for a small improvement on their present condition. If successful they will advance another point; if defeated they will wait till they are strong enough to strike again. Thus either way the public may look forward to a series of strikes, possibly extending over at least a generation, to settle a point that could be settled in a few days by Parliament.

Of the same nature, but less serious in its results, is the interruption that would be caused to the tramway and omnibus service by a strike of conductors and drivers. Every one knows that these men are so shamefully overworked that they have scarcely a moment's leisure for intercourse with their families, or for reasonable recreation. Every one knows too that immediate relief could be given to them by the same body—the Imperial Parliament—which licenses every vehicle on which they work, and which has given to their employers the privileges of monopolists. Yet this relief is withheld on the plea that it is better for the men to fight their battles by a kind of private war, and in doing so starve their families, inflict serious loss upon their employers,

* The price of coal in Glasgow rose during the Scotch railway strike of 1890-91 from 7d. to 1s. 4d. per cwt.

and untold inconvenience upon the public. The stoppage of the tramways in New York and Vienna must have been, one would have thought, a convincing object-lesson as to the impolicy of encouraging such an Armageddon.

If further illustrations are needed of the loss to the public that necessarily results from leaving labour disputes to be settled by the barbarous method of striking, we may point to the great dock strike of 1889, which for a time completely dislocated the trade of London. Happily this strike, backed up by public sympathy and generous subscriptions, was so far successful that the dockers obtained for a time greatly improved conditions of work. Whether they will be able long to retain the advantages thus gained is another matter.

Moreover, a well-supported, widespread strike in some industries could not be tolerated by any Government. If all the railways running into London were really paralysed for a fortnight, with sympathetic strikes among the seamen and carmen, it may safely be predicted that Government intervention would be necessary to prevent food going to famine prices and serious tumult ensuing. Similar reasoning applies to the gas-workers, by whose labour London is lighted; the men in the service of the waterworks, by means of which it lives; or even those servants of the community who bury its dead. In all these cases, and in many others, the proposal that the workers should gain their ends by a strike can be made only because it is assumed that they must fail. The recommendations to the workers to unite as one man, perfect their organisation, obtain the sympathetic assistance of other trades, get public opinion on their side, and then rely on their strength, would be absolutely inconsistent with the very existence of a huge city were it not for the fact that by the nature of things the recommendation can never be followed, and would not be permitted to be if it could.

This, indeed, is the explanation of the sudden conversion of capitalists to an approval of Trade Unions. It seems scarcely possible that any responsible man can really be in favour of unrestrained Trade Union dictation in matters of gas and water, railways and tramways, unless he secretly believes that it can thus be defeated.

As regards other trades the loss caused to the public by a strike is less direct than in the case of the coal and transport industries, but it is a tangible quantity. All our industries are so linked together with one another that one cannot cease without doing serious damage to others. A strike in the shipbuilding trade, for instance, would involve a stoppage of works in iron and steel trades, and this in turn would involve an immense reduction in the demand for coal. One stoppage, in fact, leads to another, and the trouble goes on spreading throughout the whole body industrial.

The objections to leaving the Eight Hours Question to be settled by Trade Unions may therefore be briefly summed up as follows:—

A Trade Union can effectively assert the will of the majority only by means of a strike. A strike involves loss of wages and physical and mental suffering to the striker, semi-starvation to his family, and the loss of the comforts and luxuries that labour and love have gathered within the home. To the tradesmen of the district it involves loss of custom, the accumulation of credit, and in not a few cases bankruptcy. To the employer it means, in the first place, the cessation of the mechanism by which he earns his living and provides for his family; in the second place, it necessitates a purely profitless outlay in order to keep that mechanism, whatever it may be, ready for future use; and thirdly, it involves as a rule considerable expense in order to start work again.

Finally, to the general public a strike means the interruption of the ordinary working of the machinery of society—an interruption which would, in some cases, be absolutely unendurable, and in all cases must entail serious personal and pecuniary troubles to thousands of individuals who are powerless to control the cause of that interruption. Trade Union action is, in fact, anti-social in proportion as it is powerful, and endurable only when it is not effective. On these grounds we suggest that Trade Union action is an objectionable method of obtaining the Eight Hours Day even in cases where it might possibly prove successful. But, as we have already shown, these cases are rare. The past history of Trade Unionism proves that even in skilled and well-organised trades the societies cannot, in the face of the short-sighted selfishness of a minority of their members, be relied upon to put down the habitual practice of overtime. In unskilled trades any attempt to carry out a serious reform in the working hours would promptly be checkmated by the introduction of blacklegs.

(*c.*) *By Legislation.*

Rejecting therefore voluntary concession as Utopian, and Trade Union action as cruel, costly, and untrustworthy, the only other method of securing an Eight Hours Day is the peremptory interference of the Legislature. To say that this method is rapidly growing in favour with the persons principally concerned—namely, the working classes—would be to understate the case. It would be nearer the truth to say that nearly all the really zealous advocates of an Eight Hours Day in the United Kingdom are in favour of obtaining it by law. It is noteworthy that the persons who oppose Parliamentary interference with the hours of labour on the ground of principle usually add to their argument the assertion that the particular form of interference proposed—namely, the establishment of an Eight Hours Day—would be fatal to the industries of the country. The economic effect of a general or partial reduction in the hours of labour would be the same however that reduction were secured. The fact that the opponents of legislation usually try thus to bolster up their position renders suspicious their assurances that they are heartily in favour of an Eight Hours Day if only the workers can get it without the assistance of the Legislature. An assurance of this sort reminds one forcibly of the Methodists who complained of Sidney Smith's "unfairness" in turning the weapon of ridicule against them. "Use argument, rhetoric, prayer, anything you like," they said, "but not ridicule." To which Sidney Smith, with justifiable brutality, retorted, "I once knew a man whose head was infested with lice. Now, the only effective means of removing lice is to use a small tooth comb. But the man thought this would be unfair to the lice. So he tried pomatums and powders, hot water and cold water, everything in fact except a small tooth comb. His head is still infested with lice."

That the organised wage-earners in the United Kingdom are rapidly coming to desire legislation is shown by the formal votes taken at the successive Trade Union Congresses. We need not go back beyond the year 1889. In this year the Congress by a small majority rejected a resolution in favour of a legal and universal Eight Hours Day, but immediately carried *unanimously* a motion for an Eight Hours Bill for miners.

But when the Congress met the following year at Liverpool, it was found that the balance of voting had turned. In the interval of twelve months, working class opinion on the importance of a general reduction in the working day had ripened, and then there was, as related in Chapter II., a majority in favour of the universal and legal Eight Hours Day.

The opposition of the minority was largely due to mistrust of Parliament as a capitalist institution. Among the older Trade Unionists the tradition still lingers of the times, of which their fathers and grandfathers used to speak, when it was a criminal offence to join a Trade Union. And themselves many of them have had experience of the more recent times when a Trade Union was still a pariah among the corporate bodies of the country, unrecognised by law and incapable of defending itself by legal process against the dishonesty of its officers. To-day, too, they see that for one labour representative who with infinite pains on the part of his fellows secures a seat in Parliament, fifty employer representatives are returned with relative ease. The few representatives of labour who do get into the House of Commons are there quite swamped and made powerless to move by the mass of landlords and capitalists around them. It is therefore perfectly intelligible that the older men among the Trade Unionists should prefer still to trust to the old method of the strike, cruel, clumsy, and inefficient as it necessarily must be, rather than appeal to a body which they regard as permanently hostile to their cause.

These considerations explain why many of the leaders among the Trade Unionists have set their faces against Parliamentary action. An equally intelligible explanation can be given of the opposition of some of the Lancashire delegates at the Congress to the resolution demanding an immediate and universal Eight Hours Day. It must not be supposed that these have any objection to Parliamentary interference. In the manufacturing districts of Lancashire and Yorkshire the duration of the day's work in a mill is already virtually fixed by law at a maximum of ten hours a day, with a half-holiday on Saturday, or a total week of 56½ hours. Thus, in the first place, the mill operative is fairly well off as compared to the mass of wage-workers, and consequently has less need to exert himself for further reform. And in the second place, every Lancashire weaver or spinner knows perfectly well that his industry is dependent for its life on the power of English manufacturers to compete with foreign manufacturers. He knows too that in other countries the hours of labour are much longer than in England, and he not unnaturally fears that any sudden reduction in the hours of working might cripple the English producer. This fear, which is not altogether reasonable, has been dealt with more fully in Chapter IV. It is only mentioned here in order to explain how the minority vote at the Trade Union Congress was built up.

One other important body of working class opponents to the Parliamentary Eight Hours Day must be mentioned, and unfortunately their opposition is less creditable to themselves than is that of the two classes already dealt with. Owing to a combination of circumstances the majority of the coal-hewers of Durham and Northumberland enjoy a working day of less than eight hours. This happy condition is glibly attributed by many persons to the strength of the miners' unions in these two counties. No evidence, however, is brought forward to show that the miners' unions in Durham and Northumberland are as a matter of fact stronger, to any considerable extent, than the unions in other counties. One palpable fact is altogether overlooked, namely, that the short working day is only enjoyed by some of the workers underground. It is the hewers, the men who win the coal from the face of the rock, who have the seven hours day; but the men and boys who convey the coal from the workings to the foot of the shaft are in the pit for ten or eleven hours a day. If the miners' union is so powerful, why has it not protected these? The answer is that the miners' union, as has already been explained in Chapter III., has little or nothing to do with the matter. The hewers work only seven hours a day, because the mine-owners find it convenient to work their pits with two shifts of hewers to one shift of auxiliary workers. The "rulleymen" can take the coal faster than the hewers can win it, and so it is necessary for the hewers to accumulate a stock. This is accomplished by keeping two shifts of hewers in the pit a total period of thirteen to fourteen hours, while one shift of rulleymen is underground for ten to eleven hours. Hence the anomaly that in Durham and Northumberland a boy sixteen years of age may be working underground several hours a day longer than his father.*

* It is objected to an Eight Hours Bill that it would upset this two-shift arrangement. It is, however, absurd to suppose that some readjustment of

Obviously a Parliamentary Eight Hours Day would get rid of this anomaly. But many of the hewers of Durham and Northumberland seem to be more anxious to perpetuate by means of this anomaly their own exceptionally favoured position, than to reduce to a moderate level the hours of labour of their comrades and their children.

These three classes undoubtedly represent a larger proportion of the minority vote at Liverpool, and may, indeed, between them comprise the whole of that vote. But on this we do not insist. It is sufficient to point out that the minority was partly composed of persons who believed, not that Parliamentary action was in itself inexpedient, but that a reduction to so short a day as eight hours was not yet applicable to all trades. Bearing this fact in mind, we are thus in a position to state that a large majority of the persons in the United Kingdom who know most about the capabilities and the limitations of Trade Unions, believe that a reduction of the hours of labour can be secured better by Parliamentary than by Trade Union action.

Such a statement, however, will not convince, nor ought it to convince, those persons who believe, on philosophic grounds, that the regulation of the hours of labour is not a matter within the province of Parliament. And the difficulty of completely combating such a view is that it is impossible to know what common premises all the holders of it are prepared to accept. It is held by an immense number of persons, whose opinions on almost every other subject of political practice or theory differ fundamentally. It is held by the Anarchist, who believes that all law is bad, and that each individual ought to be left to the guidance of his own good nature. It is held by the members of the Liberty and Property Defence League, whose nominal attachment to liberty is accompanied by a very real respect for the mass of compulsory legislation by which the privileges of property are secured. It is held by Liberals of the old school, who were brought up on the belief that nothing but the free importation of commodities, and the unrestrained sale of labour, was needed to make every one happy in the happiest of worlds. It is held by modern Conserva-

the method of working could not be made if desired, possibly at an increased cost. In other colliery districts there is no such marked difference between the hours of the hewers and those of the auxiliary workers.

tives, who believe that the panacea for Irish ills is twenty years of coercive government.

The first of them, the Anarchist, we may leave alone. He stands apart. His position is not one of argument, but of protest—protest against the cruelty and stupidity of which every Government in the world has at one time or another been guilty. As far as it goes this protest is useful, but it does not affect, and never will affect, the virtually universal belief of mankind that the harm done by cruel and foolish Governments is an insignificant quantity compared with the harm that absolutely ungoverned individuals would do to one another.

The Tory Coercionist is a much more serious person to deal with,—principally because he is more frequently met with. He believes in government; believes that the majority of human beings must not infrequently be coerced into good behaviour. But he does not believe that it is right to apply coercion to employers who persist in working adult males longer than is good for them or for the community. Such an application of coercion, he will tell you, quoting from the phrase-book of a defunct Liberalism, is an interference with individual liberty. But under what circumstances coercion is not an interference with individual liberty he will certainly be unable to explain. It is impossible to avoid the conclusion that it is not so much the interference with the individual's liberty that distresses the Tory, but, perhaps unconsciously to himself, the interference with the capitalist's profits. An Eight Hours Bill would be to him, as the Ten Hours Bill was to Sir James Graham, a piece of "Jack Cade legislation."

And here, side by side with the ordinary Tory, we may place the more philosophic individuals who constitute the Liberty and Property Defence League, and also that large body of persons who belong indeed to the Liberal party, but whose liberalism is that of the last generation. Whatever be their theories and traditions in the matter, the truth is that the real strength of their opposition to an Eight Hours Act arises from the fact that they do not want an Eight Hours Day at all, because, often from justifiable motives they dread its effect upon profits.

Nevertheless, there is a considerable number of persons drawn both from the ranks of labour, and from those of the capitalists, who honestly believe on philosophic grounds that the determination of the hours of labour is not a matter within the province of Parliament. To such persons we now address ourselves.

And as a first step towards disarming their opposition we may point out that the authority of the very political philosophers on whom they ignorantly rely is really against them. John Stuart Mill, in his essay *On Liberty*, insists that the principle of individual liberty cannot legitimately be pleaded against the jurisdiction of society in such a matter as the determination of the hours of labour. And in the same way the late Professor Stanley Jevons, in his book on *The State in Relation to Labour*, maintains that the question cannot be decided "on some supposed principle of liberty," but must be treated on the "varied and detailed grounds of expediency."

Still more emphatic is John Stuart Mill as a political economist.[*] He takes the question of the hours of labour as an illustration of the fact that individuals often cannot secure what they are all agreed in wanting except by the aid of law. Obviously one man alone cannot set the example of working short hours. He would simply be dismissed from his employment. Nor would an agreement among a number of men be more effective unless enforced by law or by a pressure of public opinion of equal power with the law. For though all the men might be convinced that their interests lay in working short hours, yet the immediate interest of each individual would be to work long hours for the sake of the extra pay. A purely voluntary agreement would consequently be liable to constant infraction, and soon the general limitation would cease to be observed. What some did from choice others would soon be obliged to do from necessity, and those who had chosen long hours for the sake of increased wages would be forced in the end to work long hours for no greater wages than before.

This question of the effect of a limitation of the hours of labour on wages is fully dealt with in another part of the present book; here we are only concerned with the theoretic justification for the interference of the State, and we may fairly ask those who object that it is not the business of Government to regulate the hours of

[*] *Principles of Political Economy*, book i., ch. xi. sec. 12. This is confirmed in the last chapter of his essay *On Liberty*, which contains admirable arguments for the interference of law, especially as regards Sunday labour.

labour, whether they possess some absolute test by which they can determine what is, and what is not, the business of Government? The great writers on the subject have no such ready rule. Bentham had none but expediency—the very point at issue. John Stuart Mill, as we have seen, had no such objection and no such rule. Even when he was diligently seeking such a rule when writing *On Liberty*, he could find nothing more definite than general expediency, and, indeed, incidentally recognises in that very volume the admissibility of legal restraints on the employment of adult labour.*

It may, indeed, on the contrary, be reasonably contended that the prevention of excessive hours of labour, for whatever object, is one of the essential duties of Government in an advanced industrial community. Even on the "glorified policeman" theory of "administrative nihilism," it is universally admitted to be the primary duty of Government to prescribe the plane on which it will allow the struggle for existence to be fought out. Of course, the fittest to survive under the given conditions will inevitably survive, but the Government does much to determine the conditions, and therefore to decide whether the fittest, by the test of conflict, shall be also the best then and there possible. We have long ruled out of the conflict the appeal to brute force, thereby depriving the strong man of his natural advantage over his weaker brother. We stop, as fast as we can, every development of fraud and chicanery, and so limit the natural right of the cunning to overreach their neighbours. Notwithstanding the ancient maxim of the market, *caveat emptor*, we prohibit the weapon of deceptive labels and trade-marks. In spite of John Bright's protest, we rule that adulteration is not a legally permissible form of competition. We forbid slavery: with Mill's consent, we even refuse to uphold a lifelong contract of service. The whole history of Government is, indeed, one long series of definitions and limitations of the conditions of the struggle, in order to raise the quality of the fittest who survive. This service can be performed only by Government. No individual competitor can lay down the rules for the combat. No individual can safely choose the higher plane, so long as his opponent is at liberty to fight on the lower. "Gresham's Law," according to which bad currency drives out good, applies throughout the industrial contest. The good

* See pages 53 and 56 of 1878 edition.

employer is liable to be ousted by the bad. The honesty which is the best policy is merely just so much honesty as will not let you fall flagrantly out at elbows with your neighbours. If sixteen hours in the gas-lit basements of the London textile warehouses is the standard of the trade for growing lads, apparently not even a Samuel Morley could venture to work his staff shorter hours. No cotton factory will dare to work only eight hours while its rival works ten. No shop dare close while its competing neighbour remains open. It is for the people collectively to decide whether the industrial tournament shall be fought to the bitter end, or shall be merely a friendly emulation, not involving wounds, degradation, and death even for the vanquished. A hundred years ago the "fittest" to survive were sturdy Virginian slaves; sixty years ago they were the maimed, distorted, and diseased factory hands who paraded before Lord Ashley in Oldham and Blackburn; a generation ago they were the "lower class brutalised" of the great apostle of culture—what they will be a generation hence depends essentially upon the legal and social limitations which we to-day set to the ape and tiger of the natural man.

The above considerations afford ample support for the positive side of the case for State interference. But it is still necessary to meet more in detail the objection that the compulsory limitation of the hours of labour is an unjustifiable interference with individual liberty.

It is, in the first place, noticeable that this objection is raised not by manual workers themselves, but by members of Parliament, barristers, journalists, and other professional men who are trying to stand between the working classes and tyrannical legislation. Without a doubt the objection is honestly and seriously felt by those who bring it forward. A law which should attempt to regulate what time a barrister should give to the study of briefs, or a journalist to the writing of articles, would be at once an impertinence, and of necessity futile. The law cannot regulate that which the workman himself cannot even measure. The real work of a barrister or a journalist is done in the brain, and no man can tell exactly when his brain ceases to work on a particular subject and gives itself up to amusement. The brain may possibly be sketching the rough draft of an article, or thinking out a legal argument, while the body is sitting in the theatre, or sauntering along the street, or lying in bed. Even were State regulation possible, there is no conceivable reason why it should be asked for. Every professional man is his own master. If he works long hours, it is to please himself only, and none of his competitors are thereby made to follow his example.*

This was also the case with the manual labourer when the weaver sat in his cottage at his own loom, and the carrier drove his own cart. But the industrial revolution which became general in the United Kingdom during the eighteenth century, and is now rapidly becoming universal, has swept away this individual liberty in all trades more highly organised than that of a chimney-sweep. The worker, in most of the great manufacturing industries of advanced communities, must now begin and leave off work at the sound of the factory bell or steam "hooter," over the times of which he feels that he has as little individual control as over the sunrise. To fix by law the working hours of a journalist or a doctor would undoubtedly diminish his personal liberty of action; to hasten by Act of Parliament the welcome signal for the close of the factory day would increase the personal liberty of the operative. At present the latter has practically no control over his working hours; it is therefore scarcely to be wondered at that he seeks even the fraction of control which his vote for an Eight Hours Bill will secure to him.

But it is not on every manual worker that the advocates of an Eight Hours Act seek to impose a legal limitation. It is not the pain of the work to the worker himself, but the effect of his action on other workers that justifies in the main the interference of the State. No one wishes to prevent a man from working as long as he pleases, provided that his working has not the effect of compelling others to work also. He may labour at his allotment far into the night if he so chooses, because no other allotment holder is thereby made to do likewise. He may spend his leisure

---

* As a matter of fact, most professional men do enjoy more leisure than the average manual worker. The workman measures his day only by the number of hours he is actually at work; the so-called Nine Hours Day really extends from 6 A.M. to 5 P.M. Few brain workers continue so long in the city. What artisan, moreover, gets a month's holiday in the summer with a week or a fortnight at Christmas? There are few professional men who refuse themselves at least this relaxation.

in constructing cathedrals out of cherry-stones, or statues out of snow. The community merely claims the right to prevent him from selling his excessive labour in such a way as to cause other workers to be compelled to work as long as he does.

Thus the advocates of State interference do not ground their case on the vague plea that an Eight Hours Day is abstractedly desirable for everybody. Their advocacy rests on the far surer basis of hard fact and practical expediency. They ask the State to coerce the employer, not because it may be good for any zealous workman to have his hours of labour limited to eight, but because as long as he is left free to work longer, his neighbours are compelled to do the same. In other words, his liberty is to be curtailed in order that the liberty of others may be extended.

Nor is there any danger that there will be any interference with the will of the majority. The natural bias of the House of Commons is altogether against legislative restriction of the hours of labour. The capitalist members of that House know that their seats depend on working class votes. Until there is no doubt left that the vast majority of the working classes have made up their minds upon the subject, an Eight Hours Bill has of course no chance of being accepted by the House of Commons. There will be virtually no coercion except by consent. When a preponderating majority in any particular industry are agreed that eight hours shall be the maximum duration of a day's work, then, and not till then, will an Eight Hours Law for that industry be possible.

Under these conditions there is clearly no infringement of liberty in the ordinary sense of the word. All that the law does is to make it impossible for the minority to continue to coerce the majority, and to hinder the individual under temptation from breaking through an arrangement which his reason has convinced him is a good one.

The next plea of the opponent of an Eight Hours Law is that the assistance given by the State to the working man as a buttress to his own resolution will destroy that spirit of self-reliance which distinguishes the English race.

No evidence is adduced to prove that the self-reliance of working men has been diminished by the long series of Factory Bills already passed into law. No suggestion is made that women workers in trades which are under effective legal protection are less self-reliant than those who toil in the unregistered laundries of Notting Hill, or "sweating dens" of East London. The cotton operatives of Lancashire, both male and female, have been longer and more thoroughly subjected to the enervating influences of the legal limitation of their hours of labour than any other workers; it will be news, to those who know them, that they are less self-reliant than less effectively protected wage-slaves, or that they possess less sturdy independence than their unprotected forefathers of seventy years ago. The actual evidence is, in fact, to exactly the contrary effect. Mr. Mundella is the best possible witness on such a point, and his testimony is emphatic. Writing in 1873, he says :—

"An argument which is freely advanced against the interference of the State with the relations of capital and labour, is that it tends to undermine the independence and self-reliance of the class which it seeks to protect, and teaches them to look to the State rather than to their own exertions to remedy evils requiring redress. My answer to this is, that the factory operatives of Lancashire and Yorkshire have made greater advances in self-reliance and independence during the past fifty years than any other class of English operatives. Building and benefit societies, co-operative associations, both for distribution and production, have taken their rise and flourish amongst them on a scale of magnitude unknown in any other part of the United Kingdom."*

It may, moreover, be added that no class of wage-earners is better organised, and that their unions have become stronger since the Ten Hours Bill became law, and not weaker.

And indeed if we examine this objection more closely we see that it has not even theoretic validity. It is merely a survival from the time when the government was an oligarchy practically free from popular control. Under such conditions any boon obtained from the government might conceivably have the effect of weakening the self-reliance of the recipients. But when the government is only the executive and administrative committee of the governed, it is difficult to see where the weakening of self-reliance comes in. A cricket club may possibly be demoralised by the gift of a set of stumps from the parliamentary candidate for the division; but when the stumps are bought out of the members'

* Introduction to E. E. von Plener's *English Factory Legislation.*

own subscriptions by the elected committee of the club, no one is demoralised thereby, or otherwise than strengthened in his self-reliance.

It may, however, be urged, and properly urged, that this argument does not cover all the cases where an Eight Hours Act would apply. Women, for instance, would be subject to the Act, but they can hardly be said to be parties to the passing of it, since they have no direct share in the choice of parliamentary representatives. But, curiously enough, there is an almost universal agreement, even among persons opposed to a general Eight Hours Act, that the State is justified in restricting the hours of labour of women. Thus, for example, in a letter written by the Right Hon. H. Childers, M.P. (formerly Chancellor of the Exchequer in Mr. Gladstone's ministry), on the Eight Hours Question, we find the following curious dictum:—

"What, I think is the dangerous notion which the State should absolutely repudiate is, that because the majority in a trade, for social reasons, or in order to raise prices or wages, desire to prohibit men from working more than a certain number of hours, the State should step in and enforce this desire. We live in a free country, and legislation of this kind is utterly inconsistent with personal liberty. The State has a perfect right to decide for how many hours it will employ men in its own workshops, arsenals, dockyards, etc., but not to decide what private employers should do. *The State has the absolute right to restrict the labour of women and children.*"

It is not worth while to criticise these remarks in detail, but in passing we may ask how the State is to impose a general restriction on the labour of women and children, without at the same time "deciding what private employers should do"? Probably Mr. Childers himself does not know, and he would be equally puzzled to explain why it is justifiable to coerce the employers of women without consulting either them or their workers, and to refuse to coerce the employers of men who ask for coercion. The usual explanation is that the women cannot protect themselves, and therefore need the assistance of the State. The Duke of Argyll* long ago exploded this fallacious defence of factory legislation, by a demonstration that women workers and youths

* *Reign of Law*, ch. vii.

were often far superior in economic strength to many classes of adult male workers. Moreover, the defence is obviously insufficient, for by Mr. Childers' hypothesis a majority of the men concerned ask for State assistance, and therefore, in their own opinion at any rate, they need that assistance. This leads to the dilemma, that if the opinion of the men themselves is taken as final, then it is decided that they do need the assistance of the State; whilst, if their opinion on a question of fact concerning themselves is set aside as valueless, the incompetence of judgment thereby attributed to them is *primâ facie* evidence that they are incapable of taking care of themselves.

We contend, therefore, that judicious assistance from the collective organisation of the community, instead of undermining the spirit and self-reliance of the individual, will often create these qualities where they did not before exist. And in support of this view, we appeal to the fact that the hours of labour of adult women have been for nearly half a century regulated by law, and that the women who have been subject to this "tyranny" are not less but more independent, more self-reliant, more progressive, than those who have been left to enjoy the "liberty" of industrial competition. The women workers in the Yorkshire cloth mills, whose hours have for two generations been rigidly fixed by law, are certainly not inferior to the female tailor hands who enjoy the comparative "freedom" of the sweater's den; or the laundresses, who are absolutely excluded from the operation of the Factory Acts. We appeal further to the fact that by the incidental operation of the Factory Laws the hours of labour of a large number of adult men have also been regulated; and these men, the mill operatives of Lancashire and the West Riding, constitute the most strong-headed and self-reliant portion of the working classes of the United Kingdom.

The contrary theory assumes that every human being is by nature strong and self-reliant; whereas, in fact, many thousands of our countrymen are by nature physical and mental weaklings. The moving force that is to enable these men of their own accord to protect themselves does not exist. To leave them simply alone, and tell them to fight their own battles, is comparable to the advice to Mrs. Dombey "to make an effort." Mrs. Dombey answered by dying.

But that unfortunately is just what our weakling class will not do. Feckless and infirm of purpose in every other direction, they have animal energy enough to breed. Half of their children die, it is true, but the other half live, and in a few generations the feeble species is almost doubled. These are the people of whom we were specially thinking when we admitted above that all the persons covered by an Eight Hours Act would not be active parties to the passing of such an Act. The application to them of a coercive law may be defended on the ground that it is the sole means of lifting them from that degradation which is so injurious to the whole community. A legal limitation of their hours of labour would raise them as it has raised the textile operatives. It will place them forcibly in an economically stronger position than they at present occupy. And though for a time they will gain thereby nothing but material profit; though for a time they will still be weaklings ready at any moment to tumble back into the slough from which they have been dragged; yet gradually the pressure of better conditions of life will tell upon them, or if not on them, upon their children. In time this feckless race will develop into a higher type, even as the men and women of Lancashire, themselves once equally degraded, have under similar coercion developed. In time it too will become sturdy and self-reliant, capable not only of standing alone, but also of joining in that higher freedom which comes with associated action for the common needs of life.

CHAPTER VIII.

ENGLISH PRECEDENTS FOR LEGISLATIVE ACTION.

A GOOD many people, otherwise well informed, have a notion that the principle of State regulation of the hours of labour proposed by the advocates of an Eight Hours legal day is an entirely novel one in English legislation. Nothing could be farther from the truth. The principle has been accepted and acted upon by the Legislature of the United Kingdom over and over again. In proof of this proposition we might if we chose go back to the numerous statutes that were passed during the Tudor period for the regulation of industry. But these examples, though interesting as showing the view of the duties of government then held by English statesmen, are not valuable as precedents for the present time. For between those days and ours a complete revolution in public sentiment on the subject of State interference passed over the country, and we may justly refuse to be bound now by principles of policy established then. But it is, however, instructive to point out in a few words how it was that the English people, who had so long recognised the compulsory regulation of industry as part of their state policy, should suddenly become converted towards the end of the last century to the doctrines of *laissez faire*.

We will go back no farther than the reign of Queen Elizabeth, when the famous Statute of Apprentices was passed (5 Eliz., c. 4). The principal object of this Act was to prevent the displacement of grown men by young lads, and to protect the latter from the possible tyranny of their masters. Its provisions may be summarised as follows :—

Whoever had three apprentices must have one journeyman, and an additional journeyman for every additional apprentice.

Journeymen must be engaged for a whole year, and must have a quarter's notice.

The hours of labour are to be twelve per diem in summer, and during daylight in winter.

Wages are to be assessed by the magistrate at every Easter Session.*

Disputes between masters and apprentices are to be settled by the magistrates, who are instructed to protect the apprentices.

It is almost superfluous to remark that many of these provisions are ludicrously inappropriate to the conditions of industry to-day. Nevertheless, this Act regulated the main industries of this country for a period of nearly two centuries, and it only broke down when the general introduction of machinery made its provisions no longer applicable. At the time it passed, the Act was little more than an authoritative statement of the rules established by the old Craft Guilds. By enforcing these rules it bolstered up the power of the Guilds. Consequently, even in Adam Smith's time, the Guilds, no longer capable of progressive action, were still powerful for stubborn opposition, while at the same time the actual provisions of the Act further blocked the way of inevitable changes. And thus the new industry, born direct from the brains of Hargreaves, and Arkwright and Crompton, found itself hampered at every turn by petty regulations once full of utility, but now stupidly obstructive. No wonder then that there was an impatient clamour for the abolition of all regulation, and a demand that industry should be left free.

Nor was this rebellion against old laws confined to this country only, or to one department of human activity. The whole current of thought that led to the French Revolution was one of bitter hostility to the tyranny of the past. Everywhere men saw the possibility of a new and wider field opening before them; everywhere they burned with eagerness to kick off their inherited fetters. And so the fetters were kicked off, and great was the jubilation. But never, perhaps, has a nation more speedily dis-

* By an Act of the next reign (1st Jac. i. c. 6) this power of the magistrates to fix wages in certain trades is extended to the wages of all labourers and workmen whatever, and it is explained that the wages are to be fixed at such a figure as to "yield unto the hired person, both in time of scarcity and in time of plenty, a convenient proportion of wages"

covered than did England then the wisdom of not despising too hastily the "old narrow ordinances" of the past. "Mein Sohn, lass uns die alten engen Ordnungen gering nicht achten. Köstlich unschätzbare Gewichte sind's die der bedrängte Mensch an seiner Dränger raschen Willen band."*

Directly the restraints of law and mediæval custom were removed, the journeyman and the small master became completely subject to the wealthy manufacturer. The new machines rendered the skill of the trained artisan and the strength of the adult no longer necessary for the production of cloth and yarn and hose. Children were brought into the factory, literally by cart-loads, while grown men who had spent the best years of their lives in learning their trade, were left to walk the streets in starving idleness. Already, early in the eighteenth century, these troubles had been felt in two important trades that had grown up since the passing of the Statute of Apprentices, and were therefore not subject to its provisions—namely, the cotton trade and the stocking trade. In the latter especially so fierce were the struggles between masters and men that in the year 1727 Parliament made it a capital offence to break a stocking frame. Half a century later, in 1779, an attempt to regulate the trade was made by Lord Carrington, who, with this object, introduced a Bill into Parliament. The Bill was thrown out on its third reading. Serious riots followed.†

Turning again to the trades subject to the Statute of Queen Elizabeth, we find that troubles began as early as 1720. By that year the assessment of wages in the woollen trade by the Justices had fallen into disuse. In consequence the masters took advantage of their men, and wages began to decline. The men tried to combine, but Parliament prohibited these combinations, and at the same time re-enacted the provision of the Statute of Apprentices requiring the Justices to fix wages. Apparently this was unsuccessful, for in 1756 the men formally appealed to the Justices to

* Advice to his son that Schiller puts into the mouth of the elder Piccolomini :—" My son, let us not despise the old narrow ordinances. Priceless fetters are they that the oppressed have forged to bind the oppressor's impatient will."

† See Brentano, *Gilds and Trade Unions*, pp. 119, 120. (London, Trübner & Co., 1870.)

carry out the law. The masters lodged a counter appeal, and the magistrates did nothing. Riots followed, causing damage estimated at £15,000. After this, the masters seem to have been more conciliatory for a time.

The object of the men was always to get the magistrates to enforce the Statute of Apprentices ; the object of the masters was to get Parliament to repeal the Statute altogether. The latter were at length victorious. In 1803 the Statute of Queen Elizabeth, so far as it affected the woollen trade, was suspended, and in 1809 repealed. Finally, in 1814, the whole Statute was formally repealed and the reign of *laissez faire* inaugurated.

The victory of the masters was apparently complete, but only apparently. For at the very time that Parliament was thus with its right hand sweeping away the laws that for more than 200 years had been the sheet anchor of the working classes, with its left hand it was creating new laws to meet the evils that had arisen out of the new anarchy. By far the most important of these new laws were the early Factory Acts, for they were the beginning of a whole system of legislation. But before dealing with these, it is interesting just to mention in passing a minor set of enactments, which, though most successful in their special object, were not sued as precedents for subsequent legislation, and have since been almost forgotten. We are alluding to the Spitalfields Acts for the regulation of the London silk trade. In this trade, as well as in others, the gradual disuse of the practice of fixing wages by the magistrates led to a decline in the wages of the workmen, and this in turn led to violence, accompanied with the destruction of property. To remedy this state of things an Act was passed in 1773 requiring the Lord Mayor, or the Justices of the Peace for the City of London, to fix the wages of the journeymen engaged in the manufacture of silk. Fines were imposed by the Act on employers who gave more or less than the wages thus fixed, and on workmen who entered into combinations to raise wages. These fines were to be applied to the relief of needy members of the trade and their families. The Act was extended in 1792, so that it should apply to a silk mixture as well as to pure silk, and in 1811 it was made to apply to women. Thus here we have as late as the year 1811 the British Parliament passing an Act for the regulation of wages by law.

And now what was the result of this effort to do by law a thing which all political economists tell us with parrot repetition that Parliament is incapable of doing? The answer is to be found in the evidence taken on a subsequent occasion before select committees of the House of Commons. From this evidence it appears* that after the enactment of the first Spitalfields Act no more strikes occurred in Spitalfields. Both masters and men were unanimous in their praise of the Acts, and an employer even declared that in case of their repeal he would retire from the trade. But that is not all. These Acts were purely local in their application. Other silk districts like Coventry, Nuneaton, and Macclesfield, were outside the scope of the Spitalfields Acts, and as soon as the general law (the Statute of Apprentices) was repealed, these districts began to suffer from all the evils of industrial anarchy. They therefore in 1818 applied to Parliament to be included in the Spitalfields Acts. A committee of the House of Commons considered their application, and after recording that the introduction of half-pay apprentices had driven the adult males to famine and the female workers to prostitution,† significantly adds, " Whilst the Statute of 5th Elizabeth was in force the distressing circumstances now complained of never occurred."

The Spitalfields Acts are thus most instructive as showing how extremely recent in our history is the last attempt to fix wages by Act of Parliament, and how remarkably successful that experiment was. We are not, however, now concerned with this particular point. For there is now no demand on the part of the working classes of this country that their wages should be fixed otherwise than by competition modified by the power of combination. Our present concern is with factory legislation properly so called. And our object is to show how this series of statutes forms a continuous precedent for the legislation now asked.

It has already been stated that with the introduction of machinery, children were brought into the factories literally by cartloads to take the places of skilled men. These children, or many of them, came from the southern counties, where children were plentiful and work scarce. They were brought to Lancashire and Yorkshire, where the new mills springing up on every hand were continually crying for more cheap labour. It was the Poor Law Guardians of the southern counties who were principally

* See Brentano, pp. 125, 126. † Brentano, p. 130.

responsible for this juvenile migration. They collected the children from the workhouses, packed them off by waggon or barge, and asked no questions as to what became of them. The manufacturer in due course received his human consignment and housed it in barracks built for the purpose close to the factory. Further, in order to economise space and bedding it was arranged that one gang of children should be at work while the other gang was in bed. And to save time the children were carried straight from the mill to beds still warm from the bodies of those who had been drafted off to work. From the manufacturer's point of view this arrangement was doubtless excellent. He kept his mill running day and night, and his labour cost him next to nothing. His profits were enormous. But a tyrannical State ventured to interfere with his divine liberty. In 1796 a Board of Health was appointed to inquire into the causes of a serious outbreak of epidemic disease among the factory population of Manchester and the surrounding district.* Nothing was done immediately. The persons on whose behalf legislation was sought were unrepresented and inarticulate. Why should Parliament bestir itself? But in 1802, on the initiative of Sir Robert Peel the elder, an Act was passed dealing with some of the worst of the evils laid bare by the Board of Health. Note, however, the extreme caution of the Legislature, its tenderness for the interests of the manufacturer. All that was done was to prescribe certain sanitary regulations, and to limit the hours of labour of these tiny children to twelve per diem. There was no eight hours nonsense in those days! Moreover, the Act only applied to pauper apprentices. Children whose parents lived in the neighbourhood were still at "liberty" to work as long as their employers chose.

Again Sir Robert Peel intervened. And this time he demanded that the freeborn British workman should not be allowed to sell the labour of his child to unscrupulous employers. In 1815 another Parliamentary inquiry took place, and from this resulted in 1819 the second Factory Act. This Act prescribed that no child should go to work in a factory before it was nine years old, and fixed the hours of labour of children between nine and sixteen at 72 hours per week, *exclusive* of meal times.

* See Plener, *English Factory Legislation*, p. 2. (London: Chapman & Hall, 1873.)

A more comprehensive measure was in 1825 carried through Parliament by Sir John Hobhouse. In this Act legal provision was for the first time made for a Saturday half-holiday.

In 1831 Sir John Hobhouse was again successful in securing an advance on the previous Factory Acts. The Act of this year consolidated and amended previous enactments. It further prescribed that in the cotton industry no person under the age of twenty-one should be engaged in night work, and that the time of labour of all persons under eighteen should be limited to 69 hours per week. This Act dealt also with the administration of the law, and provided that no owner of a cotton mill, nor any immediate kinsman of a mill owner, should be competent to act as a Justice of the Peace in cases of infringement of the Factory Law. Nevertheless, the law was constantly broken. In many cases the men were compelled to subscribe to a fund out of which the manufacturer's fines were paid.*

It was about this time that the agitation for the Ten Hours Day began among the working classes. Their great leader, Richard Oastler, who received the nickname of the "Factory King," addressed huge meetings of workmen all over Yorkshire, and his eloquence everywhere excited tremendous enthusiasm. In 1832, accompanied by Tom Sadler, he carried the agitation into Lancashire. In the same year Sadler introduced into Parliament a Bill limiting to ten hours a day the labour of all persons under eighteen years of age, and extending the protection of the law to wool, flax, and silk, as well as to cotton factories. This Bill received the fiercest opposition from the manufacturing members of Parliament. Nevertheless, a parliamentary committee was appointed to consider the Bill. The evidence taken by this committee gives a most vivid picture of the condition of the factory operatives. The principal working class witnesses were wool spinners from Yorkshire. These men enjoyed no legal protection whatever. The original Act of 1802 did not touch their case, because it applied only to pauper apprentices, and the subsequent Acts only applied to the cotton industry. In addition to these working class witnesses, numerous medical men were called. Their evidence was conclusive as to the terrible effects of prolonged labour on young children. "And then a cry was raised throughout England, and

* Plener, p. 7.

echoed all over the Continent, at the sight of the sufferings so graphically described of the poor little factory children, compelled to slave under cruel treatment from thirteen to fourteen hours a day, of young girls more wild than civilised, and of the apathetic exhaustion of men grown old at thirty."*

In spite of this damning evidence, it is only too probable that no drastic reform would have been undertaken by Parliament but for a political accident. The Tories suddenly discovered that the labour agitation of the factory operatives might be used as an effective counterblast to the purely political agitation of the middle classes. They eagerly joined in the outcry against the cruelties of the manufacturers. They held out the hand of comradeship to the champions of the factory population, and they aided in the exposure of the hideous evils brought of unrestricted competition.

In the Reform elections of 1832 the factory representative, Tom Sadler, lost his seat; but in the new Parliament Lord Ashley (afterwards Lord Shaftesbury), whose motives are now beyond suspicion, took up the cause. The Bill which he brought in virtually restricted the hours of labour of all persons employed in factories to 10 per diem.† The Whigs at once joined issue. On the motion of the Chancellor of the Exchequer, the House declared that it intended in no way to regulate the hours of labour of adults. We refuse, said the Whig House of Commons, to interfere with the cherished liberty of free-born British citizens. It is difficult to be patient with such hypocrisy. It was not the liberty of the adult labourer that the capitalist House of Commons cared about, but the profits of the manufacturer. The Government of the day knew well enough that the adult labourers were themselves the agitators for the legal restriction of their own hours. The latest Royal Commission had chronicled the fact, and ingeniously used it as an argument against the workmen. The factory operatives, said the commissioners in their report, have signed petitions in favour of the Ten Hours Bill, less out of sympathy with the sufferings of little children, than because they hope that this measure will restrict their hours of labour also.

This hope was frustrated. The Bill introduced by the Government on the report of the Royal Commission did not propose to

* Plener, p. 9. † Plener, p. 10.

establish a uniform working day, but broke up the workers into different categories. "Children," aged nine to thirteen, were to work only 48 hours per week; "young persons," aged thirteen to eighteen, were to work 69 hours; and all persons over eighteen might work as long as their employers chose. The Bill passed into law during 1833, and, though it did not satisfy the wishes of the operatives, effected, by its subsidiary provisions, a great improvement on the previous legislation. For it was under this Act that inspectors were first appointed to see that the law was carried out. And the importance of this step cannot be exaggerated. The Factory Inspectors coming to their task with the impartiality of Gallios, but with human sympathy for human suffering, gently but firmly enforced the law. More than this, these "salaried inquisitors," during the fifty odd years that have elapsed since their first appointment, have constantly pressed upon individual manufacturers and upon Parliament the necessity for progressive improvements. It is to the initiation of the Factory Department of the Home Office that nearly all the details of subsequent factory legislation have been due; and many important improvements in the sanitary condition of workshops or in the safety of machinery have had their origin in half friendly, half authoritative suggestions from individual inspectors.

We need not trouble to detail the obstacles thrown in the way of the inspectors by unscrupulous manufacturers, by interested magistrates, and by brutalised parents—parents whose only anxiety was to make the best price out of the labour of their children. These obstacles were so serious that even the "protected persons" got scanty protection from the law. Incidentally, however, the 1833 Act led to a great diminution in the number of young children employed. For the manufacturers so disliked the provisions for compulsory schooling and short hours that many of them preferred not to employ "children" at all, but only "young persons" over thirteen who might be worked sixty-nine hours a week. In this way the number of children employed in factories fell from 56,000 in 1835 to 29,000 in 1838, though the number of factories had considerably increased.*

Meanwhile the agitation for a ten hours factory day still went on, and continued to grow in strength. But it was not in factories

* Plener, p. 22.

but in mines that the next important step in the direction of State regulation of labour was taken.

In 1840 a Commission was appointed to inquire into the conditions of the employment of children in industries which had been left "free" by previous legislation. Principal among these was the mining industry, and to this the Commissioners first turned their attention. The hideous facts disclosed in their report can only be paralleled in the pages of Zola's *Germinal.* It is sufficient to state here that men, women, and children all worked together underground in a half-naked condition; that the hours of labour were usually eleven or twelve, often sixteen, sometimes more; that the whole population was sunk in a hopeless condition of ignorance and brutality.

It was in consequence of this report that the first Mining Act was passed. This Act, apart from the direct good it brought about, is interesting to us here as being the first occasion in which modern legislation interfered with the labour of adults. Under the Act of 1842 women of all ages were prohibited from working underground, and even the adult male was not allowed to enjoy any longer the "liberty" of receiving his wages in a public-house.* Underground work was also prohibited to boys under ten.

The same Commission that had reported on the mining industry issued a second report dealing with trades and manufactures other than textile industries. The report states that in many trades children commence work at 4, 5, 6, and 7 years of age; that there is no legal protection for apprentices against unmerciful masters and the greed of parents; that the hours of labour are from ten to twelve per day; that the greatest poverty and ignorance prevails. This report was published in 1843, but the evils described were not immediately dealt with.

The next legislative step was the introduction of further stringency into the Acts by which the textile trades were regulated. This was in 1844, under Sir Robert Peel's Government. In this year the principle of special regulation for adult women, already applied in the case of mines, was extended to the textile trades. This extension ought to have excited the greatest opposition from

---

* The public-houses were often owned by the employers, who also kept truck shops at which the miners were compelled to buy had provisions at exorbitant prices.

the Whig manufacturers always so disinterestedly anxious for the liberty of the subject. But they were curiously silent. And the reason for this silence is not hard to find. For the Act of 1844, though it for the first time classified adult women as "young persons," yet left to the manufacturers such a long working day, and so many loopholes for evading the law, that they thought it would be waste of energy to grumble. The real battle came three years later over the Ten Hours Bill introduced by Mr. Fielden. And with the history of this measure we must venture to deal somewhat fully, because, as we shall show, its acceptance by Parliament constitutes an undoubted acknowledgment of the principle of State regulation of the hours of labour of adults, *male as well as female*.

It is not necessary here to venture on a posthumous interpretation of the nature of this measure. It will be amply sufficient and far more to the purpose to quote the opinions of the persons who spoke for or against the Bill in the House of Commons. The most categorical statement was made early in the debate on the second reading by the Chancellor of the Exchequer, Sir C. Wood. The Government of the day had decided to allow the Bill to be an open question, and the different members of the Government who spoke only expressed their individual views. Sir C. Wood opposed the Bill, and in so doing said: "The object of the Bill before them was the limitation of the hours of labour, not of young persons and women only, but of all factory labour. To the credit of the delegates from the manufacturing districts they had fairly and openly acknowledged that such was the object. It would therefore be waste of time to discuss it on any other footing than on that of a Bill for limiting all labour in factories to ten hours a day."*

This statement is sufficiently explicit, but it is interesting to show by a few more quotations that the debate was actually conducted on these lines. For example, "Mr. Trelawny objected to the Bill because he considered it a distinct invasion of the rights of property. It would invade not only the right of capital invested in manufactures, but the labourer who with a large family desired to work fourteen or fifteen hours a day would also be affected by it."

With regard to this quotation, it is interesting to note that in 1847 the opponents of State interference frankly stated that their *first* objection was due to their tenderness for the rights of property.

* *Hansard*, vol. 89, c. 1120.

In 1891 the same party is more subtle, and only mentions the liberty of the labourer.

To proceed. Viscount Ebrington felt satisfied "that any direct interference by Parliament with adult labour was not merely useless but unjustifiable." Again, on the motion to go into committee on the Bill, Mr. Ward said: "It was his firm belief that the hours of labour could not be reduced without a corresponding reduction in the amount of wages. And he believed that there was not a man amongst the working classes who would take a ten hours Bill with ten hours wages."

Mr. B. Escott asked "whether this was a time to say to the working man, 'You shall not exert yourself to the utmost—you shall not use all the faculties with which God has blessed you—to enable you to get bread for yourself and your family.'" Among other speakers Sir James Graham (the Home Secretary) devoted a long speech to proving that the measure would have the effect of ruining our foreign trade. It is not necessary to quote his arguments here, but no doubt the opponents of the Eight Hours Day will be able to make use of them, with a few changes of date. They are to be found in *Hansard*, 3rd series, vol. 90, col. 772 to 782.

So much for the lines on which the Bill was opposed. Now for the views of its supporters. Sir George Grey said: "I do not wish to argue the question or to support the Bill on false pretences. I admit that it is a fair argument against the Bill that, looking to the number of young children and adult and females in factories, the restriction of the hours of labour for them to ten or eleven hours a day will practically restrict the working of male adults to the same period. I am not in the least disposed to deny the fact."

Lord John Manners, who strongly supported the Bill, argued that it would not reduce wages, but that it would confer a most important boon on the working classes by giving them additional leisure. This is a point to which it is well to direct the reader's special attention. It is the habit now to say that Parliament only interfered with the hours of labour in the interests of the *health* of the working classes. This is disproved by a reference to the speeches. Mr. Beckett, who was in favour of an Eleven Hours Bill, said :—"In asking for an Eleven Hours Bill they proposed to take off the hour of labour which pressed most heavily on workmen, and was the least profitable to the manufacturer. One hour taken off would permit the family of the working men to enjoy around their own domestic hearths the relaxation from labour which they did not now possess."

It would be impossible to express more concisely the ultimate moving reason of the demand made to-day for a legal reduction in the hours of labour. One last quotation from the debate on this Bill must be made—namely, from the speech of Mr. John Bright. The Tribune of the People, who has since ended his long political career honoured by all his countrymen, was then member for Manchester. In the course of his impassioned speech against the Factory Bill, he did not disguise the fact that he spoke as a manufacturer in the interests of manufacturers. He denounced the wickedness of noble lords who were attempting by this measure to transfer some of the profits of employers to the employed. He proved by quotations from American Blue Books that factory operatives were better off than almost any people on the face of the globe. He declared that the Bill was an interference with the dearest rights of the working classes; that they did not want the Bill, and had only been deceived by agitators. He quoted piles of figures to show that our trade must infallibly be ruined if the Bill passed, and he wound up his speech with the following impassioned peroration:—" Believing that the proposition was most injurious and destructive to the best interests of the country—believing that it was contrary to all principles of sound legislation—that it was a delusion practised upon the working classes—that it was advocated by those who had no knowledge of the economy of manufactures—believing that it was one of the worst measures ever passed in the shape of an Act of Parliament, and that if it were now made law the necessities of trade and the demands alike of the workmen and of the masters would compel them to retrace the steps they had taken—believing this, he felt compelled to give the motion for the second reading his most strenuous opposition."

In spite of these terrible forebodings the Bill passed and became law. And now what happened? It was soon discovered that owing to complications with the previous Act of 1844 it was possible to evade the 1847 Act. Consequently, on representations made by the Factory Inspectors, a new Bill was introduced in 1850 to make the Ten Hours Day peremptory. This was to be accomplished by compelling manufacturers to stop their machinery and close the factory altogether when the ten hours limit, as determined by a public clock, had elapsed. A good deal of negotiation took place over this Bill, and ultimately a compromise was arrived at, by which, in return for the greater efficiency of the present measure, an extra two hours a week should be conceded to the manufacturer. It is interesting to note that Mr. Disraeli opposed this compromise as a breach of faith with the operatives. "I strip this question of all hair-splittings. The working classes of this country imagined that when they gained the Act of 1847 they succeeded in restricting the hours of their labour to ten a day."

Apart from this question of pledged faith, the debate followed much the same lines as in 1847. But the tone was totally different. Perhaps the change in Mr. Bright's attitude was the most remarkable. On the motion for leave to bring in the Bill, he made a conciliatory speech, urging the promoters of the measure to come to terms with the manufacturers, and pointing out that owing to the mistakes made by the Parliamentary draughtsman adult males were put in a worse position than they had been in before. The supporters of the 1847 Act were jubilant over the success already achieved. Evidence was quoted to show that many manufacturers had frankly accepted the Act, and that the operatives "preferred the ten hours' system to the twelve, even if they only got ten hours' wages." Sir George Grey reasserted in the most explicit terms that the object of the previous Act had been to secure leisure for the working classes:—"The objects of the limitation of the hours of labour were in his opinion twofold—to promote first the physical, and secondly the social improvement of the classes to which it applied."

A few members, notably Mr. Hume, still opposed the Bill on general grounds, because it was an interference with that sacred creature the adult male; but they did not venture to carry their opposition to a division. All three readings were allowed to pass unchallenged, and in Committee the most important division that took place was on the question whether the hours of labour should be fixed at 58 or 60 per week.

So far therefore from it being true that the principle of interference with the hours of labour of adult males is unknown to

Parliament, the supporters of the principle are entitled to claim that it has been accepted by a unanimous vote of the House of Commons.

"In the thirty years that followed," as Mr. John Morley approvingly observed in 1883, "the principle has been extended with astonishing perseverance." *

Omitting several years and several minor Acts, we come to the important Factory Act of 1864. The object of this Act was to subject all manufactories of earthenware, percussion caps, lucifer matches, cartridges, paper staining, and fustian cutting, to the factory law. Here again the law, while professedly and formally applying only to women and children, would practically and effectually regulate the hours of labour of men. Whether the House of Commons of 1864, like the House of Commons of 1850, foresaw this result it is impossible to gather from the debate as reported in *Hansard*, for the point is hardly raised It seems indeed to have been assumed as a matter of course.

The fact is that the whole House combined in a chorus of congratulation on the success of the previous legislation, and aided the passing of the present Bill as its logical corollary. Mr. Roebuck, for example, confessed† that he had been quite converted by seeing the success of the previous Acts, and mentioned that Sir James Graham had told him that he also was going to make a "recantation" of his errors. In the same way Mr. Potter "admitted that he had been opposed to the Factory Acts before their introduction, but that he had become a convert on seeing their beneficial working."

It is almost superfluous to go further into the history of the Factory Acts. But a brief allusion must be made to what happened in 1867. In that year two Bills were introduced, the Factory Acts Extension Bill and the Hours of Labour Regulation Bill. These were referred together to a Select Committee of nineteen members, among whom were Lord John Manners, Mr. Bright, Mr. Fawcett, and Mr. Potter. When the Bills as re-drafted by this Committee came before the House, Mr. Moffatt, who had been a minority member of the Committee, opposed the Bills in a general resolution, and in the course of his speech said :—" He believed that they

* *Life of Cobden*, vol. i., c. xiii., p. 303.
† *Hansard*, vol. 175, col. 1942.

might interfere very beneficially in many cases in reference to the labour of children, but this Bill interfered with and touched the labour of children, young persons, and males in every large factory where they employed more than one hundred men."

Mr. Fawcett, in reply, said :—"It had been argued that this measure was an undue interference with the rights of capital and labour, but as a question of political economy it was easy to prove that there was no contravention of the principle of economy in legislation such as was proposed in this Bill. . . . With respect to the working classes his own experience among them had been that working men were glad to welcome this kind of legislation." Both Bills were carried without any division being challenged.

Further Acts were passed in 1870, 1871, and 1874. In the debates on the latter Bill, all the old arguments were brought up by Professor Fawcett, who once more pointed out to the House of Commons that the measure would apply to the hours of men. "Although," said he, "the Bill nominally applied to women only, its real effect would be to place a Parliamentary limit on the length of the day's work, and its general application would be precisely the same in a great majority of cases as if in every clause after the word 'woman' they had inserted the word 'man.'"* Notwithstanding this explicit statement, Parliament reduced the hours of labour in textile factories from 60 to 56½ hours per week. Four years later the whole body of factory legislation was codified in the Factory and Workshop Act of 1878. This Act confirmed the statutory week of 56½ hours in textile factories, and of 60 hours in non-textile factories, with a certain margin of overtime for the latter only. Workshops—*i.e.*, places where no steam or other power is employed—are on much the same footing as non-textile factories, but the provisions of the law are slightly less stringent. In each case the limitation of hours nominally applies only to women and children : practically, wherever men are engaged in work requiring the assistance of women or of children, their hours of labour are also limited. That this result was foreseen at the time the original Acts were passed has been amply proved by the above quotations. Therefore those politicians who make a business of opposing an Eight Hours Bill, must cease to assert that such a measure involves a new principle of State policy. They must

* *Hansard*, vol. 219, page 1422.

instead be content to argue that it is undesirable to extend the application of this already established principle.

Moreover, the precedents furnished by the Factory Acts are not the only precedents to which we can appeal in favour of the restriction of freedom of contract. They are indeed the most important, for they bear directly on the question of State regulation of the hours of labour. But equally suggestive are such collateral precedents as the Truck Acts. Here we have a whole series of Acts, extending from far back in our history down to modern days, every one of which constitutes a serious interference with freedom of contract between master and man. These Acts prohibit the master from paying wages in any other form than in coin of the realm, even if the workman desires it. Scores of cases can be thought of where it would be more convenient for both parties that at any rate part of the wages should be paid in kind. For instance, a miller's labourer requires flour for the consumption of his family, and as a rule will spend at least half his weekly wages in this one commodity. Why should not the miller hand over to him the quantity of flour he requires, and reckon that part of his wages? The arrangement seems simple enough, but the law does not allow it. By law the miller is required, possibly at great inconvenience to himself, to find sufficient cash to pay the whole of his weekly wage bill. This cash, according to the strict letter of the law, must be paid over to the men in full. And then, but not till then, according to the law, they are at liberty to repay as much of it as they choose for new purchases of flour or for the liquidation of old debts.

It is not our business to explain why successive British Parliaments, in successive generations and in successive centuries, should have repeatedly passed such laws as this. That is a matter which we will leave to those politicians who contend that the interference of the State between employer and employed is opposed to the principles of English Government.

Of this school of politicians one of the most prominent has recently died—Mr. Charles Bradlaugh. This powerful representative of a bygone Liberalism was perhaps the most strenuous of all the opponents of the Eight Hours Movement. In Parliament and without, with "tongue, pen, and vote," he was constantly attacking the proposal for the establishment of an equal

Eight Hours Day. But, curiously enough, Mr. Bradlaugh had not the least objection to the Truck Acts. On the contrary, he was an energetic supporter of these Acts, and was the author of more than one valuable amendment. Nor did his interest end with the making of the law. He busied himself also about its enforcement. It is a fact not generally known that Mr. Bradlaugh was constantly writing to the Home Office to report breaches of the Truck Acts. Let all posthumous credit be given to him therefor. But at the same time it is worth while to point out, not from disrespect to the dead, but for the sake of the living, the inconsistency of this conduct. For there is no difference in principle between saying to free-born British adults—You shall not work more than a certain number of hours a week; and saying—You shall not, even if you wish it, take your wages in the form of tea and sugar, bacon and flour. You shall take only hard cash.

The Truck Acts, however, as a piece of State tyranny, pale into insignificance compared with the "Payment of Wages in Public Houses Act." This, by the way, was Mr. Bradlaugh's own pet child. But its authorship is now of less consequence than the fact that it is the law of the land, "enacted by and with the consent of the Lords Spiritual and Temporal and of the Commons in Parliament assembled." Anything more tyrannical than this law can scarcely be imagined. A man who has honestly earned his wages is not allowed to seek the shelter of a public-house while they are being counted out to him! On what ground could Parliament be induced to pass such a law? On the ground of practical necessity.

Experience had proved that when workmen are left to enjoy the liberty of receiving their wages in a public-house, employers would take advantage of this liberty to the serious detriment of men and their families. The workmen in their sober moments hated the system. They knew that it meant degradation to them and semi-starvation to their families. But by themselves they had no power to change it.

It was on these facts and these allegations that Parliament decided to interfere. The men could not protect themselves from an insidious evil, and therefore the State had to protect them, even though Mr. Herbert Spencer should blaspheme.

PRECEDENTS FOR LEGISLATION. 209

To pass to another parallel of still wider application, we may note the State regulation of the sale of intoxicating liquors. Why, asks the opponent of an Eight Hours Act, should a man not be allowed to work as long as he likes? Why, we may ask in return, should a man not be allowed to drink as long as he likes? The publican is willing to sell the liquor, the man is willing to buy it, why should a tyrannical State interpose between them? Why should we deliberately limit the hours of labour of adult male barmen and publicans, and refuse to do the same for the assistants in other shops? This question we will leave to be answered by the Whig and Tory members of Parliament who almost every session give legal force to some amendment or extension of the licensing laws.

It may be pleaded, however, that the licensing laws are no precedent for an Eight Hours Act, for the sale of liquor is a State-created monopoly. Parliament may control that which it has created. Accepting for a moment this plea, let us point out that it at once justifies the demand that the State should limit the hours of labour of railway servants, of tram drivers and conductors, and of gas stokers; for railways, tramways, and gasworks are also monopolies created by Parliament.

But the above plea is a false plea. It is not true that Parliament has imposed strict regulations upon public-houses and railway companies, because these are statutory monopolies. The regulations have been imposed because they were thought to be in the public interest.

For further illustration of this fact, we may turn to the case of hackney cabs. Here there is no pretence of a monopoly. Yet by a tyrannical law a uniform fare is established in every borough in England, and a cab-driver can be criminally prosecuted for demanding more. Can this be justified? Undoubtedly it can, on the double ground that it is a convenience to the public and a safeguard to the driver to have fixed fares. If the determination of cab fares were left to free competition, they would at times be run up to half a guinea for a short drive, while at other times drivers would be bidding against one another for fares that would barely pay for carriage oil. Each fare would be the subject of a special bargain, generally negotiated under circumstances not conducive to calm consideration.

But exactly similar evils to these follow the freedom that is left to masters and men to settle the length of the working day. At times men are driven to the utmost limit of human endurance. At other times they are told that there is no work for them at all. If it is of importance to the cab-hiring public that there should be a uniformity of fares, it is of far more importance to the working classes that there should be a reasonable regularity in their work. This the establishment of a uniform working day would tend to promote. The work that is now crammed into a few months would be spread out more evenly over the year. The public at first would grumble as it did in the case of cab fares, but it would soon fall in with the arrangement. Orders for season goods would be given in advance, just as house-wives now make provisions in advance for the wants of Sunday.

From cab fares to Irish rents is a far cry, but the principle which has induced the State to interfere is the same in each case. A wealthy Londoner cannot on a wet night protect himself against the extortion of a cab-driver; the starving Irish peasant cannot protect himself from the extortion of an absentee landlord. In each case the State interferes to enforce a fair bargain.

We need not however prolong this list of precedents. We have already quoted more than enough for the needs of our argument. We have shown that the State regulates the fares of cabs, the rates on railways, the rents of Irishmen; that it fixes the hours during which public-houses shall be open; that it determines the material in which wages shall be paid; that it prohibits their payment in places where liquor is sold.

And as regards the English workman, "We have to-day," as Mr. John Morley himself enthusiastically tells us,[*] "a complete, minute, and voluminous code for the protection of labour: buildings must be kept pure of effluvia; dangerous machinery must be fenced; children and young persons must not clean it while in motion; their hours are not only limited but fixed; continuous employment must not exceed a given number of hours, varying with the trade, but prescribed by the law in given cases; a statutable number of holidays is imposed; the children must go to school, and the employer must every week have a certificate to that effect; if an accident happens, notice must be sent to the proper authorities;

[*] *Life of Cobden*, vol. i., ch. xiii., p. 303.

special provisions are made for bakehouses, for lace-making, for collieries, and for a whole schedule of other special callings ; for the due enforcement and vigilant supervision of this immense host of minute prescriptions there is an immense host of inspectors, certifying surgeons, and other authorities, whose business it is 'to speed and post o'er land and ocean' in restless guardianship of every kind of labour, from that of the woman who plaits straw at her cottage door, to the miner who descends into the bowels of the earth, and the seaman who conveys the fruits and materials of universal industry to and fro between the remotest parts of the globe."

No words of ours could more fully express the universality of the labour code of Great Britain. Nor would any one reading these words dream that the author of them opposes to-day, on the *ground of principle*, any extension of this code which should explicitly regulate the hours of labour of adult men as well as of adult women. That this regulation does already exist in practice, if not in theory, is a matter of fact beyond question. And further, as we have now shown by indisputable evidence, this effective regulation of adult men's labour is not the accidental result of a statute really intended or expected to apply to women and children only. It was foreseen at the time each Act was passed, protested against by the employers, denounced by the political economists, thoroughly debated in the House of Commons, and eventually accepted without a dissentient vote.

CHAPTER IX.

PRACTICAL PROPOSALS.

IT is made a matter of complaint by some opponents of the Eight Hours Movement that there exists no "authoritative" definition of what is meant by an Eight Hours Bill, and that no precise statement is made as to the details of its application. Is the limit, they ask, to be eight hours per day, or forty-eight hours per week; are shifts to be allowed; are meal-times, times of "standing by," and of passage to and from work, to be included or excluded; is overtime to be permitted, and what provision is made for accident or other emergency; how will it be applied to season trades, to times of pressure, to brain-workers, to sailors, to sick-nurses, and so on? This series of questions implies a complete misapprehension of the Eight Hours Movement. If that movement were the product merely of a few agitators, there would be some ground for asking whether it was based upon a definite and explicit scheme that could be worked into an Act of Parliament. But the Eight Hours Movement is primarily a vague and spontaneous desire on the part of the workers for some shortening of their hours of labour. That desire is only now crystallising into definite shape, and it is scarcely to be expected that the great mass of working people should be prepared with the details of a complicated extension of the already complicated Factory Acts. It was not made a matter of reproach against the unenfranchised agricultural labourers that they had not drafted their own Reform Bill. Nor is it in any case the business of the multitude to elaborate Acts of Parliament. There is for this work a special class of workers known as statesmen, politicians, and Parliamentary draughtsmen, whose duty it is to throw into practicable legislative form as much as they can understand of the desires of their less articulate fellow-citizens.

Politicians and statesmen have, however, been very slow to attempt to find suitable legislative expression for a movement of opinion to which both great parties, in the United Kingdom as well as in the United States, are instinctively hostile. In the United States, indeed, we are not aware that any serious attempt has been made to put into legislative shape anything beyond the definition of a normal day, and the limitation of hours in some public departments as well as in a few monopolies. In Australia there are useful models as regards the closing of shops and the limitation of the hours of labour on public works, on tramways, and in connection with mines. On the Continent we find not only laws applying to particular industries, but also to all employment of hired labour. England, the mother of Factory Acts, supplies most of the practical experience of their efficient working. These legislative models have, however, not been made much use of by popular advocates of an Eight Hours Law. We are not acquainted with any serious or practicable drafts of Eight Hour Bills outside the United Kingdom, and even there such drafts date only, so far as we are aware, from 1887 for the coal-miners, and from 1889 for industries in general.*

Such drafts have since been multiplied, but it is of little use to describe them in detail. By the very nature of the case, they have been, as yet, merely the preliminary sketches of the shape which legislation, according to the fancy or knowledge of the draughtsman, might possibly take. Indeed, they have been published rather as propagandist documents than as actual legislative proposals. The opponent who seeks for an "authoritative" expression, in bill form, of the Eight Hours Movement, must still be reminded that such is not the way with which to deal with a genuinely popular movement.

The so-called "practical proposals" with which we are acquainted begin with a mere definition of the normal day, and reach up to a general limitation of the period of employment in all occupations to eight hours out of any twenty-four.

* The Eight Hours Bill of the Fabian Society was published in the middle of November 1889.

I. Partial Proposals.

(*a.*) *The Fixing of a Normal Day.*

The Bill of the Queensland Premier, referred to in the Introduction, furnishes a detailed model of a statutory definition of the normal working day. As some of its clauses are suggestive, we give it in full :—

" 1. This Act may be cited as '*The Eight Hours Act of* 1890.'
" 2. In this Act—
"The term 'workman' means any person employed in manual or clerical labour :
"The term 'manual or clerical labour' includes any kind of work except as herein expressly excepted, but does not include the work of sailors when the ship or vessel is under way or on a voyage, or the work of domestic servants, or the work of persons employed in ships or vessels to do similar work to that of domestic servants, or the work of persons employed in work of an intermittent character in connection with agricultural or pastoral pursuits :
"The term 'domestic servant' means any person employed in or about a house in doing the necessary daily work of the household, or in attending to horses, cows, or other animals kept for the purposes of the household, or in driving carriages or other vehicles kept for such purposes, or in other similar avocations :
"The term 'employer' includes any agent or servant of an employer who is entrusted with the duty of supervision, or of engaging or discharging servants.
" 3. Whenever in any contract of hiring, whether verbal or in writing, reference is made to a day's labour, or it is stipulated that the rate of payment for labour shall be calculated by the day, or at a fixed price for a day's labour, or otherwise calculated by reference to a day's labour, such day shall be taken to be a day of eight hours, and such day's labour shall be taken to be labour for eight hours, unless in any case a shorter period than eight hours is, by the usage or practice of the trade or business in connection with which the labour is performed, the ordinary duration of a day's labour.
" 4. Whenever in any contract of hiring provision is intended to be made for the work of any workman being continued for more than eight hours in any one day, it shall be necessary that a special stipulation be made with regard thereto.

PRACTICAL PROPOSALS.

"5. Except in the case of a contract made as prescribed by the last preceding section, and then only in accordance with its provisions, it shall not be lawful for any employer to require any workman to work, without his own consent, for more than eight hours in any one day. And except as aforesaid no employer shall dismiss a workman by reason of his refusal to work for a longer period than eight hours in any one day.

"Any employer who offends against the provisions of this section shall be liable to a penalty of five pounds."

We add two briefer models of a similar kind :—

"In contracts for the hire of labour or the employment of personal service in any capacity, a day shall, unless otherwise specified, be deemed to mean a period of *eight* working hours, and a week shall be deemed to mean a period of *forty-eight* working hours." *

"Eight hours of labour constitute a day's work, unless it is otherwise expressly stipulated by the parties to a contract."†

The above specimens sufficiently indicate the scope of the proposal to define the normal day. Similar laws have been passed in various States in the American Union, and are usually said to have been a dead letter. But obviously the mere legal definition of the normal day's labour, in the absence of any agreement to the contrary, has no coercive effect. The object of such a definition is only to influence public opinion, with a view to bringing about a voluntary shortening of the hours of labour. Since the enactment of these laws in the United States many thousands of American workmen have obtained an Eight Hours Day, and the movement in favour of its general adoption has grown enormously. We do not intend to attribute the whole of this result to the passing of these statutes, but no one could seriously assert that they have had no effect whatever. Still less could it be said that similar laws would be ineffective in the United Kingdom, where statutes do much more to modify public opinion than in America. A declaration by the Imperial Parliament in favour of an Eight Hours Day would virtually compel all public and quasi-public authorities to adopt the same working day, and would quicken the conscience of philanthropic employers. Those who desire to see the hours of

* Fabian Society's Eight Hours Bill, clause 3.
† *Statutes of California*, sec. 3244. See *Foreign Office Report*, C—5866, p. 88.

labour brought down to eight, but who are impressed by the difficulties in the way of doing this by coercive law, ought to be eager to accept such a simple, if only partially effective, method of promoting voluntary action. As to precedent for such an Act of Parliament, we may point out that it is not uncommon for terms used in contracts to be defined by general law, in the absence of stipulation to the contrary. A familiar instance in the United Kingdom is the Conveyancing Act of 1881, by which the ordinary terms used in legal documents are made to import, in the absence of express stipulation to the contrary, a whole host of covenants and reciprocal engagements.

(b.) The Limitation of Hours of Public Employés.

A good example of an existing statute limiting the hours of labour of public employés is furnished by the State of California:—

"Eight hours labour constitute a legal day's work in all cases where the same is performed under the authority of any law of this State, or under the direction, control, or by the authority of any officer of this State acting in his official capacity, or under the direction, control, or by the authority of any municipal corporation within this State, or of any officer thereof acting as such; and a stipulation to that effect must be made a part of all contracts to which the State or any municipal corporation therein is a party."*

The best draft of a law to effect the same purpose in the United Kingdom has been prepared by the Fabian Society:—

"No person employed under the Crown in the United Kingdom in any department of the public service, other than military or naval, or by any county council, municipal corporation, vestry, local sanitary authority, school board, board of guardians of the poor, dock or harbour trustees, district board of works, district council, improvement commissioners, commissioners of sewers, of public libraries, or of baths and wash-houses, or by any other public administrative authority, shall, except in case of special unforeseen emergency, be employed for a longer period than *eight hours* in any one day, nor for more than *forty-eight* hours in any one week: provided that in cases of public emergency a Secretary of State shall have power, by order published in the *London Gazette*, to suspend, for such

---

* *Statutes of California,* sec. 3245. See *Foreign Office Report,* C—5866, page 88.

PRACTICAL PROPOSALS.

employments and for such period as may be specified in such order, the operation of this section.

"Any public officer ordering or requiring any person in public employment to remain at work for a period in excess of either of those herein specified, except in case of special unforeseen emergency, shall be liable to a fine not exceeding *ten pounds*.

"Any public authority, or the principal officer of any department of the public service, employing or permitting to be employed by reason of special unforeseen emergency, any person in excess of either of the periods herein specified, shall report the fact within *seven days* to a Secretary of State, and a complete list of such cases shall be laid before both Houses of Parliament once in each year."*

A law limiting the hours of public employés would—(1) improve the position of the men primarily affected; (2) enable other men, now out of work, to obtain regular employment; (3) influence public opinion.

It is urged, even by those who object to a law coercing private employers, that the community must necessarily fix the hours during which those workers who are directly in its service should work, and it may therefore, if it chooses, fix that limit at eight per day. A formal statute is not necessarily required for this purpose, as the working day in Government departments is fixed by mere executive order.†

But in the United Kingdom it is certain that the executive government would not take any such step, except at the express command of the House of Commons. This command might be given, without the formality of an Act of Parliament, by a mere resolution of the House.

Besides preventing excessive hours in any one department, a rule is needed to put a stop to the practice which prevails in the Post Office, Inland Revenue, and Customs Departments in London, of taking on, as casual workers or "glut men," or even for the performance of the regular work of the department, persons who have already done a day's work in one of the other departments. This re-engagement of exhausted workers is evidently a fraud on the public, and limits the area of employment. To the credit of

* Fabian Society's Bill, clause 4.

† In the United States, for example, President Van Buren did much to promote the Ten Hours Movement by instituting a Ten Hours Day in the Navy Department (see page 46).

the London County Council be it said, this body has already dealt with the evil, and has made a strict rule that a man who has been at work in one department shall not be taken on for a fresh spell of work in another department.

That the moral effect of a law defining a nominal working day would be very great is believed by such an opponent of the Eight Hours Movement as Mr. George Howell, M.P. "Custom," he says, "has the force of law, and a State regulated day, and a fixed rate of wages for such working day, would, in effect, govern the labour market generally, certainly for the same kind of labour, in all parts of the country." *

This brings us to the question whether an Act of Parliament, establishing a maximum working day for Government workshops, should be made to apply also to workshops belonging to local authorities. There is much to be said on both sides of the question. On the one hand it is said that this is a matter where the independence of local authorities ought not to be interfered with by the central government. Working men, both in the United Kingdom and the United States, have at least as direct control over county and borough councils as they have over the national legislature.

These considerations however only apply to the proposal that an exceptional Eight Hours Law should be made for local authorities. But if Parliament were to pass a general Act limiting the hours of labour in all employment, local authorities would properly come within its scope. In exactly the same way the existing Factory Acts in England, being of a general character, apply to public as well as private employers.

On the other hand, many of the economic and juristic difficulties in the way of enforcing an Eight Hours Law against private employers do not apply in the cases of public bodies. For the expenses of public undertakings fall upon the ratepayers, and they by their electoral privileges have the ultimate power of making or rejecting laws. Consequently the national Parliament is as fully entitled to restrict by law the hours of labour of municipal employés, as it is to impose a general tax.

It may here be mentioned that in 1868 the United States Legislature enacted that eight hours should be a day's work in the

* *A Plea for Liberty*, p. 129.

Government navy yards. This law was however set aside by the action of the Executive Government, which insisted that wages should be reduced in proportion. The men were neither strong enough to resist, nor willing to submit to this deduction. They therefore sullenly acquiesced in the retention of the Ten Hours Day at the old wages.*

It may be noted that, in 1890, some of the men petitioned the Senate for arrears of pay, claiming an addition to their wages of one-fourth, since the law of 1868 declared eight hours to be a day's work. The petition was rejected in January 1891.

The first step in the United Kingdom would be the prohibition, by resolution of the House of Commons, of the present practice of habitual overtime in the Woolwich and Enfield factories.† By the same method it would be possible to secure the insertion of stipulations against excessive hours of labour in all Government contracts.‡ The House of Lords Committee on the Sweating System vaguely recommended the tentative adoption of some such principle in the Government contracts for clothing. Compare Mr. Sydney Buxton's resolution in the House of Commons in January 1891, as amended by the Government, and accepted by the House of Commons without a dissentient voice:—" That, in the opinion of this House, it is the duty of the Government in all Government contracts to make provision against the evils which have recently been disclosed before the House of Lords Sweating Committee, and to insert such conditions as may prevent the abuses arising from sub-letting, and make every effort to secure the payment of the rate of wages generally accepted as current for a competent workman in his trade."—(*Times*, 14th January 1891)

* See page 48. It is not easy to see what valid analogy the so-called failure of this law offers to the opponents of a law applying to individual employers. The United States Executive—the most independent in the world—proved stronger than the Legislature in a matter which, at that time, failed to excite sufficient public interest to warrant the workers in resisting their powerful employer. The circumstances were peculiar to the United States.

† See page 155.

‡ The Glasgow Town Council, in leasing out its tramways, stipulates that the working day of conductors and drivers shall not exceed an average of ten hours. The Municipality of Toronto (Canada) has done the same thing in the new lease concluded in January 1891.

(c.) The Limitation of Hours by way of stipulation in the grant of Exceptional Statutory Powers.

This is a further extension of Parliamentary action which would be calculated greatly to influence public opinion. A suggested enactment is appended :—

"No person or company hereafter obtaining statutory powers or privileges of any description by private or local Act of Parliament shall employ any person for hire for more than *forty-eight* hours in any one week; and this section shall be deemed to be incorporated in every subsequent private or local Act of Parliament granting statutory powers or privileges of any description to any such person or company that employs labour of any description for hire, and to apply to all the operations of the said person or company under statutory powers or privileges, whether by that or any other Act.

"Any person, or the principal manager or other chief officer of any company, employing or allowing to be employed any person in contravention of this section shall be liable to a fine not exceeding *one hundred pounds* for each such contravention."*

Conditions of this kind have been imposed by the Victorian Legislature in granting special statutory powers. The instances of the Melbourne Harbour Works and the Melbourne Tramways have been already cited.† Bargains of a like nature, but not dealing with the hours of labour, have frequently been made with railway, tramway, and gas companies, who have sought statutory powers from the Parliament of the United Kingdom. Hitherto such bargains have had relation to the interests of the ratepayers or the consumers. There is no reason why the same consideration should not be shown to the interests of the working class. During the session of 1890 several notices were given in the House of Commons of resolutions to add stipulations against excessive hours of labour in private bills, but no action was taken.

We now come to the proposals relating to a compulsory shortening of the hours of labour in particular trades. Such proposals are usually made for miners, railway and tramway workers, and shop assistants.

* Fabian Society's Bill, clause 9. † See page 40.

PRACTICAL PROPOSALS.

(*d.*) *An Eight Hours Bill for Miners.*

We have already given the Victorian law limiting to eight per day the hours of labour of persons employed underground, or employed aboveground in charge of steam machinery in connection with any mine. Various attempts have been made since 1887, in the Parliament of the United Kingdom, to enact a similar law for underground workers. Nearly all these have emanated from men who have spent a large part of their lives actually labouring in coal mines, and may be assumed to have a practical knowledge of their working.

We give, as a specimen, the form in which Mr. W. Abraham, M.P. (Glamorgan), introduced his Eight Hours Bill for Mines in 1891 :—

"A person is not, in any one day of twenty-four hours, to be employed underground in any mine for a period exceeding eight hours from the time of his leaving the surface of the ground to the time of his ascent thereto, except in case of accident. Whenever any employer or his agent employs, or permits to be employed, any person in contravention of this enactment, he is to be liable to a penalty not exceeding 40s. for each offence. This penalty is to be recovered in the same manner in which any penalty under the Acts relating to factories and workshops is recoverable."*

The proposal of the Fabian Society aims at greater precision :—

"No person shall be employed underground for hire in any mine for a longer period than *eight* hours in any one day, nor than *forty-eight* in any one week.

"The period of employment underground in a mine shall, for the purpose of this section, be deemed to be the whole period from the time of leaving the surface of the ground to descend the mine, to the time of return to the surface of the ground after cessation of work.

"The manager of any mine employing or permitting to be employed any person in contravention of this section shall, on conviction thereof, be liable to a fine not exceeding *one hundred pounds* for each such contravention.

"In any cases in which, through accident or other unforeseen emergency, any person may be employed underground for a longer period than is prescribed by this section, a special report may, within *seven days* thereof, be made to a Secretary of State by the manager of the mine, and

---

* House of Commons Bill, No. 13, 1890-91.

a Secretary of State may, if he thinks fit, thereupon direct that no prosecution shall be instituted in respect of the particular offence so reported.

"A list of the cases in which such direction has been issued by a Secretary of State under this section shall be laid before both Houses of Parliament once in each year."*

The Austrian Law of the 21st of June 1884, for regulating the hours of work and the Sunday rest in mines, provides—

"That the duration of a shift is not to exceed twelve hours, and the actual working time during the same ten hours.

"Exceptions may be made by the Minister of Agriculture in the case of mines situated in the High Alps, under the condition that the number of sixty actual working hours per week be not exceeded.

"In extraordinary cases, or under temporary pressing necessity, the Head Office of the mining district can allow a limited prolongation of the shift.

"On Sundays no work is to be done in a mine except that which is absolutely necessary, and the Sunday rest must begin not later than 6 A.M., and last twenty-four hours at least.

"In cases of imminent danger to life the above provisions do not apply."†

This foreign example suggests that it might possibly be of advantage to incorporate in any future enactment a provision enabling the hours to be extended on the occurrence of any emergency, or in mines of special difficulty. For example, collieries are occasionally stopped owing to snowstorms or fogs, which impede in some cases the actual drawing, in others the transportation of the coal from the pit's mouth. In exceptionally prolonged winters, too, occasion might arise for longer work. There is, however, no difficulty in providing for any such contingency in the manner suggested by the Austrian law. Nor does this proposal exclude resort to arbitration or a "Board of Conciliation." It would be quite possible to require all proposals for fixing the working day in any coal-mining district or particular mine to be first thrashed out by a Joint Board, before being acted upon by the Home Secretary.

* Fabian Society's Bill, clause 6.
† *Foreign Office Report*, C—5866.

(e.) An Eight Hours Bill for Railway Workers.

The two Unions of railway workers in the United Kingdom agree in asking that the hours of labour for signalmen should be limited to eight per day, and those of other workers to ten per day.

The demand of the men in the Scotch strike of 1890-91 was for a maximum limit of 60 hours per week.* The clause drafted by the Fabian Society adopts a weekly limit of 48 hours, with power to extend any day's work (except for signalmen) to twelve hours.

"No person employed wholly or mainly to work railway signals or points shall be employed continuously for more than *eight* hours, nor for more than *forty-eight* hours in any one week.

"No person employed as engine-driver, fireman, guard, or wholly or mainly in shunting, on any railway, shall be employed continuously for more than *twelve* hours, nor for more than *forty-eight* hours in any one week.

"The General Manager of any railway company employing or permitting to be employed any person in contravention of this section shall be liable on conviction thereof to a fine not exceeding *one hundred pounds* for each such contravention.

"Provided that in any case in which the employment of persons to work railway signals or points, or as engine-drivers, firemen, or guards, or in shunting, for longer periods than is permitted by this section is by reason of some special and unforeseen emergency necessary for the public safety, it shall be lawful for a Secretary of State, on a report made within *seven* days by the General Manager or Secretary of the Railway Company acting in contravention of this section, to direct that no legal proceedings shall be taken in the case of the particular contravention so reported.

"A list of the cases in which any such direction has been issued by a Secretary of State under this section shall be laid before both Houses of Parliament once in each year."†

It is obviously necessary to fix some daily maximum as well as a weekly or fortnightly one. For the object aimed at is to prevent, not only overwork on an average, but also overwork on any one day. A period of eighteen or twenty hours' work at a stretch is not adequately compensated for by a couple of days of idleness. As a Scotch engine-driver observed, "A man can't wind up his

---

* *The Scottish Railway Strike*, 1891, by Professor James Mavor.
† Fabian Society's Bill, clause 5.

physical system to run in weeks. We want regularity to do justice to ourselves and our families." But the daily maximum need not be rigidly fixed at eight hours for all classes of workers, if this is found inconvenient in practice.

In rural stations many railway servants have comparatively light work, and it is urged that they may well be required to put in longer days than the men in a busy goods yard or urban signal-box. It is, of course, not absolutely necessary that a uniform rule should be applied to all cases, but it should not be forgotten that one main object of the Eight Hours Movement is to enable the workers to discharge better their duties as parents and citizens. A man who is at work away from home for fourteen hours a day has little personal freedom, even if his duties be light. The monotony of prolonged waiting to work, especially if, as with signalmen, it be in solitude, is scarcely less wearing than the work itself.*

A proposal which found much favour in the House of Commons during a debate in February 1891 was, not to fix by law any limit of the hours of labour of railway workers, but to empower the Board of Trade peremptorily to order any company, in whose service the hours were generally excessive, to take prompt steps to reduce them. This might form a useful beginning of compulsory action, and would probably do much in relief of the worst cases. But the Board of Trade could hardly be expected to order any reduction of hours below the present average, and this would still leave the 400,000 railway workers on duty for twelve hours a day.

A more definite proposal is contained in the Bill brought into the House of Commons in February 1891, by Mr. Donald Crawford, which provides that, if an application be made by any ten *employés* or any ten shareholders of a company, or by any person authorised by the majority of the company's *employés* to represent them, alleging that the hours of work in any branch of the service are excessive, the Board of Trade is required to obtain a report from one of their inspectors, and should they be of opinion that there are probable grounds

* A signalman at an unfrequented rural station, with fourteen hours daily duty and very few trains, complained to one of the present writers that nearly his whole waking life was passed in solitary confinement—a treatment now considered too rigorous for our felons.

PRACTICAL PROPOSALS. 225

of complaint, they are directed to hold an inquiry. If the Board of Trade are then satisfied of the truth of the allegation, they may require the company to submit a draft scheme providing for shorter hours. When a draft scheme is approved by the Board of Trade, they may order it to be carried out. If within three months a draft scheme is not presented that meets with the Board's approval, the Board may itself make a scheme. Should default be made in compliance with such an order, the Railway Commission may, on the application of the Board of Trade, enjoin obedience to the order with all their powers of enforcing it. When a scheme is prepared by the Board itself, a copy of it is to be placed before Parliament; and if either House pray Her Majesty that the order shall not continue in force, it is to be deemed to have expired.

(*f.*) *An Eight Hours Bill for Workers on Tramways and other local monopolies.*

Services of a local nature might be left to the regulation of the local authority. A detailed suggestion to this effect is made in the Fabian Society's Bill:—

"The Council for the administrative county of London, and elsewhere the sanitary authority, shall have power to make, and from time to time to amend, by-laws restricting the hours of labour of persons employed for hire in or in connection with any docks, harbours, tramways, telephones, markets, establishments for the supply of electric light, or of electric or hydraulic power, gasworks and waterworks, within the area under its jurisdiction, whether owned by a public authority or not.

"Any by-laws made in pursuance of this section shall be submitted for confirmation to a Secretary of State, and shall, when confirmed by him, be deemed to be incorporated in this Act: provided that no such by-law shall fix a maximum number of hours of labour in excess of *fifty-four* per week."*

On the other hand, the State of New Jersey has kept the control of local monopolies in its own hands. A law passed in 1887 enacts that twelve hours' labour, to be performed within twelve consecutive hours, with reasonable time for meals, not less than half-an-hour for each, shall constitute a day's labour in the operation of all cable,

* Fabian Society's Bill, clause 8.

traction, and horse-car street surface railroads, and of all cable, traction, and steam elevated railroads, owned or operated under the laws of New Jersey. Provision is made that, in case of accident or unexpected contingency demanding more than the usual service, extra labour may be permitted and exacted for extra compensation.*

Similar laws exist in New York and Maryland. This is the course advocated by the English Tramway Workers' Union, whose draft Bill contains the following clauses :—

"No person shall be employed in, upon, or in connection with the working of a tramcar for a longer period than twelve hours in any one day.

"No person shall be employed in, upon, or in connection with the working of an omnibus for a longer period than twelve hours in any one day.

"These periods shall include two hours rest for meals for each person, so that the actual work shall not exceed ten hours per day.

"Any corporation, company, manager, or other person who employs any person falling within the provisions of this Act shall upon demand, when any workman leaves his employment, give to such workman a writing containing a true description of his conduct, ability, truthfulness, and honesty.

"Every corporation, company, manager, or other person who employs any person falling within the provisions of this Act shall affix a copy of the Act in a conspicuous part of every tramcar and omnibus within his control, and he shall keep a time-book containing a true daily record of the hours at which every person in his employment begins and finishes his work.

"Every corporation, company, manager, or other person falling within the provisions of this Act shall upon demand show to any local chief constable, superintendent, or inspector of police, and to any person in the employment of the said company or person, the time-book referred to; provided that the request be made between the hours of 8 A.M. and 4 P.M., and that not more than one request per month be made.

"This Act shall apply to every tramway company's plant in the United Kingdom as to tramcars, and as to omnibuses shall apply only to places with a population exceeding one hundred thousand."

A more drastic suggestion is made by Mr. Hyndman in his *Draft of an Eight Hours Bill*:—†

* *Foreign Office Report,* C. 5866, p. 51.
† London, 337 Strand, W.C. Price 1d.

"No person shall be employed on any line of tramway, omnibuses, cars, waggons, or other conveyances for the purpose of the transport of goods or persons, except in case of special unforeseen emergency, for a longer period than *eight working hours* in any one day, or *forty-eight working hours* in any one week.

"The general manager or manager of any company or firm, or individual firm, or employer employing or permitting to be employed, any person in contravention of this section, shall be liable, on conviction thereof, to a fine of not less than fifty pounds for each such contravention; and one-half of all fines so imposed shall be paid over, without any deduction whatsoever, to the person or persons directly or indirectly affected, whose action and evidence shall be the means of bringing home such offence to the perpetrator."

Whatever provisions are adopted as to these local monopolies might usefully be embodied in the general Acts by which they are regulated, such as the Waterworks Clauses Act, the Tramways Act, etc., so as to be incorporated as a matter of course in any Act establishing a new service.

(*g.*) *The Compulsory Early Closing of Shops.*

The regulation of the hours of business of retail shops appears to call for the exercise both of local option and trade option. Diversity in the habits of the people in different towns, and diversity of requirements for each trade, stand in the way of any uniform or centralised action. The Bill introduced into the House of Commons by Sir John Lubbock accordingly proposes to enable the shopkeepers in any trade in any locality to decide, by a majority, whether they will adopt the measure. The Victorian Act of 1885 goes, however, much further, and throws the onus upon the shopkeepers of exempting themselves, by a majority, from its operation. It also suggests a convenient means of ascertaining the result of their decision:—

"CLOSING OF SHOPS.

"All shops other than those of the kind specified in the Third Schedule hereto, and other than such as may be licensed to remain open at night under any by-law made under the authority of this Act, shall be closed on each and every evening of the week except Saturday at the hour of seven of the clock, and on Saturday evening at the hour of ten of the clock, provided that on the day immediately preceding any public holiday any such shop may be kept open until ten of the clock in the evening.

"45. Any Municipal Council may, if it think fit, from time to time make, alter, and repeal by-laws in and for the municipality for all or any of the following purposes:—

"For limiting the hours during which shops mentioned in the Third Schedule hereto may be kept open, but no by-law shall be made limiting such hours unless a petition, certified to by the Municipal Clerk as being signed by a majority of the shopkeepers keeping shops of the class within such municipal district to be affected thereby, has been previously presented to such Municipal Council.

"For permitting shops of any particular class (not included in the Third Schedule hereto), on obtaining a licence, to keep open after the hours hereinbefore mentioned, and during such hours as shall be specified in such licence; but no by-law shall be made authorising the issue of such licence unless a petition, certified to by the Municipal Clerk as being signed by a majority of the shopkeepers keeping shops of such class within such municipal district, have been previously presented to such Municipal Council.

"Requiring shops (not included in the Third Schedule hereto) to close before the hours hereinbefore mentioned, but no such by-law shall be made except on receipt of such a petition as aforesaid. For limiting the total number of hours persons may be employed during the day and night in shops licensed to remain open at night, provided that such limit shall not be less than eight hours in each full day and night.

"For imposing penalties not exceeding ten pounds on any shopkeeper failing or neglecting to close his shop in accordance with the provisions of this Act, or of any by-law made in pursuance hereof.

"For closing all shops within its municipality other than those mentioned in the Third Schedule for one afternoon in each week, provided that before any such by-law be made a petition, certified to by the Municipal Clerk as signed by a majority of the shopkeepers substantially interested and affected thereby, shall be presented to such Municipal Council.

"If in any shop any trade or business is carried on or any goods dealt in of such descriptions or kinds as would, under the provisions of this Act or of any by-law made hereunder, necessitate such shop being closed during certain hours, unless licensed to remain open, then such shop shall, unless a licence be obtained, be closed for all purposes during such hours as may be directed by this Act or by such by-law.

"*Third Schedule.*

Chemists' Shops.	Fruit and Vegetable Shops.
Coffee-Houses.	Restaurants.
Confectioners.	Tobacconists' Shops.
Eating-Houses.	Booksellers' and News-Agents'
Fish and Oyster Shops.	Shops."

Both these proposals are, however, so far defective that they leave the decision entirely in the hands of the shopkeepers. Clearly the shop assistants have a right also to be consulted. We are, however, not acquainted with any practical proposal for giving to shop assistants any voice in the decision as to the early closing of the shops in which they work; nor would it be easy to obtain their votes without exposing them to intimidation.

More drastic proposals are contained in the Draft Bill promoted by the Shop Assistants' Union, which contains the following clauses :—

"No assistant or other person (other than members of the occupier's family) shall be employed in, about, or in connection with any shop on week-days for longer periods than—

"(a) Fourteen hours on one day of the week, which period shall be between the hours of 8 A.M. and 10 P.M.

"(b) Twelve hours on four days of the week, which period shall be between the hours of 8 A.M. and 8 P.M.

"(c) Six hours on one day of the week, which period shall be between the hours of 8 A.M. and 2 P.M.

"These periods shall include meal times, and shall not in the aggregate exceed sixty-eight hours' employment per week for each assistant."

II. GENERAL PROPOSALS.

More ambitious are those who seek to extend an Eight Hours Law to all industries by one general enactment. It is true that the Factory and Workshop Acts in the United Kingdom now extend to all manufacturing industries. But this universality has only been reached after two generations of legislation. Even now it requires for its embodiment an Act of 107 sections, and six schedules filled with complicated exceptions and qualifications.

A universal Eight Hours Bill was introduced into the House of Commons in 1891, backed by Mr. Cunninghame Graham, Mr.

Randell, Mr. W. Abraham (Rhondda), Dr. Clark, and Mr. Conybeare. It ran as follows :—

"1. On and after the first day of January one thousand eight hundred and ninety-two no person shall work, or cause or suffer any other person to work, on sea or land in any capacity under any contract or agreement, or articles for hire of labour, or for personal service on sea or land (except in case of accident), for more than eight hours in any one day of twenty-four hours, or for more than forty-eight hours in any week.

"2. Any employer, manager, or other person who shall knowingly cause or suffer any person subject to his or her authority or commands, or in his or her employment, to work on sea or land in any capacity under any contract or agreement, or articles for hire of labour, or for personal service (except in case of accident), for more than eight hours in any one day of twenty-four hours, or for more than forty-eight hours in any week, shall, on conviction, be liable to a penalty of not less than ten pounds nor more than one hundred pounds for every such offence."*

This measure is understood to have been drafted by the Parliamentary Committee of the Trade Union Congress, as an attempt to carry out the resolution passed at the Liverpool meeting of the Congress in 1890. If it ever became law, it could not be universally enforced. The sudden and simultaneous adoption of a rigid limit of eight hours in all trades might seriously dislocate industry. As regards, too, many classes of workers, such as seamen, domestic servants, and many others, the law must inevitably become a dead letter, as being inconsistent with the habits of these industries.

It should however be remembered that a law fixing a uniform maximum day for all workers in all industries is in force in Switzerland, where it is said to be effective. But in this case the limit is ten hours a day (eleven hours, less one for meals), and provision is made for possible extensions of the working time.† The French general Twelve Hour Law now applies only to factories, mines, and the larger workshops, and is largely evaded owing to the insufficient number of inspectors and the weakness of the Trade Unions.‡

A more cautious attempt to place an Eight Hours Day within the reach of all those classes of workers who might consider it practicable

* House of Commons Bill, No. 85 of 1891.
† An abstract of this remarkable law is given in the Appendix.
‡ *Foreign Office Report*, C—5866.

in their own industry is made in the well-known "Trade Option" clause of the Fabian Society's Bill, which runs as follows :—

"Where it is proved to the satisfaction of a Secretary of State that a majority of the persons employed throughout the United Kingdom in any one trade or occupation are in favour of the maximum hours of labour per week in that trade or occupation being fixed by law, or, if already so fixed, being altered by law, he may by order made under this part of the Act declare a maximum number of hours per day or per week for such trade or occupation, and after the expiration of *three months* from the date of publication of such order any person employed in contravention thereof shall be deemed to be employed in contravention of this Act, and the person so employing him, or permitting him to be so employed, shall be liable on conviction thereof to a fine not exceeding *ten pounds* for each such contravention.

"A Secretary of State shall have power, in order to satisfy himself of the desire of the persons employed in any trade or occupation as aforesaid, to cause a public inquiry to be held in the principal district or districts in which such trade or occupation is carried on, or to cause a poll to be taken of the persons employed in such trade or occupation, or to take such other means as he may deem fit.

"For the purpose of this section, persons employed in any trade or occupation shall be taken to mean all persons employed for hire, or actually performing labour in any capacity, in such trade or occupation, whether already subject to the provisions of the Factory and Workshop Act, 1878, or of this Act, or not.

"No order made in pursuance of this section shall declare a maximum number of hours of labour per week in excess of *fifty-four* (or less than *forty-five*).

"It shall be the duty of a Secretary of State to institute an inquiry, in such manner as he may deem fit, with a view to the consideration of the expediency of making an order under this part of the Act, in each of the following cases, viz. :—

"(a) Whenever he shall have reason to believe that excessive hours of labour prevail in any trade or occupation.

"(b) Whenever he shall be requested to do so by the Committee or other Executive body of any duly registered trades union, or, in the case of there being no duly registered trades union in the trade or occupation in respect of which the application is made, by the Committee or other Executive body of any trades council, trades union congress, or other association or federation of trades unions.

"Provided that a Secretary of State shall not, except for special reasons approved by him, institute any such inquiry within a period of *twelve months* from the date of the holding of any previous inquiry in respect of the same trade or occupation."*

This clause enables the legal limitation of the hours of labour to be introduced in any trade as soon as a majority of the workers desire it. It provides for the case in which a majority of the workers are compelled to work long hours against their wish, by the obstinacy or disloyalty of the minority, which prevents an effective strike. In such a case, as John Stuart Mill pointed out,† the interference of law is required, and on similar grounds Mill supported the continuance of the legal enforcement of a weekly day of rest.‡ The principle involved has also received the endorsement of Professor Henry Sidgwick.§

The Fabian clause could not practically be put in force in any trade until a prolonged discussion had convinced a considerable majority of the workers of its advantage; and by that time the minority would have become prepared to acquiesce in the law, and the employers would have been able to make arrangements to avoid any inconvenience from the change.

The clause provides that the labourers, and all other workers in the trade, should be able to take part in the decision, and share in the benefit. By this means the advantages which the skilled and organised workers can now sometimes obtain by combination, would be extended to their less fortunate colleagues. The employer, if actually performing labour in the trade, is not excluded from participation in the decision.

By providing that the initiative may be taken by the workers themselves approaching the Home Secretary through some representative organisation of their own, the clause will promote the organisation of labour, and make the aid of the State practically conditional upon the workers first using their opportunities of self-help, as far as is possible and—having regard to the interests of the rest of the community—socially expedient. At the same time it permits the Home Secretary to step in to the relief of those

* Fabian Society's Bill, clause 7.
† *Principles of Political Economy*, book v., ch. xi., § 12, pp. 581-82.
‡ Mill's *Liberty*, p. 53, cheap edition.
§ *Principles of Political Economy*, book iii., ch. ii., p. 422, 1883.

exceptionally unfortunate workers who, by their condition, or the circumstances of their employment, are hindered from associating for the purpose of discussing their position.

The final decision is left with a Secretary of State (meaning the Home Secretary), because his subordination to the House of Commons affords, at present, the only practicable means of exercising public supervision and control over the award. The Home Secretary is the officer entrusted with the general administration of the existing Factory Acts. Under these Acts he possesses and exercises very large discretionary powers, and can issue orders for the special regulation of different industries.

One suggested difficulty in the way of applying the above clause is, that no register of the workers in any particular trade exists, and thus it would be impossible to take a poll. It is, however, not proposed that the decision should necessarily depend on the result of an actual ballot. It is for the Secretary of State to satisfy himself as to the desire of a majority of the workers, and he may use such means as he thinks best for this end. In some great works an actual ballot might take place. In other cases, one of Her Majesty's Factory Inspectors might hold a local inquiry on the lines of those frequently held by Inspectors of the Board of Trade and of the Local Government Board. Further, the Home Secretary would always consult the Trade Union concerned and representative employers, and would discuss the matter with the Labour Correspondent of the Board of Trade. If after these or other inquiries he was not satisfied that a clear and indisputable majority desired his intervention, nothing would be done. Thus the Secretary of State would not take action unless a considerable preponderance of opinion had been made manifest. But in cases like those of the railway and tramway workers, and the coal miners, there is already no doubt as to the existence of a huge majority in favour of a legal limitation of the hours of labour.*

* It is interesting to record two instances in which an effort was made to adopt essentially the same principle as that advocated by the Fabian Society. In the case of the railway workers, Mr. Channing's resolution in the House of Commons, in January 1891, proposed to empower the Board of Trade, in any case in which they thought it necessary in the public interest, to direct a railway company to shorten the hours of its workers. The abortive Conference of coal miners and coal owners, which met in London in January and February

The advantage of the Fabian Society's proposal is that it avoids the evil of a rigid universal rule. The order of the Secretary of State, like those which he already issues under the Factory Acts, might be framed so as to meet the circumstances of each industry, with the exceptions, qualifications, and exemptions that its needs seemed to require. If the limit was found inconvenient, or any of the conditions became unsuited to the industry, a new order of the Home Secretary could be easily and promptly obtained, making the necessary alterations. To the objection that the proposal places too great discretion in the hands of a single official, we reply that his action has both an upper and a lower limit. He may not prescribe more than 54 hours or less than 45 for the normal working week. Thus the clause, while giving trade option through the Home Secretary, in regard to an Eight Hours Day, makes compulsory the establishment of a nine hours limit in all trades. On this a word or two is necessary. Under the existing Factory Acts, in the United Kingdom the hours of labour in textile factories are absolutely limited for all women and all persons under eighteen to 56½ hours a week. No overtime is permitted on any condition.* It has already been explained that these restrictions, though nominally applying only to women and young persons, practically extend to men. Thus in all the great textile trades of England the working week is rigidly fixed by law at 56½ hours. In non-textile factories the law is less strict. The nominal week here extends to 60 hours, and overtime is in many cases permitted.† This difference of treatment is important, but we assert, without fear of contradiction, that in the majority of cases it is absolutely devoid of justification. The sole reason why textile factories are more rigidly regulated than non-textile factories is that the former class first attracted the attention of Parliament. The first English Act affecting textile factories was passed in 1802; non-textile factories escaped all control until 1864. During this long interval the powers of resistance of the textile manufacturers had been

---

1891, to consider the possibility of a voluntary adoption of the Eight Hours Day, had it in view to request the Home Secretary to embody any decision they might arrive at, in a "rule" to be made by him under the Coal Mines Regulation Act, which would have had the force of law.

* Except for mills driven by water power. See p. 157.
† See p. 158.

gradually overcome, and the laws had been made progressively more stringent. When Parliament came to deal with non-textile factories it encountered an entirely fresh opposition. A whole new set of manufacturers rose in protest against any interference in each and all of their special cases. It was necessary to conciliate their opposition, and consequently the law was made as liberal as possible. The favourable exemption thus established has since been maintained by force of precedent.

That is the sole explanation of the general distinction made between textile and non-textile industries. The distinction is not only worthless, it is unjust. Work in most non-textile factories is just as exhausting as in textile factories; it is often even more exhausting. The employés in non-textile trades are, as a rule, not more but less able than those engaged in the textile industries to protect themselves against economic pressure. The employers have not more but less reason to ask for a long working day. For in a textile factory an immense mass of fixed capital is standing idle every hour that the operatives are not at work. In many non-textile trades machinery is only used to a comparatively small extent. Finally, on the ground of foreign competition, textile manufacturers may with perfect justice contend that their working day ought to be not shorter but longer than the working day in non-textile trades. Of all English industries the textile manufactures are the most sensitive to foreign competition, while many of the non-textile trades are purely domestic in their character, and cannot be affected by competition from abroad.

We therefore contend that, as a first step to the reform of the Factory Acts, the legal distinction between textile and non-textile industries must be abolished. The only sound distinction to make is between those trades in which occasional overtime should be permitted and those in which it is unnecessary. This distinction is dealt with elsewhere. Subject then to proper provision for overtime in those trades where it is necessary, our proposal is that all trades and occupations should be brought under the same working day as textile factories, and that the law should be made to apply explicitly to men as well as to women.* Our next point is

* In many occupations great injustice would be done to women by a one-sex law. For example, the mere extension of the present Factory Acts of

that this working day, or rather this working week, might probably, without any inconvenience, be reduced from 56½ to 54 hours. We have already pointed out elsewhere in this volume the disadvantages which follow from the practice of working before breakfast. The operatives are not in the heart for good work till they have had their morning meal, and the break for that meal entails loss of time in leaving and resuming work. The law at present prescribes a gross working day in textile factories of twelve hours, with two hours for meals. On Saturdays the gross working time is eight hours, and one and a half hours are deducted. In this way a net week of 56½ hours is made up. But if instead of coming to work at six in the morning, and losing two hours for meals, the mill hands came to work at seven, and only lost one and a half hours, they could get in a net day of nine and a half hours before six o'clock in the evening.* By a similar arrangement on Saturday, the working week would be brought down to 53½ hours. It may safely be asserted that this re-adjustment of times, while it would give an extra hour's liberty each day to the operatives, would not, in the long run, perceptibly influence the output of work.

In special justification of this suggestion we may point to the fact that artisans who have won a Nine Hours Day do not in many cases begin work before seven. It may thus easily happen that a little girl, or her mother, working in a mill, has to be there by six o'clock, whilst the father or husband employed about the mill as an artisan does not put in an appearance till an hour later.

This leads us to the point that since employers have in many industries conceded a nominal 54 hours week to their male employés, it is impossible for them to contend that a 60 hours week is necessary in non-textile factories and workshops. The limit of 54 hours is, we believe, one which any industry could safely adopt to-morrow. As to the further reduction to 50, 48, or 45 hours a week, we suggest that it should generally be left to trade option, in the manner proposed in the Fabian Society's Bill.

Great Britain to public-houses, would throw out of employment thousands of young women now honestly earning their living as barmaids, and lead to their replacement by barmen.

* Non-textile operatives have to get in a net day of ten and a half hours between six in the morning and six in the evening.

The letters we print in the Appendix prove conclusively that even the lowest limit would in some trades be a net gain to employer as well as to employed.

There are, however, certain occupations in which the direct interference of Parliament is justifiable and desirable, in order to secure at once a maximum 48 hours week, accompanied with a maximum 10 or 12 hours day. These occupations are the following:—all government work, whether direct or by contract; all work in mines; all work on railways, tramways, gasworks, and other local monopolies. To refuse the Eight Hours Day in these cases, on the ground that it is inapplicable in other cases, is childish. Nor generally need we delay to embody in law, wherever practicable, the declared wish of the workers in any particular industry, merely because we are in doubt as to the wishes of the workers in other industries, or as to the wishes of the general community with regard to a general law.

CHAPTER X.

CONCLUSION.

FEW words are necessary by way of conclusion. In the course of the present volume we have shown that the Eight Hours Movement is no new fad of a few agitators. It is a movement that directly results from the growing prosperity and intelligence of manual workers throughout the civilised world.

It is now recognised that all social organisation is the product of a long series of actions and reactions on each other of opinion and law. In matters industrial, the factor of law was, after the dissolution of the mediæval order, almost entirely neglected, with the result that, as one eminent economist tells us, "we have been suffering for a century from an acute outbreak of individualism, unchecked by the old restraints, and invested with almost a religious sanction by a certain soulless school of writers."* The "true inwardness" of the Eight Hours Movement is an assertion of the necessity of the legal recognition of the general social interest in every labour contract, quite as much for the sake of the influence upon public opinion of such legal recognition, as for the immediate social advantages sought.

That the assistance of the law is necessary we claim to have shown on the double ground that the hours of labour ought to be reduced, and that no other power but that of Parliament can secure an effective reduction. For though working classes collectively, or the members of any particular trade collectively, may see clearly enough that it would be to their advantage to reduce the hours of labour, yet by themselves they are powerless to effect this change. Should it come to an open rupture between employer

* Professor H. S. Foxwell, p. 249 of essay in *The Claims of Labour*. (Edinburgh Co-operative Printing Co., 1886.)

and employed, the essential weakness of the wage-worker's position instantly flashes out. In the majority of cases he is entirely dependent for his weekly livelihood on his weekly wages. When a strike comes two alternatives present themselves to him—to remain true to his class and live on a small and precarious strike allowance; or to turn blackleg, receiving double pay while the strike lasts and a permanent situation when it is over. It is a matter for astonishment that relatively so few workmen at once accept the latter alternative. But as the strike continues, the number of blacklegs inevitably grows. Men cannot starve and see their families starve. Public subscriptions may at first flow in to help the cause of labour, but this source of strength soon begins to run dry. And while it lasts it is not necessarily effective. For even if the men first concerned in the dispute are enabled to hold out, other workmen will be brought from a distance to take their places. The simple fact is that in labour disputes the last word rests with the man who has the longest purse, and that man is not usually the labourer or the artisan of Great Britain.

Moreover, whatever additional strength the labouring classes obtain by combination is also obtainable by their employers. Since the days when Adam Smith wrote, and before, the open "conspiracies" of the men have ever been met by the tacit conspiracies of the masters. When a workman takes the lead on behalf of his fellows, he renders himself liable to be relentlessly boycotted by every employer in the trade, to be driven from town to town in search of work, only to find that the employers' "black list," with his name upon it, has preceded him.

And beyond this old-fashioned, though still most efficient, weapon of the employers, there is the power of direct and open combination. The employers are closing their ranks. Organised strikes are met by organised lock-outs; the union of labourers by the consolidation of capital. The two parties now stand face to face. On the one hand are the legal owners of the land we live upon, and the legal possessors of the implements that are essential to modern industry; on the other hand are a landless folk who can only live by selling from day to day the strength or skill of their bare hands.

As to the issue of the conflict there could be no doubt, were it not that the landless labourer now possesses a new power. He is no longer a mere worker; he is also an elector. The power of the

State is now his. It is this power which secures to the landlord and capitalist the value of their property. There is no injustice in asking that the same power shall be used to secure to the labourer the leisure which he has earned by his toil.

This is the new demand which is perplexing politicians and disturbing the calculations of statesmen. Yet, as we have repeatedly shown, the same issue has been raised before on many occasions.

Forty-five years ago Mr. Greville wrote in his diary:—

"I never remember so much excitement as has been caused by Ashley's Ten Hours Bill, nor a more curious political state of things—such intermingling of parties, such a confusion of opposition. . . . John Russell voting for 'ten hours,' against all he professed last year, has filled the world with amazement. . . . The Opposition were divided—Palmerston and Lord John one way, Baring and Labouchere the other. It has been a very queer affair. Some voted not knowing how they ought to vote, and following those they are accustomed to follow, many who voted against Government afterwards said they believed they were wrong. Melbourne is all against Ashley; all the political economists, of course; Lord Spencer strong against him. Then Graham gave the greatest offence by taking up a word of the *Examiner's* last Sunday, and calling it a *Jack Cade legislation*; this stirring them to fury, and they flew upon him like tigers. . . . The whole thing is difficult and unpleasant."*

Since that date about forty Acts of the nature of Factory Acts have been passed in the United Kingdom alone, and the world is richer by forty-five years of experience of the result of such legislation. Nevertheless, when next year, or the year after, Lord Ashley's successor in "Jack Cade legislation," whoever he may be, seriously pushes forward the Eight Hours Bill, which the rising Democratic tide is now making inevitable, it can easily be foreseen that the House of Commons of to-day will be little better prepared for the proposal than was the House of 1844. It may be safely predicted that the division will again be, to the unseen political Greville of the hour, "a very queer affair." The Opposition will be once more divided; Individualist Radicals like the Mr. Labouchere of to-day may not improbably follow in the cautious footsteps of his uncle, while some very sturdy politicians will be found voting in favour of the Bill, even "against all they professed" some time ago. The Home Secretary will possibly

* *Journal of the Reign of Queen Victoria*, vol. ii. p. 236 (March 31, 1844).

not venture to repeat his predecessor's unhappy epithet, but some representative of the Liberty and Property Defence League will doubtless supply the omission, and it is quite certain that every political wire-puller will once again regard the whole thing as "difficult and unpleasant." Even as we write (February 1891) the Conservative Government announces, greatly to the disgust of the surviving capitalist Liberals of the old school, that the relations of capital to labour are to form the subject of inquiry by a Royal Commission. And to sum up, just as the Ten Hours Bill passed within three years of Mr. Greville's entry, so every politician knows in his heart of hearts that a reasonable Eight Hours Act will probably be one of the earliest fruits of the next general election.

How soon the question will come to a decisive issue in other countries we make no pretension even to guess. \England has, indeed, already lost her honourable lead in labour legislation. Already in some respects Switzerland, in others Germany, in others France, far surpass the United Kingdom in the extent to which they have pursued the path marked out by Robert Owen, Tom Sadler, and Lord Shaftesbury. But for them, as well as for the United Kingdom and the United States of America, the Labour Problem demands even more pressingly its solution.

Fifty years ago that solution would have been promised in the name of Absolute Freedom of Trade and Industry. But that crude vision has long since been demolished. Cobden himself scarcely maintained it, and Cobden's biographer gives us the judgment of statesmen on the opposition to the principle of factory legislation of the great apostles of Free Trade. Speaking of Cobden's preference for the latter panacea, Mr. John Morley, in words pregnant of import, asks:—

"How are you to settle the mutual relations of capital and labour to one another? Abolition of restriction may be excellent in the sphere of commodities. Is it so clear that the same condition suffices for the commonwealth when the commodity to be settled is a man's labour? Or is it not palpably false and irrational to talk of labour as a commodity? In other words, can the relations between labour and capital be safely left to the unfettered play of individual competition? *The answer of modern statesmanship is, that unfettered individual competition is not a principle to which the regulation of industry may be entrusted.* There may be conditions which it is in the highest degree desirable to impose on industry, and to which the public opinion of the industrial classes may be entirely favourable. Yet the assistance of law may be needed to give effect to this opinion, because—in the words of the great man who was now preparing the exposition of political economy that was to reign all through the next generation—only law can afford to every individual a guarantee that his competitors will pursue the same course as to *hours of labour* and so forth, without which he cannot safely adopt it himself." *

How far the application of this principle may ultimately be carried does not here concern us. In the present volume we deal only with one well defined proposal for improving the labourer's position through his own collective power. In general terms that proposal is:—That the hours of labour of all classes of manual wage-workers should be limited by law, in order that those men and women who are now overworked may have leisure, and that those who are now idle may have work. Incidentally we contend that this measure would put the working classes in a better position to bargain with their employers, and thus tend to raise the wages and the general status of those who live by selling their labour.

As to detailed proposals, they are discussed at considerable length in the preceding pages. Briefly our suggestions are—

First, that the Eight Hour Day should be introduced as soon as may be into all Government work and Government contracts; not because the employés of the central and of the local governments are on the average worse off than the employés of private firms, but because it is the duty of the State to set an example in its treatment of the persons who work for it.

Secondly, we propose that the worst cases of overwork should, wherever practicable, at once be dealt with, and some limit imposed to the hours of labour. The worst sufferers at present are the persons employed on omnibuses, trams, and railways, in shops and public-houses, bakeries and gasworks; and as it happens these persons by the very nature of their occupation are completely shielded from all danger of foreign competition. It is therefore at once possible to limit the hours of labour in all these cases. The actual limitation need not necessarily involve a uniform Eight Hours Day, but should be a period adapted to the present circumstances of each case.

* Morley's *Life of Cobden* (Chapman & Hall, 1881), vol. i. ch. xiii. p. 298. The reference is to John Stuart Mill. (Italics added.)

CONCLUSION. 243

Thirdly, we suggest that to the other industries of the country the principle of "trade option" should be applied. By this means we shall avoid the danger of imposing restrictions which, in the opinion of those most concerned, would be unsuited or dangerous to the industry.

There are many who will be unconvinced by our arguments, and who will continue to resist the ever-growing phenomenon of State interference. To them we would in conclusion say that this phenomenon after all is nothing more than an incident of the general process of the differentiation of functions, or in the simpler and older-fashioned phrase, of the division of labour, which is everywhere going on. The progress of mechanical invention and the growing complexity of industrial organisation necessarily compels each individual to take an increasingly circumscribed part in the general work of the world. Taken alone, these economic causes are infinitely more potent to limit individual capacity than is the comparatively superficial action of the thing we call Government. The hope for the future, however, lies in this, that the power of Government may be used to make good the loss of individual liberty caused by economic development.

This is the final justification for State interference. The State is compelled to interfere between machinery and man, because otherwise man would be crushed by the demon of his own creation. This demon to-day still stands fronting him. It tells the English operative—the descendant of the English artisan—that he shall no longer, as his fathers did, take a pride in his work or feel delight in the exercise of his muscles and brain. Instead, he shall be tied set hours to a great thing of steel and iron that moves and reasons for him; in front of it he shall dance about within the limits of his tether; and when he has done his day's dancing he may go drown himself for all the demon cares. And to this the modern State—collective man—replies :—If we cannot resist the power of machinery, we can neutralise its bad effects. If machinery lowers human beings below the level of monkeys in order that they may earn their living, we can at any rate limit the period of monkeydom. If we cannot make the work manly, we can insist that the workers shall have leisure to become men.

APPENDIX I.

HOURS OF LABOUR IN DIFFERENT TRADES.

Railway Servants.

The following details of the hours of labour of employés of the North British Railway Company were collected at the beginning of the year 1891 by personal inquiry:—

A FIREMAN.—Hours on duty during the sixteen fortnights preceding December 22nd, 1890.

1st fortnight	. 174 hours	9th fortnight	. 168 hours
2nd „	. 174 „	10th „	. 193 „
3rd „	. 156 „	11th „	. 190 „
4th „	. 186 „	12th „	. 192 „
5th „	. 193 „	13th „	. 198 „
6th „	. 188 „	14th „	. 155 „
7th „	. 193 „	15th „	. 167 „
8th „	. 254 „	16th „	. 194 „

Average, 185¾ hours per fortnight.

It will be noticed that in ten instances the fortnightly duty exceeded 190 hours. On some days the man was on duty 20 hours. In one case only 8 hours.

A DRIVER.—Hours of duty during the four fortnights preceding December 22nd, 1890.

1st fortnight	. 202 hours	3rd fortnight	. 204 hours
2nd „	. 186 „	4th „	. 172 „

APPENDIX.

I. F.—Hours on duty during the days specified.

	H.	M.		H.	M.
24th November 1890	13	45	8th December 1890	13	20
25th ,, ,,	11	45	9th ,, ,,	14	10
26th ,, ,,	14	0	10th ,, ,,	16	20
27th ,, ,,	12	55	11th ,, ,,	13	15
28th ,, ,,	14	0	12th ,, ,,	15	0
29th ,, ,,	11	35	13th ,, ,,	14	5
Sunday.			Sunday.		
1st December 1890	16	5	15th ,, ,,	17	5
2nd ,, ,,	14	30	16th ,, ,,	12	50
3rd ,, ,,	16	55	17th ,, ,,	13	35
4th ,, ,,	14	30	18th ,, ,,	13	40
5th ,, ,,	23	0	19th ,, ,,	14	25
6th ,, ,,	13	0	20th ,, ,,	13	25

Daily Average, 14½ hours.

Pawnbrokers.

Extract from a letter from a pawnbroker's assistant in Belfast to a member of Parliament :—

"It's no wonder employés are thin pale-looking boys and men. In this city there are firms doing business from 7.30 A.M. till 1.30 A.M. the following morning. If the Attorney-General is thinking of legislating upon this subject, I suggest that the hours should be from 9 A.M. to 6 P.M., and until 8 P.M. on Saturdays. . . . Every man, woman, and child is paid before three o'clock ; but when they know that they can get into the 'pawn' up till midnight, they sit in public-houses drinking."

In order to get reliable information on the subject of the actual working hours at the present time, we issued during the preparation of this book a circular-letter to the secretaries of some fifty or sixty different trade unions. Extracts from the answers received are printed below.

Amalgamated Engineers.

The standard time for a week's work is 54 hours, except on the north-east coast, where it is now 53 hours. All time above this is overtime, and a great deal of overtime is now being worked both in London and more or less in all other parts of the United Kingdom.

Bakers, Liverpool.

It would be near the mark to average the hours at 80 per week. We are unanimous in favour of a 10 hours working day, and with that object have just (November 17th, 1890) issued a manifesto to the master bakers.

Extract from Circular.—"The men's committee have come to the unanimous conclusion that a day's work shall consist of 10 hours, all necessary meal-time included, and a week's work 60 hours, Sunday work included."

Blast Furnacemen, Scotland,

"Whom he represented, were, he was sorry to say, at present worked 12 hours."—(Speech by Mr. Patterson at the Trades Congress, 1890.)

Boiler Makers and Iron Ship Builders.

On the north-east coast of England 53 hours per week; elsewhere, 54. We do not allow overtime except in cases of great necessity.

Bookbinders, London.

The hours are nominally 54 per week, but as this is in a great measure a season trade, overtime is of necessity worked, and is paid an eighth extra. In consequence of the extension of the Factory Acts to the females in this trade, there is not so much overtime worked as formerly. But a fixed eight hours would be inapplicable to us. For instance, just now (November 1890) the trade is very busy, the men working in some shops from 7 A.M. to 10 P.M., and in all our shops more or less overtime is being made, and all our hands are in work. This has been the case for the last two months, and will be for a few weeks longer. Then for a few months the trade will be normal, and in the summer slack, till the autumn comes round again.

Bookbinders, Glasgow.

I enclose a list of our branches; give wages and hours per week wrought at the towns mentioned. The list is interesting as showing that at Birmingham and Nottingham we have men working for 28s. per week, whereas *the same men* would get 32s. for the same work and time at London, Manchester, Liverpool, and Dublin. Where the union is weak, wages are low. The hours named in the list (usually 54 per week) do not include overtime, which differs greatly in different shops. The hours of women and children (as fixed by the Factory Act) do not affect the men materially, as when pressure comes it is common to give the women work to take home after their day's work in the workshops.

Bookbinders (Women), London.

In some firms the women work 54 hours per week, in others 51 hours. Only in one or two they work 48. This is independent of overtime.

Book Folders and Sewers (Women), Liverpool.

Men bookbinders and finishers serve seven years, after which their wages are 32s. to 42s. per week of 54 hours; overtime 8d. an hour. From October to February there is a deal of overtime worked by men and women. The women and girls work exactly the same hours as the men, and in some shops two hours more, with no extra pay. One of the largest firms in Liverpool only pay their women 8s. or 9s. per week. In many shops we are compelled to go out for our meals, no matter how severe the weather, and, often with poor clothing on, go back to work and sit for five hours with wet boots and clothes.

Brass Fitters, Newcastle-on-Tyne.

The normal working hours are 53 per week—*i.e.*, for the first five days commence at 6 A.M., leave at 5 P.M., with 1½ hours for meals; Saturday commence at 6 A.M., leave at noon, with half-an-hour for breakfast. There is not much overtime worked regularly except in a few shops, when there may be a pressure of work for the time being.

Brickmakers, Nottingham.

From April 1st to September 30th, 55 hours a week; from October 1st to March 31st, 47½ hours a week. These are the hours of work, weather permitting. But we cannot work in frost, rain, or snow, so you may take off ten hours each week. We do not work overtime unless it is a case of necessity, for our union is very strict against overtime.

Card and Blowing Room Operatives.

Upwards of 70 per cent. of the operatives engaged in the above branches of factory labour are females, and their hours of labour are restricted to 56½ hours per week by the "Factory Acts." Male labour in our cotton mills work the same number of hours, "overtime" working being of very rare occurrence—in fact, the work in cotton mills is so arranged that it is almost impossible for the males to work more hours per day than the females and young persons.

Carpenters and Joiners.

Hours vary in different towns from 50 to 60 per week. They are generally (but not always) longer in summer than in winter. In Dublin the working hours have been recently (November 1890) reduced to 54, after a strike had occurred to enforce the reduction. Respecting overtime, I cannot give you any information except that we detest it, and in most towns it is paid for at an increased rate.

Compositors, Edinburgh.

We work 9 hours 50 minutes per day, equivalent to a working week of 54 hours. It would be difficult to say how much overtime is worked, as the system is being considerably done away with.

Compositors, Manchester.

The average hours of our members are about 55 per week for day work, and 52 for night work. Overtime is not habitually worked.

Coopers, Burton-on-Trent.

The majority of our labour is performed by the piece, and the hours vary in accordance with demands for casks. What few there are engaged by the day work 54 hours per week. We are not in any way affected by the labour of women or children.

Felt Hatters, Denton.

Our regular working hours are 56 per week, with overtime limited to two hours per day five days a week during the busy season from March to August. Any member working beyond the two hours limit is heavily fined.

APPENDIX.

File Cutters, Sheffield.

There are about 2000 men, women, boys and girls in the trade, and not above one-third of them work in the factory. The others fetch their work and take it to little shops, principally in back yards, and some in their own houses. All those who work outside the factory can work as many hours as they like, and do work very late at nights. The factories generally close about seven o'clock at night.

Iron Founders, London.

"The hours of labour in the iron moulding industry are 54 per week; on the Tyneside and the north-east coast generally, 53 hours constitute a week's work. All time worked after the ordinary hours is paid for at a higher rate." To this statement of the Secretary may be added the following table, showing the progressive improvement in the hours of labour during the last forty years, and showing also that the reduction in the hours of labour has been accompanied with a progressive *rise* in wages.

FRIENDLY SOCIETY OF IRON FOUNDERS—11,710 MEMBERS.

Years.	Hours of Labour.	Average Wages.
1845–54	59½ to 63	£1 3 1
1855–64	57½ to 60	1 4 6
1865–74	56½ to 60	1 6 3
1875–84	54 to 58½	1 6 6

Lithographic Printers, Manchester.

The hours worked are 55 per week; in Scotland, 51 only. Overtime is worked extensively at the end of the year, or rather the last two months of the year.

Millers, Liverpool.

About a year ago—the end of 1889—a union was formed in this trade, and has succeeded in reducing the hours of labour to 58 per week.

Mill Sawyers, London.

This trade is divided into two sections—namely, saw mills that do sawing for timber merchants, cabinet makers, etc., and mills that belong to box and packing-case making firms, who do their own sawing and employ the largest number of men. In the first the normal working day is 10 hours, or 59 per week; but by systematic overtime this is brought up to 67 hours, and even 73 and 74. In the second class things are somewhat better, as the working hours are only 56 per week, scarcely any overtime being worked. If you should require further proof of the scarcely credible long hours worked in first-class mills, I should be pleased to show you some of these mills that start work at 6 A.M. and go on to 9.30 and 10 o'clock at night.

Plumbers.

The Operative Plumbers' Association has a membership of nearly 5000 workmen, scattered all over the country. Both the hours of work and the rate of wages vary in different towns. Thus at Kettering the hours are 59 per week, winter and summer, and at Inverness 57, while in most districts of London the hours fixed by the Society are only 47 in summer, and 44½ in winter. Between these limits there is every possible variation. With regard to overtime the Secretary writes :—" We do not approve of overtime under any conditions, but we are obliged to allow it on board ships that are timed to leave by certain dates, or in repairing breakdowns of various kinds in mills, which to delay would cause serious loss to a large number of workpeople."

Riggers, Cardiff.

A week's work is 55 hours. There is considerable overtime in this district, paid for at the rate of a shilling an hour.

Shipwrights, Hull.

During the summer months the hours are 53 per week; in winter rather less. This rule only applies to the largest centres of our trade; in places where no society exists the men work from six to six during the summer, and perhaps during the winter also when they can. Taking our trade all round, what with lost time through bad trade and bad weather, the best of our men in the large yards do not average five days a week.

APPENDIX.

Shirt and Collar Makers, Islington.

The hours average between 9 o'clock in the morning till 7 or 8 o'clock in the evening. There is very little overtime worked in West End and City houses, but the plain workers and button-holers are often allowed to take work home with them.

Steam Engine Makers, Manchester.

The established hours in all districts in the engineering trade are 54 per week, except on the north-east coast, where they are 53 per week. Overtime is extensively worked in some localities, but not in others. The Factory Acts do not apply to adult labour, as you must be aware, in relation to hours, but are beneficial in sanitary matters and the fencing of machinery.

Steel Smelters, England.

The normal working day is 12 hours and 6 days per week. The furnaces begin charging for the week on Sunday at 6 P.M., some of the furnaces finishing for the week at 10 A.M. Saturday morning, others as late as 5 P.M. From careful observation I place the average for the week as follows :—

First hand smelters, 69 hours. Second hand smelters, 72 hours.

The three hours difference being due to the fact that this second class have to bring the furnaces up in heat on the Sunday and previous to charging.

Third hands, 69 hours.   Charge-wheelers, 66 hours.
Pitmen . 69 ,,   Gas producermen, 80 ,,

This last class work all the week round, with the exception that on Saturday nights a proportion of the men get relieved in turn, as a smaller quantity of gas is requisite than when the furnaces are on full swing, thus reducing the normal week of 84 hours to an average of 80.

There is no such thing as overtime, the reason being apparent from the fact that the furnaces work continuously from the time of charging on the Sunday to the Saturday by two staffs of men, who work night and day week about.

In the case of the producermen, at the end of the week they work a long turn to accomplish the change of shift—viz., 24 hours.

It is the general custom in all three countries to work from 7 A.M.

to 5 P.M. on the day shift, and from 5 P.M. to 7 A.M. on the night turn. This, of course, is an arrangement by the workmen themselves, and necessitates a 14 hours shift on nights, but only 10 on days.

All the workmen are paid tonnage except charge-wheelers and the producermen, who are paid day wages.

The men have agitated for the past five years for the hour of charging on Sunday nights being 12 midnight generally. This would be accomplished could the obstinacy of the Consett Iron and Steel Company, County of Durham, be overcome. The agitation will be continued till successful.

Steel and Iron Workers, Wednesbury.

The iron and steel workers in this district are working 12 hours per day in most mills and forges. They work six days one week and five nights on the alternate week. There is no opportunity for overtime.

Stevedores.

When at work we do 10 hours a day. But very often we do not work more than a few hours. In the event of rain our employers can pay us off at any minute. Our work does not average more than three days a week; it is laborious and at times dangerous, especially in dark and foggy weather. We do not work much overtime as a rule. It is only when a ship is behind her time of sailing.

Stone Masons, London.

Hours vary in different towns from 48 to 58 per week, and are generally longer in summer than in winter. "I am a great advocate of the Legal Eight Hours Day, and so also is my society. Overtime is strictly prohibited except in cases of breakdown. So thoroughly opposed are the masons to overtime that we inflict a penalty varying from 50s. to 10s. on any member working in opposition to the local rule on the subject."

Tailors, Bradford.

We have no fixed hours in our trade except in a few towns. The sweating system and home working has obtained so much hold, and in many shops the work is so irregular, that the adoption of a system of regular hours is almost hopeless. The in and out workers are pitted against each other by our foremen and employers. We do not expect to do any good until all firms are compelled to find workrooms for all whom they employ. I am sorry we are in such a plight. I feel the position very keenly, and I put a very large amount of blame on the sweater.

Tailors, Edinburgh.

The average hours for the week may be put down at 60. The proper hours are 57, but this number is exceeded very generally, and no overtime is paid, except in one or two shops.

While the present volume was being prepared for press a Parliamentary Return of the hours of labour in various trades was issued. This return—originally moved for by Mr. Broadhurst—is, like many of the publications of the British Government, more bulky than valuable. From it we briefly summarise the following statements as to the hours of labour in the trades specified during the year 1890:—

Agricultural Labourers.—Normal week's work in different districts: in winter, lowest 45 hours, highest 54 hours; in summer, lowest 57 hours, highest 63 hours; in harvest time, 70 to 80 hours.

Dock and Riverside Labour—
    Dock Labourers—lowest 48, highest 63 hours.
    Coal Trimmers—lowest 63, highest 72 hours.
    Lightermen—72 hours.
    Wharfingers—54 to 72 hours.

Bakers—Normal week's work varies in different districts from 50 to 80 hours.

Brickmakers—From 38 to 69 hours.

Bricklayers—48 to 54 hours.

Carpenters and Joiners—In winter, from 45 to 61 hours; in summer, from 49 to 61 hours.

Cement Workers—53½ to 60 hours.

Coopers—52 hours.

Painters and Decorators—54 to 60 hours.

Plasterers—In winter, from 39 to 60 hours; in summer, from 49 to 60 hours.

Plumbers—In winter, from 40 to 60 hours ; in summer, from 49 to 61 hours.
Slaters—In winter, from 41½ to 56½ hours ; in summer, from 49 to 65 hours.
Stone Masons—In winter, from 42 to 60 hours; in summer, from 49 to 62 hours.
Timber Trade—54 to 59 hours.
Cabinetmakers—50½ to 60 hours.
Chemical Workers—50 to 84 hours.
Tobacco Trades—44 to 60 hours.
Boot and Shoe Trades—49 to 56½ hours.
Fur Dressing—52 hours.
Hat Manufacture—51 to 60 hours.
Hosiery—55 to 56½ hours.
Tailoring—50 to 72 hours.
Coachmaking—53 to 60 hours.
Engineering Trades—53 and 54 hours.
Glass Trade—36 to 67 hours.
Iron Manufacture—47 to 96 hours.
Pottery Trades—48 to 60 hours.
Printing and Bookbinding—51 to 56 hours.
Railway Porters—60 to 80 hours.

It is to be noted that in all cases these figures refer solely to the *normal* week's work, no account whatever being taken of overtime ; but, as elsewhere shown in this volume, overtime working is in many trades an habitual practice.

APPENDIX II.

LETTERS, Etc., RECEIVED FROM FIRMS WHICH HAVE ALREADY ADOPTED AN EIGHT HOURS DAY.

In order to obtain as full information as possible with regard to the practical working of the Eight Hours System, the authors wrote to all the firms where they heard that the system had been tried asking for information on the following particulars :

APPENDIX.

1. Effect on amount of work produced in a week.
2.   ,,   cost of production.
3.   ,,   amount of overtime worked.
4.   ,,   time wages of the men.
5.   ,,   piece wages.
6.   ,,   relations between employer and employed.

The following letters and memoranda of conversations are the replies:—

From BURROUGHS, WELLCOME, & CO., *Importers, Exporters, and Manufacturing Chemists, Snow Hill Buildings, London, E.C.*

16*th* December 1890.

Replying to your inquiries of the 11th inst., regarding our experience with the Eight Hours System, we beg to say that our impressions are:—

1st. We believe the amount of work produced in a week is very nearly, if not quite, as great as when we were working nine hours a day.

2nd. We think that the cost of production is not materially increased.

3rd. At first there was a considerable amount of overtime work, which was perhaps largely due to the fact (*a*) that we were very short of stock, owing to our fire at Wandsworth, (*b*) that we had engaged a good many new and inexperienced work people at Dartford. Now, however, we have been able to avoid overtime work almost entirely.

4th. Wages. We are glad to have been able both to reduce the hours of work and to increase the amount of wages at the same time. Of course, in the first instance, this was money out of pocket and a loss to us, but it is our opinion that in the long run the loss will be made good to us on account of the hearty and friendly interest which all our employés manifest in our business.

5th. Piece wages. None of our employés are paid in this manner. We rely upon their honour to do the best they can for our business during the eight hours of work per day.

6th. The relations between employer and employed are, we believe, most friendly and cordial. On account of the general interest manifested by our employés in our business, we decided some years ago to reward them with a present or bonus, consisting of a fixed percentage of the profits. After four years' experience with this system, we are perfectly satisfied with it, and wish to increase the percentage as soon as our profits will permit. We doubt if it would be possible for more friendly and cordial relations to exist between employer and employed than in our business, and we desire to do everything we can to perpetuate it.

We believe that increased intelligence and efficiency follow upon limiting the hours of labour to eight, because opportunities are thus afforded for intellectual and physical development and recreation. We believe that the proper employment of such opportunities tends to elevate the general tone of life, to improve the health, and to cultivate a taste for good society, and precludes that excessive fatigue which demands unnatural stimulant and vicious pleasures. It is therefore our opinion that the general adoption of the Eight Hours System would powerfully tend (1) to increase the amount of work produced in a given time, by reason of the improved physical and mental conditions; (2) to decrease the cost of production for the same reason, and also, on account of the improved mental elasticity, lead to inventions in labour-saving machinery; (3) to improve relations between employers and employed, brought about by the disposition evinced by the former to give the employé opportunities for recreation and social advancement.

From BRUNNER, MOND, & CO., LIMITED, *Manufacturers of Alkali and Soda.*

NORTHWICH, 23*rd December* 1890.

In reply to your letter of December 14th, we cannot give you the details asked for with regard to the effect of the Eight Hours System, but we can assure you that we are in every way satisfied with the change which we have made. You may perhaps be aware that our process of manufacture is of necessity continuous, and that the works never stop, and our adoption of the Eight Hours System means that the work is carried on in eight hours shifts. All artisans and labourers employed by us work the usual hours in this district. The effect on the health and physique of the men of this change has been most beneficial, and we expect still further improvement when the men have got really used to having time to spare between sleep and work.

Memorandum of a conversation with Mr. T. W. SMITH, *of the firm of Caslon & Co., Typefounders, Chiswell Street, E.C.*

December 15th, 1890.

The circumstances which gave rise to the Eight Hours System in our business are in many ways exceptional. To begin with, all our men are paid "stab" or regular time wages, and I personally consider this system far more satisfactory than piece wages. It puts a man upon his honour to do a fair amount of work for a fair day's wage. At any rate it answers with us. But possibly if our men had been on piece wages they would have been less anxious for a reduction of hours.

The change to the Eight Hours System came about in this way:—The improvements effected in type-founding machinery during the last twenty years have made it possible for our men to turn out the same quantity of work as formerly with much less exertion. We knew this and they knew it. A few months ago there was some stir among the men in sympathy with the general movement which has been going on among the working classes. We thereupon had a friendly talk with the men in a general meeting, and told them that if they would undertake to send us down the same quantity of work as before, we were perfectly willing to reduce the hours, and still pay them the same wages. This arrangement was agreed to, and has worked perfectly since.

Our day is from 8 A.M. to 6 P.M., with an hour for dinner; and from 8 A.M. to 1 P.M. on Saturdays. So that the week is 50 and not 48 hours. But we credit each man with his odd two hours, and allow him to add them up and take an equivalent holiday on full pay.

I may mention that the most friendly relations have always existed between the firm and its employés. We have men with us now who have been here for fifty years, and some of our people can trace back their connection with the firm, passing from father to son, almost to our origin in 1716.

From S. H. JOHNSON & Co., *The Engineering Works, Carpenters' Road, Stratford, E., London.*

December 12*th*, 1890.

In reply to your favour of yesterday, we beg to say that there can be no universal rule as to the applicability or practicability of what is now being agitated as the Eight Hours System, and we desire it to be clearly understood that we are in no way advocates of external pressure being brought to bear so as to affect the relationship of employers and employés, and we would strenuously resist any attempt of the kind in our own case. The great majority of employers are fair-dealing men, and there is every reason to believe that a like proportion of the employés are the same, provided they are not interfered with by professional agitators. If masters and men cannot settle their differences between themselves, it is little likely that an outsider knowing nothing about the matter should be competent to give an opinion. The most self-seeking men are the agitators, who take their pay in money; or posing as a philanthropist, or both, they are generally partisans, and without experience to qualify them to make opinions of any weight or value. We are glad to say that our employés have thrown off that Old Man of the Sea, the Trade Society, and time has proved that both sides have profited in consequence. If our men were society men it would not be possible for us to make the concessions we have done hitherto, nor to have given them the Eight Hours Day.

What we have done is to make the week 48 hours instead of 54, and we give the nine hours' pay for the eight hours day, provided full time is punctually worked, otherwise we pay for eight hours only per day. It would appear from this that for time work we pay 12½ per cent. more than formerly, and this is to the employés' advantage. But we are recouped in this, we believe, in several ways.

1st. We do away with the breakfast-hour, as the men come to work with their breakfast done at eight o'clock.

2nd. Our men are more punctual.

3rd. There is only one break in the day—viz., for dinner. Every break means practically a quarter of an hour lost time, getting ready for going and getting ready for work on returning.

APPENDIX. 259

4th. Our men are fitter for work after breakfast than they were formerly when they came to work at six o'clock without breakfast, and consequently do more in a given time. Formerly before breakfast very little work, comparatively, was done. In winter especially the men were cold, the light (artificial) bad to work in, and unpunctuality led to this.

5th. The men are saved the walk home and back again, which means a further saving of time to them of a quarter of an hour or twenty minutes per day—an important saving to them. They have more energy for their work in consequence, and use it.

6th. The men have more time for improvement and recreation; in fact, they are not only better men but better animals.

The sum of all these considerations justifies the change, and we consider more than balances the account. Our men, we need scarcely say, appreciate the difference to themselves fully, and reciprocate in their efforts to show us that we shall lose nothing by it.

If we had been in the toils of the society this would not have been possible. Now we have confidence in our men and they in us.

We are glad to give our experience in this matter, as it may help other employers to see it in the same light as we do at present.

From GREEN, McALLAN, & FEILDEN, LIMITED, *Printers and Engravers, St. Andrew Street, London, E.C.*

December 18*th*, 1890.

In reply to your queries as to the effect of the Eight Hour Day in our firm, I have to confess, with very deep regret, that so far it has been a failure financially. Less work is produced, cost is increased, more overtime in proportion has to be worked, and lastly, and most important, rent presses more heavily. I have given it a most patient trial for seven months—a term long enough to enable one to form a fair opinion in the matter—and am now most reluctantly compelled to face the question of reverting to the usual week of 54 hours. My experience has convinced me that no firm in our trade of any size, employing only regular time hands, can compete successfully, on a 48-hour week basis, with houses working full time. No one deplores this more than myself, but unfortunately the fact remains. I have one of the best staffs in London—experienced, quick, and willing, and filled with a desire to render me assistance in every possible way—and yet I have not been successful. It might have been otherwise had the Trade Unions supported us by giving some at least of their work our way; but with the honourable exceptions of Miss Black, the L.S.C., the Printers' Labourers' Union, and Mr. Tom Mann, we have received no help from them, showing how selfish is the cry from the workmen of an Eight Hour Day when they refuse a chance to help some of their brethren to get it, and by giving their work to the lowest estimator, do their best to perpetuate a system which every right-minded man ought to deplore.

P.S.—Am going to introduce profit-sharing as a substitute.

From GREEN, MCALLAN, & FEILDEN, LIMITED.

December 19*th*, 1890.

You have correctly put my position. In our trade the profits are so small, and subject to so much leakage, that one, and only one, person ought to bear the brunt, and that person is the customer. My experience has shown me that it is not easy to induce him to take the same view, and that as a rule he will buy in the cheapest market. I may say that several customers left me when I started the 48-hour week, concluding—and quite rightly—that prices would go up. Three of them told me so plainly.

I am most strongly of opinion that legal enactment is the only way by which a better state of affairs can be brought about. I know that in taking this view I differ from many of our leading trade unionists, who talk of having got the 54 hours by their own efforts (but at what cost and friction?). These gentlemen, however, talk very glibly. If we take the compositors of London, I would venture to say that they work on an average nearer 60 hours a week—a condition of things which they are powerless to prevent. Many of them are rather glad of it; and to a man who has a wife and family, 6s. or 10s. per week extra means more comfort, although the head of the family may be untimely killed by the drain on his constitution. Many of them are too ignorant to see that if a legal day were enacted they would still have the same necessities, and that they would ultimately get as much for the shorter day as they now get for the longer one.

From H. W. MASSINGHAM, *then Editor of the "Star,"*
Stonecutter Street, London, E.C.

December 12*th*, 1890.

The Eight Hours System has been carried out in our office with ease and with little friction, owing largely to the excellent organisation of our printing staff, and the great ability of our foreman and his careful attention to the interests of the men. With regard to the specific points you raise—

1. The effect upon the amount of work produced per man per week is small, owing to the fact that our twenty-eight piece workmen were in the habit of working 48 hours a week before the new arrangement came into effect, the foreman giving each man a weekly half-holiday in turn. Our four time workmen worked about 49 hours a week before the eight hours regulation, so that we had practically only about four hours a week to make up in order to bring the office within the eight hours rule. This was done by occasionally putting the piece workman on time and paying him as a time hand, the necessary piece work being accomplished by a little additional speed. No difficulty has arisen in accomplishing this, and there has been no necessity for employing extra labour.

2. From the foregoing it follows that there has been practically no increase in the cost of production. I may add that since its establishment the eight hours rule has been maintained with but one trifling exception—the production of the double number. Even on this occasion the time work only came to about an hour over the 48 hours per week.

3. Overtime is not allowed on the *Star*.

4. Wages of the ordinary time workers vary from £2 16s. a week to £2 18s.

5. The wages of our piece workers vary from about £2 18s. to £3 and over.

6. The relations between employer and employés on have always been excellent, and have been in a measure improved by the introduction of the Eight Hours System. It is the custom

of the firm to allow a yearly holiday of one week to each employé with full wages.

The foregoing remarks apply purely to the case-room. In other departments the Eight Hours System has been organised without much difficulty. I need not add that the system does not apply to the editor.

From the (*late*) FREETHOUGHT PUBLISHING COMPANY, 65 *Fleet Street, London, E.C.*

December 17*th*, 1890.

We found the Eight Hours Day answered all right. People deal with you when your shop is open; and I do not think it makes any real difference in the amount of custom.

Memorandum of a Conversation with Mr. MARK BEAUFOY, M.P., *Manufacturer of Vinegar, British Wines, and Jams.*

When I first obtained control of the business, I found that during the months of October and November overtime was habitual. The men often worked till 8 or 9 at night, and sometimes even till 11. I realised that they were doing no good to themselves or to me, for such long hours rendered them physically incapable of doing good work. I put a stop to the system, and in order to compensate the men for the loss of overtime pay, I revised the scale of wages in their favour. It was some years later before I began to think of an Eight Hours Day. The men were now coming to work at six in the morning and leaving at five in the evening. But the hours before breakfast were almost wasted, because the men were too cold and hungry to set to work with a will. In the middle of the morning too there was a ridiculous break of a quarter of an hour for lunch. Every break involves loss of time, both in going and in coming. The total working day was 9¼ hours. I proposed to the men that they should come to work at eight, that they should work without any stoppage till 12, and again from 1 to 5; that for this Eight Hours Day I should pay them the same wages as before. This they agreed to willingly. They were delighted with the system, and so was I. It has now been in working since June 1889. Our

APPENDIX. 263

financial year ends in September, so we have one complete year's experience. During this year, from September 1889 to September 1890, we did more business than in almost any year I can remember, but *not one hour of overtime was worked*. The work was done by the same staff as before, with the exception of three or four men added to relieve the gate porters and watchmen, who had previously been on duty 12 hours at a time, and were now reduced to 8 hours.

The Saturday half-holiday has been preserved, so that our working week is only 45 hours.

I am so thoroughly convinced about the success of the experiment, that I would as soon argue about the multiplication table.

HUDDERSFIELD CORPORATION TRAMWAYS.

Town Hall, Huddersfield, 18th Dec. 1890.

In reply to your letter of the 11th inst., I am authorised by the Chairman of the Tramways Committee of my Council to forward you the enclosed memorandum, prepared by Mr. Pogson, the Tramways Manager, as to the hours of employment of drivers and conductors engaged upon the tramways.

It is necessary for me to add that the arrangement adopted in 1888 was not intended by the Corporation or their tramway servants as an adoption of an Eight Hours Day System.

If in the future the public convenience demands a further extension of the services, the eight hours arrangement will not necessarily be adhered to, but the men will divide the extra work.

Yours truly,

H. BARBER, Town Clerk.

Memorandum by Manager, 17th Dec. 1890.

Previous to May 1st, 1888, the trams were run 14 hours per day, and the drivers and conductors were allowed one hour for dinner and one hour for tea (a working day of 12 hours).

On the above date the service of cars was increased to 16 hours per day, and instead of increasing the working hours of the men, or of having an extended and complicated system of relief, the

Tramways Committee determined to try the experiment of a double set of men, working 8 hours each, for a period of 6 months.

The results of the experiment were very satisfactory, both to the management and also to the men.

The wages paid to the men under the long hours were—drivers 32s., and conductors 23s. per week of 6 days.

Under the present arrangement drivers are paid 26s., and conductors 21s. per week of 6 days.

Huddersfield Corporation Tramways Committee — Financial Report for six months ended 30th September 1890 and 1889. During both of these periods the drivers and conductors were employed on the Eight Hours System :—

Expenditure, Six Months ended 30th September 1890.			Revenue Account.	Expenditure, Corresponding Period last Year.		
£	s.	d.		£	s.	d.
2117	8	2	............Locomotive Power.............	2073	5	2
638	18	1	........................Traffic...................	605	16	1
976	11	7	...Maintenance of Ways and Works...	689	12	6
1324	18	2	..... Repairs to Engines and Cars	1136	6	1
261	6	10	................Management..................	359	5	4
250	0	0	.........Rents, Rates, and Taxes.........	172	13	3
216	16	4	...............Miscellaneous...............	125	8	5
5785	19	2	....................Total.....................	5162	6	10
2750	13	10	..............Gross Profit................	2772	14	3
8536	13	0	....................Receipts...................	7935	1	1
1778	11	8	Interest & Sinking Fund, 4¼ % on Loans	1558	11	2
880	0	0	........Depreciation, 2% on Capital......	753	6	0
2658	11	8		2311	17	2
2750	13	10	................Gross Profit..............	2772	14	3
£92	2	2	.... Balance Profit...............	460	17	1

Capital Account, £88,039. Depreciation Account, £3285. Loan Account, £84,000.

APPENDIX. 265

APPENDIX III.

REPORT ON THE SWISS LEGISLATION REGULATING THE HOURS OF ADULT LABOUR.*

The legislative measures affecting the hours of adult labour in Switzerland are contained in the Federal Factory Labour Law of 1877, which received the sanction of a popular vote by the exercise of the Constitutional right of *referendum*.

Article 1 defines "factory" to be "any industrial establishment in which a more or less considerable number of workmen are employed away from their homes in an inclosed locality."

The Federal Council has in the course of the last ten years given several decisions to prevent evasion of the law on the part of employers.

Article 11.—*A Maximum Ten Hours Day.*—The duration of a normal working day must not exceed eleven hours, and on Saturdays and public holidays it shall be reduced to ten hours.

The duration of a working day shall be comprised within the hours of 5 A.M. and 8 P.M. during the months of June, July, and August, and during the remainder of the year between 6 A.M. and 8 P.M.

The hours of labour shall be regulated by the town clock, and notified to the local authority.

In the case of unhealthy industries, the duration of the normal working day shall be reduced by the Federal Council in accordance with the requirements of the case.

Applications for authority to prolong exceptionally or temporarily the duration of a working day must be made to the competent district authorities, or, if no such authorities exist, to the local authorities, provided always that the duration of such prolongation is not to exceed the term of two weeks; otherwise the applications must be made to the Cantonal Government.

The labourers shall be allowed in the middle of each working day an hour's rest at least for their meal; suitable localities, heated

* *Foreign Office Report*, C—5866, 1889. See also C—5896-18 of 1890.

in winter, and outside the ordinary working rooms, shall be placed gratuitously at the disposal of such labourers as may bring or have their meal brought to the factory.

The Federal Council has decided that the intervals of rest are to be regular and simultaneous for all hands employed.

Article 12.—*Exceptions.*—The provisions of the foregoing Article do not apply to accessory works which ought to precede or follow the labour of manufacture properly so called, and are executed by men or by unmarried women above the age of 18 years.

Article 13.—*Night Work.*—Work between the hours of 8 P.M. and 6 A.M. is only permissible as an exception, and the working hands cannot be employed on it without their full consent. In all cases excepting that of urgent repairs necessitating exceptional night work for one night only, the permission of the authorities is requisite ; if this night work is to be prolonged beyond the term of two weeks, the Cantonal Government is alone competent to give such authority.

Regular night work may however take place in such branches of manufacture as, by their nature, require uninterrupted work.

Manufacturers considering themselves entitled to the benefit of this legal provision must satisfy the Federal Council that their industry necessitates this kind of work.

At the same time, they must submit to the Federal Council a scheme of Rules providing for the distribution of the work, and the number of working hours obligatory on each working hand ; this number must, in no case, exceed eleven hours in twenty-four for each workman.

Article 14.—*Sunday Labour.*—Except in cases of absolute necessity, Sunday labour is prohibited, with the exception of such establishments as by their nature require uninterrupted labour, and have received the authority provided for in the foregoing Article from the Federal Council.

In the case of these establishments, each working hand must have one free Sunday out of every two.

Holidays.—The Cantonal Legislature has the right to determine other holidays on which work is to be prohibited as on Sundays. These holidays must not exceed in number eight in one year.

Article 15.—*Special Rules for Women.*—Women cannot, under any circumstances, be employed in night or Sunday labour.

APPENDIX. 267

When they have a household to look after, they shall be free to leave their work one half-hour before the midday rest, if the latter is of less duration than one hour and a half.

After and before childbed a term of eight weeks in all is set apart during which women cannot be admitted to work in factories.

After their confinement they are not to be readmitted into the factory without furnishing proof that six weeks, at least, have elapsed since the date of their delivery.

The Federal Council shall designate the branches of industry in which women in pregnancy are not to be allowed to work.

Administration.—The Federal Council controls the enforcement by the Cantonal authorities of the foregoing provisions.

For this purpose the Federal Council has appointed Federal Inspectors of Factories.

Infringements of the law are punishable by fines varying from 5 fr. to 500 fr. Judging from the annual Reports of the Federal Inspectors, the provisions affecting the hours of labour appear to have been very carefully enforced.

Supplementary.—The Federal Council has decided that the exceptional or temporary prolongation of hours of labour is only admissible in case of a determined external cause or necessity, and not simply to suit the convenience of the employer, and that permission to prolong the working hours cannot be given except for a fixed term; that all such permissions must be issued in writing, must be communicated to the local supervising authorities, and must state a fixed term of hours; and further, that the permission must be made public, for the information of the workmen, by being posted up in the work-rooms.

All such permissions are to be communicated to the Factory Inspectors.

The local authorities are forbidden to grant the permission in question in such a manner as to enable the employers to evade the control of the Cantonal Government by obtaining an immediate or periodical renewal of such permission.

With reference to Article 12, the Council has addressed a Circular to the Cantonal Governments defining some of the works which are to be classed as "accessory" in the sense of this Article—*e.g.*, the cleaning, greasing, and sweeping out of the work-rooms, but not the periodical dismounting of machinery for the purpose of repair or thorough cleaning, etc., an operation requiring several hours' work.

In breweries, by Article 12 the provisions of Article 11 do not apply to stokers, machinists, and the staff of clerks, nor to maltsters, workmen directing the process of fermentation, or working brewers employed in the clerks' office, provided that, in the case of these three last categories, the total number of hours of work does not exceed eleven in every twenty-four.

APPENDIX IV.

PUBLICATIONS RELATING TO THE EXISTING FACTORY LEGISLATION AND THE EIGHT HOURS BILL.

No attempt has been made to compile an exhaustive list, or to include the very numerous German publications on the subject.

The main law now in force is contained in the Act of Parliament 41 Vic., c. 16, "The Factory and Workshop Act, 1878." Copies can be obtained from Eyre & Spottiswoode, and elsewhere, price 2s. 6d. An edition, with notes by Mr. A. Redgrave, C.B., is published by Shaw & Sons, price 5s.

The law relating to labour in coal mines will be found in the Act 50 and 51 Vic., c. 58, "The Coal Mines Regulation Act, 1887;" and that relating to other mines in the Act 35 and 36 Vic., c. 77, "The Metalliferous Mines Regulation Act, 1872." "The Agricultural Gangs Act, 1867," "The Canal Boats Act, 1884," and "The Merchant Shipping Acts," also minutely regulate the employment of labour. The labour of persons under eighteen in shops is regulated by the Act 49 and 50 Vic., c. 55, "The Shop Hours Regulation Act, 1886." The other Acts in force, such as 46 and 47 Vic., c. 53 (Factories); 38 and 39 Vic., c. 39; 44 and 45 Vic., c. 26; and 45 and 46 Vic., c. 3 (Mines), effect only minor alterations. The hours of work on railways are referred to in the Railways Regulation Act, 1889 (52 and 53 Vic., c. 57, sec. 4).

The chief Parliamentary Reports are the Select Committee's

APPENDIX. 269

Report of 1816, and those of the Royal Commissions of 1832, 1840-3, 1862-8, and 1876. All but the last two are summarised in Engel's "Condition of the Working Class in England" (Reeves) and Karl Marx's "Capital" (Sonnenschein). More recent information will be found in the Report of the House of Lords Committee on the Sweating System (H.L. 62, 1890).

The laws of foreign States are given (imperfectly) in Foreign Office Report, "Commercial, No. 25," C—5866, price 5d. The *Board of Trade Journal* contains valuable information on the subject in nearly every month's issue during 1890 and 1891. Other particulars are given in the Report of the Berlin Labour Conference (May 1890). The Swiss law, in many respects the most minute and stringent of all, is briefly described (p. 202) in "The Swiss Confederation," by Sir F. O. Adams and C. D. Cunningham (Macmillan, 1889), and is given more fully in the Foreign Office Report, C—5866 of 1889. The first Annual Report of the Federal Commissioner of Labour (Washington, 1886) gives a valuable summary of American labour laws.

The history of English factory legislation is best found in E. E. von Plener's "English Factory Legislation" (Chapman & Hall, 1873). Alfred's "History of the Factory Movement" is a practically contemporary chronicle of the movement down to 1847. Lord Shaftesbury's work is described in his "Life and Work," by E. Hodder (Cassell, 1886), and "Speeches" (Chapman & Hall, 1868). Besides Lord Shaftesbury's speeches, those of Sir Robert Peel (Routledge, 1853), John Bright (Macmillan), Fawcett (Macmillan, 1873), and Lord Macaulay (Longmans, 1854), are historically interesting, and the speech of the latter on the Ten Hours Bill rebuts the arguments against regulation of adult labour with great oratorical force. The early history of the regulation of labour is well given in Professor L. Brentano's "Gilds and Trade Unions" (London: Trübner, 1870). Colonial precedents are described in Sir C. W. Dilke's "Problems of Greater Britain" (Macmillan, 1890). Important information is contained in the Report and Evidence of the Royal Commission in Victoria (1882-5) on the working of the Factory Law, and of the Royal Commission in Canada (1889) on the Relations between Capital and Labour.

The chief factory law in some of the principal Colonies may be found as under:—Victoria (49 Vic., No. 862); New Zealand (Act No. 23, of 1891); Ontario (47 Vic., c. 39); Quebec (Code, sec. 3026).

The subject is omitted from Cobden's "Speeches" (Macmillan, 1870) and "Political Writings" (Ridgeway, 1867). It is scarcely mentioned in Torrens' "Life of Sir James Graham" (Saunders, 1863).

The arguments for and against factory legislation are given in W. S. Jevons' "The State in Relation to Labour," ch. iii. (Macmillan, 1882); John Morley's "Life of Cobden," vol. i., ch. xviii., pp. 298, 303; H. Ll. Smith's "Economic Aspects of State Socialism," ch. iv., sec. ii. (Simpkin, 1887); J. S. Mill's "Principles of Political Economy," bk. v., ch. xi., sec. 9 and 12, and essay "On Liberty," ch. v.; Duke of Argyll's "Reign of Law," ch. vii. (Strahan, 1867); Gunton's "Wealth and Progress" (Macmillan, 1888). They are admirably summarised in the "Political Manual" by Mr. Sydney Buxton, M.P. (new edition, Cassell & Co., 1891, price 1s.), where 34 pages out of a volume of 168 pages are devoted to the question.

The whole system of factory legislation is examined and criticised in Herbert Spencer's "Man *versus* the State" (1887), Mackay's "The English Poor," ch. xiv. (Murray, 1889), Wordsworth Donisthorpe's "Individualism" (Macmillan, 1889), and "A Plea for Liberty" (by various writers; Murray, 1891).

The prohibition of Sunday labour is specially referred to with approval in Mill's essay "On Liberty," ch. v., and in Sidgwick's "Principles of Political Economy," bk. iii., ch. ii., p. 422, 1883.

The economics of an Eight Hours Day are discussed in the magazine articles given below, and also in the paper read by Prof. J. E. Crawford Munro at the Leeds meeting of the British Association for the Advancement of Science, 1890, and printed in full in the proceedings. Professor Marshall briefly refers to the subject at the end of his "Principles of Economics" (Macmillan, 1890).

A Dutch socialist view is given in "De Normale Arbeidsdag," by F. Domela Nieuwenhuis (The Hague: Liebers & Co., 1889).

The pamphlet of the Fabian Society, "An Eight Hours Bill in the form of an Amendment of the Factory Acts" (John Heywood, Deansgate and Ridgefield, Manchester; or from the Secretary, 2 Hyde Park Mansions, London, price 1d.), contains numerous references. Mr. Hyndman's "Draft of an Eight Hours Bill" is published by the Social Democratic Federation, 337 Strand, London, price 1d.

The Reports of the Trade Union Congress for 1887, 1888, 1889, and 1890, and those of the International Trade Union Congress for 1886 and 1889, contain useful information.

A small international journal, *The Eight Hours Working Day*, is published in two languages at Zürich (Cantonsrath Carl Bürkli, Zürich-Fluntern; subscription 5s. per annum).

Among the popular pamphlets on the subject, mostly at a penny, are the following :—

- Tom Mann, "The Eight Hours Movement." (Modern Press, London).
- Charles Bradlaugh, "The Eight Hours Movement." (Freethought Publishing Company, London, 1889. Price 2d.)
- H. H. Champion, "The Parliamentary Eight Hours Day." (Reeves, London.)
- A. K. Donald, "The Eight Hours Work Day." (Labour Press, 57 Chancery Lane, London, 1890.)
- George Gunton, "The Economic and Social Importance of the Eight Hour Movement." (American Federation of Labour, 21 Clinton Place, New York.)
- James Leatham, "An Eight Hours Day with Ten Hours Pay." (15 St. Nicholas Street, Aberdeen, 1890.)
- Report of the Bradlaugh-Hyndman Debate on the Eight Hours Bill. (Freethought Publishing Company, London, 1890. Price 6d.)
- Maltman Barry, "The Labour Day." (John Avery & Co., Aberdeen, 1890. Price 2d.)
- John Burns, L.C.C., "The Liverpool Trade Union Congress." (Green & McAllan, London, 1890.)
- The Fabian Society's "Plea for an Eight Hours Bill" (1891).

The best discussion of the subject is, however, to be found in recent magazine articles, such as the following :—

- George Gunton, "The Eight Hours Law: shall it be adopted?" (*Forum*, 1886, p. 136).
- Harold Cox, "The Eight Hours Bill" (*Nineteenth Century*, July 1889).

Anonymous (H. de B. Gibbins), "Some Economic Aspects of the Eight Hours Movement" (*Westminster Review*, July 1889).
H. M. Hyndman, "Eight Hours the Maximum Working Day" (*New Review*, August 1889).
Charles Bradlaugh, M.P., "The Eight Hours Day" (*New Review*, September 1889).
H. H. Champion, "The Eight Hours Movement" (*Nineteenth Century*, September 1889).
Sidney Webb, "The Limitation of the Hours of Labour" (*Contemporary Review*, December 1889).
R. B. Haldane, M.P., "The Eight Hours Question" (*Contemporary Review*, February 1890).
C. Bradlaugh, M.P., "The Eight Hours Question" (*Fortnightly Review*, March 1890).
J. Murray Macdonald, "The Case for an Eight Hours Day" (*Nineteenth Century*, April 1890).
John A. Hobson, "The Cost of a Shorter Day" (*National Review*, April 1890).
Dr. Delon, "Encore les lois de fabrique" (*Revue Soc.*, May 1890).
P. Boilley, "La Journée de huit heures et le travail intensif" (*Revue Socialiste*, June 1890).
Francis A. Walker, "The Eight Hour Law" (*Atlantic Monthly*, June 1890).
C. Bradlaugh, M.P., "Eight Hours a Day by Law" (*Universal Review*, August 1890).
Edward Atkinson, "Eight Hours" (*North American Review*, vol. cxlii., No. 354).
Dr. B. W. Richardson, "Working Hours and Working Men" (*Longman's Magazine*, October 1890).
Benoit Malon, "La Legislation Internationale du Travail" (*Revue Socialiste*, December 1890).
F. Pincott, "The Eight Hours Movement" (*National Review*, December 1890).
L. Ramsay, "The Eight Hours Movement" (*Westminster Review*, December 1890).
Rev. Professor Symes, "Some Economic Aspects of the Eight Hour Movement" (*Economic Review*, January 1891).
Rev. H. B. Brown, "How many Hours a Day shall we Labour?" (*Nationalist*, January 1891).

INDEX.

Abraham, W., M.P. ("Mabon"), Eight Hours Bill for Miners, 221; for all trades, 230
Accidents in mines, 129; on railways, 80
Adult male labour, Early regulation of, 191; by the Factory Acts, 198; generally, 210
Adulteration Acts, 183
Aerated water making, Overtime in, 158
Agricultural labourers, Awakening of, 2; hours of, 92, 253
Alfred (King), division of his time, 14
Almanac making, Overtime in, 158
Amalgamated Society of Carpenters and Joiners, unemployed, 169; hours of, 172
Amalgamated Society of Engineers, Formation of, 16; overtime circular, 153; unemployed in, 169; hours of, 172, 245, 254
American competition, 125
American Eight Hours Movement, 44
American Federation of Labour, 52
American laws relating to labour, 8, 45, 215, 216, 219, 226; alleged failure of, 48, 219
Anarchists, Continental, 12; objection to legislation, 180
Argyll, Duke of, 188
Artificial flower making, Overtime in, 158
Ashley, Lord, see Shaftesbury, Lord
Ashton, Thomas, J.P., works for Factory Act of 1874, 20
Ashton, Thomas (Miners' Secretary), 86
Australia, Eight Hours Day in, 8; history of the movement in, 38; legislation in, 39, 214, 227; competition of, 127; results in, 150
Austria, Political position of, 9; legislation in, 64; reduction of hours in, 99; miners' law in, 222

Baker, William Robert (Factory Inspector), 96
Bakers, Hours of, 89, 246, 253; in Melbourne, 40
Baltimore, Ten Hours Strike at, 46; congress of workmen, 47
Bargemen, Mortality among, 143
Barmaids, Hours of, 72; danger of legislating for, 236
Beaufoy, Mark, M.P., experience of Eight Hours System, 262; as to overtime, 154
Beckett, Mr., on Ten Hours Bill, 202
Belgium, Movement in, 63; legislation in, 64; proposal as to women employed during menstrual periods, 65
Bentham, Jeremy, quoted, 183
Berlin Labour Conference, Effect of, in England, 33; in Germany, 62; report of delegates to, 269
Bevan, G. Phillips, statistics of strikes, 19
Bibliography, 268
Biscuit making, Overtime in, 158
Blacklegs, 175
Blacksmiths, Mortality among, 143
Blanc, Louis, 56
Blastfurnacemen, Hours of, 80, 246
Bleaching, Overtime in, 158
Boards of Conciliation, 222
Board of Trade, railway regulations, 224; statistics as to hours, 253
Boilermakers, Hours of, 90, 246; unemployed amongst, 169
Bonbon making, Overtime in, 158
Bookbinders, Hours of, 90, 246; condition of, in 1780, 15; overtime among, 158
Bookfolders and Sewers, Hours of, 247
Boot and Shoe Trades, Hours in, 254
Booth, Charles, 170
Box making, Overtime in, 158

18

INDEX.

Boys in coal-mines, 179
Bradlaugh, Charles, opposition of, 207; publications of, 272; debate by, 32
Brain-workers, 184
Brassfitters, Hours of, 90, 247
Breakfast, Work before, 144, 165, 258, 262
Brentano, Professor Luigi, quoted, 193
Brick and tile making, Overtime in, 158
Bricklayers, Hours of, 90, 91, 253
Brickmakers, Hours of, 247, 253
Bright, Right Hon. John, opposes Ten Hours Bill, 203, 205; opposes Adulteration Act, 183
British Association, Meeting of, 1890, 34
British Consul-General for France, Report of, 59
Brunner, Mond, & Co., experience of Eight Hours System, 256; wages, 102, 113
Burns, John, L.C.C., speech on the Liverpool Trade Union Congress, 35, 271
Burroughs, Wellcome, & Co., experience of Eight Hours System, 255
Buxton, Sydney, M.P., 219; *Political Manual* by, 270

Cab fares fixed by law, 209
Cabinet-makers, Hours of, 254
Cairnes, Professor J. E., quoted, 112
Californian Eight Hours Bill, 50, 225, 226
Canada, Movement in, 54, 55; experience as regards production, 55, 104; Royal Commission, 55, 148, 269
Capital, Increase of, 120; export of, 121; shifting of, 124
Card and blowing-room operatives, Hours of, 248
Cardwell, Right Hon. Viscount, on Ten Hours Bill, 95
Carpenters and joiners, Hours of, 90, 91, 172, 248, 253; ditto in Dublin, 16; unemployed among, 169
Caslon & Co., experience of Eight Hours System, 257
Caveat emptor disregarded 183
Cement workers, Hours of, 253
Champion, H. H., editor of *The Labour Elector*, 23
Channing, F. A., M.P., on railway hours, 36, 233
Chemical workers, Hours of, 254; in Brunner, Mond, & Co.'s, 102, 113, 256.
Chicago, Outrages at, 52
Childbirth, Employment of women at, 65
Childers, Right Hon. H. C. E., letters of, 188
Children in factories, 196, 199; in America, 45, 46; in Germany, 61; in Belgium, 65
Chili, Movement in, 64
Christmas, Overtime for, 158, 160

Cigar factory, Hamilton, Reduction of hours in, 55, 104
Cigar-makers, United States, 50; in Canada, 54; effect of Eight Hours Day, 101
Citizenship, Need of leisure for efficient, 151
Claims of Labour, The, quoted, 238
Clark, Dr. G. B., M.P., bill, 230
Clerks, Hours of, 72
Clothing trades, Overtime in, 158
Coachmaking, Hours in, 254
Coal, Production of, 128; price of, 126; South African and Australian, 127
Coal-mines, Accidents in, 129; boys in, 179; rental of, in Great Britain, 127; legislation as to, 23, 200; in Australia, 39
Coal Miners Conference at Jolimont, 33; desire for an Eight Hours Day, 23; probable effect, 126
Coal-mining industry, Effect of Eight Hours Day upon, 126
Coal Mines Regulation Act Amendment Bill, 1887, Debate on, 23
Cobden, Richard, Views of, 241; *Life* of, quoted, 205, 210, 241; writings of, 270
Colonial coal, Competition of, 127
Combination, Weakness of, 239; among capitalists, 239
Combination Laws, Repeal of, 1824, 15
Commercial deadlocks, 5; Crisis of 1866, 18; of 1873, 49
Competition, American, 125; Indian, 125; Colonial, 127; Foreign, 115, 116; limitation of, 183
Compositors, Hours of, 16, 90, 173, 248, 254; unemployed among, 169; overtime, 158; at Leipzig, 62
Condensed milk making, Overtime in, 158
Conflicts of Capital and Labour, by George Howell, M.P., quoted, 155
Connecticut, Legislation of, 47
Conservative objections, 181
Consumption, Result of increased, 150
Conveyancing Act, 1881, 226
Conybeare, C. A. V., M.P., bill, 230
Coopers, Hours of, in 1825, 16; at present, 90, 248, 253
Cotton, Prices of, 96
Cotton goods, Exports of British, 97
Cotton-spinning, Profits of, 125; difficulties of Eight Hours Day in, 125
Crawford, Donald, M.P., bill, 224
Customary prices, 114

Daily limit, Need for, 223
Deakin, Hon. Alfred (Victoria), 40
Decree of February 1848 (France), 56
De la Warr, Lord, railway hours, 28
Delegates to Trade Union Congresses, opinions of Bailey (Preston), 18;

INDEX.

Drummond (London), 22; Kane (Darlington), 18; Marks (London), 34; Matkin (Liverpool), 34; Mawdsley (Manchester), 25; Parnell (London), 22; Patterson (Durham), 34; Ritchie (Dundee), 28; Swain (Manchester), 18; Swift (Manchester), 22
Demand, Restriction of, 118; increase of, 149
Democracy, Growth of, 9
Demonstration on May 1st, 1890, 59
Demoralisation due to law, 187
Denmark, Political position of, 9; legislation in, 64
Denton, Hat industry at, 91
Dilke, Sir Charles, quoted, 38, 43, 55, 150, 269
Disciplined employment, Advantages of increasing, 110
Disraeli, B., supports Ten Hours Bill, 204
Dock labourers, Mortality amongst, 143; work of, 144; hours of, 253
Dombey, Mrs., 189
Dublin carpenters, printers, and painters, Hours of, 16
Durham miners, Hours of, 83; opposition to Eight Hours Bill, 179

Early Closing Association, Melbourne, 41; England, 69
Early Closing Bill, England, 71; Victoria, 42, 227; Sir J. Lubbock's, 227
Early morning work, 144, 258, 202
Ebrington, Viscount, quoted, 202
Economics of the question, 93; results of previous reductions, 94; of the Ten Hours Bill, 96; in Massachusetts, 97; in Austria, 64, 99; among artisans, 99; in New York, 100; in coal mining, 100, 101; on the Huddersfield tramways, 101, 263; in German glass works, 101; in chemical works, 102, 256; in manufacturing chemists, 255; in type-founding, 257; in engineering, 258; in printing, 259, 261; in vinegar making, 262; on the export trade, 97; on wages, 100, 110; on productivity, 103; in absorbing the unemployed, 108; on prices, 114; on growth of capital, 120; on interest, 118; summary, 122
Economic effect on particular trades, 123; on employment of capital, 123; on the textile trades, 125; on coal mining, 126; on the railway service, 129; on the tramway service, 132; on retail trade, 134; on Government work, 136
Education, Need of leisure for, 147
Eight hours the sanitary limit, 141, 143; exact number not essential, 3; drafts of bills, 212, 229, 230

Eight Hours Working Day, The, newspaper, 68
Elizabeth, Condition of labourers during reign of, 15; statutes of, 190
Ely, Dr. R. T., quoted, 45-54
Employers' opposition, 112
Employment, Better distribution of, 108
Engineers, see Amalgamated Society of
Engine-drivers, Hours of, 78, 244, 245; limitation of, in Minnesota, 51
Enfield small arms factory, Hours at, 136; overtime at, 155, 219
Envelope making, Overtime in, 158, 161
Escott, B., M.P., quoted, 202
Expansion of wants, 2, 148, 149
Explosions in coal-mines, 129
Export trade, Effect of Eight Hours Day upon, 117

Fabian Society, 11, 167, 213, 214, 217, 222, 223, 225, 232, 270, 271
Factory Acts, United Kingdom, Gradual growth of, 122; overtime under, 157; effects of, 96, 187, 189; history of, 196; reforms needed in, 235; advances in, 241
Factories and Shops Act (Victoria), 1885, 42, 227
Factory Law, Austria, 64, 99, 222; Belgium, 63, 64, 65; Denmark, 64; France, 55-61, 230; Germany, 61, 62, 65; Hungary, 64; Italy, 64; Netherlands, 64; Russia, 65; Spain, 64; Sweden, 65; Switzerland, 62, 65, 230, 265
Factory Law, Canada, 54; New Zealand, 270; Ontario, 54, 270; Quebec, 54, 270; Victoria, 38-44, 227, 270
Fairfield, C., insolvency of Victoria, 43
Family life, 146
Fawcett, Professor H., M.P., 206
Felt hatters, Hours of, 248
Fenwick, J., M.P., at Paris, 28; on mining accidents, 129
Fifteenth century, Hours in, 14
Figure "eight" not essential, 3
File cutters, Hours of, 90, 249
"Finding" work, Notion of, 110; Experiments in, 108
Firemen, Hours of, 78, 244
Firewood cutting, Overtime in, 158, 161
Fish curing, Overtime in, 158
Flax scutch mills, Overtime in, 158
Forum, The, 52, 271
Foundries, Overtime in, 159
Foxwell, Professor H. S., 238
France, Eight Hours Movement in, 55-61
Freethought Publishing Co., experience of Eight Hours System, 262
French law, 55-61, 230; inquiry of Chamber of Deputies, 60
Fruit preserving, Overtime in, 158
Fur dressing, Hours in, 254

INDEX.

Gas stokers, result of shorter hours, 107, 108, 143
George III. and London bookbinders, 15
Germany, Political position in, 9; Eight Hours Movement in, 61; legislation in, 61, 64, 65; experience in, 101
Giffen, R., quoted, 167
Gilds and Trade Unions, by Professor L. Brentano, 193, 195, 269
Glasgow Town Council, 219
Glass-bottle makers unemployed, 169
Glass trade, Hours in, 254
Glue-making, Overtime in, 158
Golden age of English labour, 14
Gompers, Samuel, 52
Goods guards, Hours of, 73-80
Government servants, Hours of, 88, 136; effect of reduction, 136; overtime among, 137, 155; proposals to restrict hours of, 216
Grad, Charles, quoted, 144
Gradual growth of English factory legislation, 122
Graham, Cunninghame, M.P., Bills of, 23, 202, 205
Graham, Sir James, 95, 181, 202, 205; *Life* of, 270
Green, McAllan, & Feilden, experience of Eight Hours System, 167, 259
"Gresham's Law" in industrial life, 183
Greville's diary, 240
Grey, Sir G., 202
Griffith, Sir S. W., 1
Gunton, George, quoted, 52, 149, 270, 271
Guilds, 192
Guy's Hospital, Hours of nurses at, 87

Hague, the, Removal of the International from, 49
Hamilton (Ontario) cigar factory, 55, 104
Hansard's Parliamentary Debates, quoted, 201, 202, 205, 206
Hat manufacture, Hours in, 254; effect of Factory Act on hours of, 91
Havana, Movement at, 64
Hobhouse, Sir J., 197
Hobson, J. A., quoted, 150
Hosiery trade, Hours in, 254
Hospital nurses, Hours of, 87
Hours of work, Local differences in, 172; in various trades, 89-92, 244-254; among shop assistants, 68-71; in public-houses, 72; on railways, 73-80, 241; on tramways and omnibuses, 81; in mines, 82-87; in hospitals, 87; for Government employés, 88, 136
House of Commons, debate on Berlin Conference, 33; on hours on railways, 36; on Government "sweating," 210; on the Factory Acts, 201-206
How an Eight Hours Day can be obtained, 165
Howell, George, M.P., 14 137, 155, 218

Hozier, J. H. C., M.P., 23
Huddersfield Tramways, wages, 101, 102, 132; Eight Hours Day on, 23, 82; financial results of, 263
Hume, Joseph, M.P., 204
Hyde Park Demonstration, May 1890, 32
Hyndman, H. M., proposed Eight Hours in 1881, 21; draft clause for tramways, 226; as to overtime, 163; words quoted, 21, 270; debate with C. Bradlaugh, 32

Illinois, Legislation in, 48
Increase of capital, 120
Increase of wages following reduction of hours, 92, 95, 96, 98, 99, 100, 101, 102, 111, 112, 130
Independence, Loss of, 187
Indian competition, 125
Indiana, Legislation in, 50
Industrial revolution, Effect of, 7, 185
Intemperance caused by long hours, 148
Interest, how affected by an Eight Hours Day, 120; result of a fall of, 121
"International," The, on the Eight Hours question, 13; removes to America, 49; influence in France, 58
International trade, Effect of Eight Hours Day upon, 115; theory of, 116, 117
International Trade Union Congress, 13, 25, 28, 58
Interstate Commerce, Report of U.S. Senate Committee on, 130
Irish rents fixed by law, 210
Iron founders, as to overtime, 154; hours of, 90, 249, 254; unemployed among, 169
Iron mills, Overtime in, 159
Iron ship builders, Hours of, 90, 246

"Jack Cade legislation," 181, 240
Jeans, J. S., quoted, 167
Job dyeing, Overtime in, 158
Johnson, S. H. & Co., experience of Eight Hours System, 258
Joiners, see Amalgamated Society of Carpenters and Joiners
Juristic aspect of legal prohibition of overwork, 9, 183, 185

Knights of Labour, 49
Knights of St. Crispin, 47

Labouchere, H., M.P., Attitude of, 240
Labour Code in England, 210
Labour-saving machinery, Distribution of, 110; effect of, upon worker's life, 243
Lakeman, John, quoted, 162
Lancashire objection to Eight Hours Bill, 178

Lawson Tait, Evidence of, 68
Law, Need for, in industry, 238
Legislation, Need of, 177; desire for, 178; opposition to, 178; justification of, 182
Legrand, Daniel, 56
Leicester stocking makers, Hours of, 16
Leipzig, Movement in, 61, 62
Letterpress printing, Overtime in, 158
Levi, Leone, quoted, 169
Lewis, Dr. Waller, quoted, 140
Liberty, Interference with, 185
Liberty and Property Defence League, 180, 241
Licensing Laws, 209
Life and Labour in East London, quoted, 170
Life of Cobden, by the Right Hon. J. Morley, M.P., 205, 210, 241, 270
Lithographic printing, Overtime in, 158; hours of, 249, 254
Local authorities, 218, 225, 226
London, Brighton, and South Coast Railway, Hours under, 74
London builders' strike, 1879, 172
London County Council, hours of labour, 27, 136, 218
London dock strike, 175
London Liberal and Radical Union in favour of Eight Hours, 31
London Trade Unionists' Conference, 1887, 22
London tramways, 133
Low-priced commodities, Social cost of, 118
Lowell textile workers, 45, 47
Lubbock, Sir John, M.P., 43, 70

Macaulay, Lord, on Ten Hours Bill, 93, 269
Macclesfield silk weavers, 16
Machine-ruling, Overtime in, 158
McCulloch, on tax, on labour, 114
Manchester, Sheffield, and Lincolnshire Railway, 75
Manchester School, 20
Mann, Tom, pamphlet, 22, 271
Manners, Lord John, 202, 205
Marx, Karl, 13, 21, 44, 269
Maryland, Legislation in, 50, 51, 226
Masons, Hours of, 90, 91, 254; in Middle Ages, 14, 104
Masonry in Middle Ages, 104
Massachusetts, Hours of textile workers in, 45; movement in, 46; legislation in, 50; result of Ten Hours Law in, 98; competition of, 117, 126
Massingham, H. W., experience of Eight Hours System, 260
Mavor, Professor James, quoted, 223
Mecklenburg, Political position of, 9
Melbourne, Eight Hours Movement at, 38; hours at, 38, 41; Royal Commission at, 41; Early Closing Association of, 41; tramways, 40, 220; harbour, 40, 220; overtime at, 164; legislation at, 39, 40, 41, 164, 220
Menstrual period, Prohibition of work at, 65
Mental health, Need of leisure for, 145
Metropolitan Radical Federation, 33
Midland Railway Company, 80
Mill, John Stuart, 182, 183, 232, 242
Millers, Hours of, 90, 249
Mill sawyers, Hours of, 89, 249
Mines, Hours of work in, 17, 82, 85; Durham and Northumberland, 83, 84; state of, before legislation, 200; laws relating to, in Victoria, 30; in Austria, 222; in Germany, 61, 62; in Belgium, 63; in Hungary, 64; maximum production of, 104; probable effect of Eight Hours Day in, 126; rental of British, 127; practical proposals as to, 221
Miners, Draft Eight Hours Bills for, 221; Austrian Law, 222; hours of, 85, 86
Miners' Federation of Great Britain, 31, 86
Minnesota, Legislation in, 51
Morley, Right Hon. John, M.P., 27, 210 241, 270
Morley, Samuel, 184
Mourning orders, Overtime for, 160
Mundella, Right Hon. A. J., quoted, 187
Munro, Professor J. E. C., 34, 109, 113, 270

National Labour Federation, 1886, 21
Newcastle Daily Leader, 83
New England mills, Hours in, 45, 47, 53; progress of, 98; effect on wages in, 98
New Lanark, Hours at, 15
New South Wales, Movement in, 30; social results in, 150
New Unionism, Influence of the, 26
New wants, Effect of, 2; economic results of, 149, 150
New York, Movement in, 47, 48, 49; result upon wages in, 100, 101; legislation in, 51
New Zealand, Eight Hours Bill in, 44
Nine Hours Day, Real length of, 185
Nine Hours Movement, Origin of, 13; result of, 168; overtime, 153
Normal Day, Laws fixing, 214, 215, 216; alleged failure of, 215
North British Railway, Long hours on, 75, 244, 245
Northumberland objection to Eight Hours Bill, 179; coal miners in, 127; hours in, 85; shift system in, 179
Nurses in hospitals, Hours of, 87

Oastler, Richard, Work of, 197
Oil mills, Hours in, 89
Omnibuses, Hours on, 81, 82; draft bill for, 227
On Liberty, by J. S. Mill, quoted, 182, 232, 270
Ontario, Hours in, 54; legislation in, 55, 270
Output, Reduction of, in coal mines, 128; maximum at eight hours, 104
Overtime, 153; at Woolwich and Enfield, 155; under Factory Acts, 157; from bad weather, 159; from press of work, 160; proposals as to, 163, 164; Victorian legislation as to, 164; in Government works, 219
Owen, Robert, originates Eight Hours Movement, 15

Painters, Hours of, 253; in Dublin, 16
Panacea, Eight Hours Bill no. 11
Paper mills, Overtime in, 159
Paradox, The, of international trade, 116
Parliamentary Committee of Trade Union Congress, Action of, 23; bill of, 230
Parti ouvrier, The, 58
Passenger guards, Hours of, 76
Paviors, Work of, 144
Pawnbrokers' assistants, Hours of, 245
Payment of Wages in Public Houses Act, 208
Peel, Sir Robert, 196
Pennsylvania, Movement in, 46; legislation in, 48
Peru, Demonstration in, 64
Petticoats, Women's, protecting men's labour, 20
Physiology of Industry, by Hobson and Mummery, quoted, 150
Piece-work, Economics of, 113
Pile-drivers, Work of, 144
Plasterers, Hours of, 253
Playing-card making, Overtime in, 158
Plea for Liberty, quoted, 137, 218
Plebiscite of Trade Unions on Eight Hours Question, 24, 25; of Paris workmen, 60
Plener, E. E. von, quoted, 187
Plumbers, Hours of, 90, 250, 254; mortality among, 142
Post Office, Hours of labour in, 88; ill-health at, 140; overtime at, 217
Potter, T. B., M.P., 205
Potters, Mortality among, 143; hours of, 254
Powderley, president of the Knights of Labour, 53
Practical proposals, 212
Precedents for legislation, in England, 191; in United States, 47; in Canada, 54; in Australia, 39; in France, 56; in Austria, 64, 222; in Switzerland, 62, 266

Prices, Effect of Eight Hours Day upon, 114; of cotton goods, 96
Principles of Political Economy, by J. S. Mill, quoted, 182, 232, 242, 270; by Professor H. Sidgwick, 232, 270
Productivity under Eight Hours System, of tramways, 102; of coal mines, 100, 104; of glass works, 101; of chemical works, 102, 255, 256; of printers, 260, 261
Profits of English cotton industry, 97, 125; of coal-mines, 127; of railways, 131; of tramways, 133; effect of Eight Hours on, 119
Prophecies of ruin to foreign trade, 5, 64, 202, 203; fallacy of, 115, 116
Provand, A. D., M.P., 75
Public-houses, Hours in, 72; effect on, 136; rent of, 136; present limitation of hours in, 209
Pyramid making, Cause of extinction of, 125

Quebec, Hours in, 54; legislation in, 55, 270
Queensland Eight Hours Bill, 1, 224; movement in, 44

Railways, Accidents on, 80, 130; capital of, in United Kingdom and United States, 131; effect of Eight Hours Day on, 129; increase of capital in, 124; hours of workers on, 36, 73-80, 244, 254; House of Commons on, 36; profits of, 131; result of nationalisation of, 132; rates, how fixed, 115, 130, 131; regulation of, by law, 28, 36, 223; in Switzerland, 63; in Minnesota, 51; shunters, work of, 103, 107; strikes on, evils of, 174; working expenses, effect on, 130; workers' wages, effect on, 139; workers, draft bills for, 223
Railway capital, 131
Railway industry, Effect of Eight Hours Day upon, 129
Railway capital, Increase of, 124
Randell, David, M.P., bill, 230
Rate of interest, Effect of Eight Hours Day on, 119, 120
Rates, railway, Effect of Eight Hours Day on, 115, 130, 131
Reaney, Mr., and tramway directors, 21
Reduction of hours, Effects of, 98, 99, 100, 101, 102, 107, 108, 130, 255-264
Reduction of output in coal-mines, 128
Reign of Law, by the Duke of Argyll, quoted, 188
Rent of coal-mines, 127; of public-houses, 136
Restaurants, Hours in, 72

Restriction of demand, 118
Retail trade, Effect on, 136
Richardson, Dr. B. W., quoted, 68, 140, 143
Riggers, Hours of, 90, 250
Roby, Dr. H. J., M.P., Election of, 35
Rockhampton, Movement at, 44
Roebuck, Right Hon. J., 205
Rogers, J. E. Thorold, 14, 104, 115
Rope works, Overtime in, 158
Roubaix, Strikes at, 59; demand of workers at, 146
Royal Mint, Hours at, 136
Rulleymen, 179
Ruskin, John, quoted, 150
Russia, Legislation in, 9

St. Albans, Duke of, and railway servants, 21
St. Crispin, Knights of, 47
St. Etienne, Miners' Congress at, 59
Sadler, Tom, 197
Sanitary results of an Eight Hours Day, 139
Saturday half-holiday, Result of, 148
Savings Bank (Post Office), Overtime working in, 88
Sawyers, Hours of, 89
Saxony, Movement in, 61
Scotch Railway Strike, 7, 174
Season trades, Overtime in, 160
Seed crushers, Hours of, 89
Self-reliance, Danger to, 186
Seligman, Dr. E. R. A., quoted, 131
Shaftesbury, Lord, 12, 120, 198
Shift system, 99; in Northumberland and Durham, 127
Shipbuilders, Hours of, 90, 250
Shipton, George (Secretary of London Trades Council), 33
Shirt and collar makers, Hours of, 251
Shop assistants, Hours of, 66-71; effect on, 134; legislation, 41, 42, 70, 229
Shop Assistants' Union Bill, 229
Shops, Early closing of, 134, 229; in Victoria, 41, 42, 229; in England, 69
Shop Hours Labour League, 66
Shop Hours Regulation Act, 1886, 70
Shunters on railways, Work of, 103, 107
Sidgwick, Professor Henry, quoted, 135, 232, 270
Signalmen, Solitary confinement of railway, 224; hours of, 79
Silesia, Hours in, 61
Silk trade, Regulation of, 194
Silk-weavers, Macclesfield, Hours of, 16
Slaters, Hours of, 254
Smith, Adam, 192, 239
Smith, T. W., Experience of Eight Hours System, 257
Social results of an Eight Hours Day, 139
Social Democratic Federation, Formation of, 1881, 21

Social Science Association, inquiry into Trade Unions, 1860, 17
Solacroup, M., quoted, 131
South African competition, 127
Spencer, Herbert, 208, 270
Spitalfields' Acts, 194
Stacey, J. A., 70
Standard of comfort, Rise of, 148
Star, Experience of Eight Hours System, 261
State in Relation to Labour, by W. S. Jevons, quoted, 182, 270
State interference, Principles of, 183; justification of, 243
Statistical tables, exports of cotton goods, 97; hours on railways, 76-79; miners' hours, 85; strikes, 19; votes of Trade Unions on Eight Hours, 24, 30
Statutory powers, Condition on grant of, 220
Statute of Apprentices, 191
Steam engine makers, Hours of, 90, 251; unemployed among, 169
Steel and iron workers, Hours of, 89, 251, 252, 254
Stevedores, Hours of, 252
Stocking Frame Acts, 193
Stocking makers, Leicester, Hours of, 16
Stone-masons, Hours of, 90, 91, 252, 254; in Melbourne, 38; in Middle Ages, 14, 104
Strike, Evils of, 171; general, impossible, 175
Strikes, in America, 1886, 51; 1890, 53; Boston, 45; Belgian miners, 63; bookbinders, London, 16; cotton operatives, Preston, 95; cloth-lappers, Glasgow, 17; engineers, 1851-2, 16; Glasgow masons, 17; Glasgow cotton-spinners, 16; London building trades, 1858, 17; 1879, 172; London gas men, 1889, 26; masons at Huddersfield, 18; painters at Glasgow, 18; Paris gas workers, 59; Roubaix, 59; Scotch railways, 36; statistical table of, 19; Tyneside, 18; Westphalia, 61
Struggle for existence in industry, 183
Sunday labour, 182
Sunday holiday, 135
Survival of the fittest in industry, 183
Sutherst, Thomas, 66
Switzerland, Movement in, 62; federal constitution of, 10, 62; legislation in, 63, 230, 265
Symmetry not sought for, 10

Tailors, Hours of, 89, 252, 254
Tait, Lawson, Evidence of, 68
Ten Hours Bill, 13, 95, 197
Ten Hours Day, 13, 21, 95, 98, 197

INDEX.

Textile trades, Demand for a shorter day in, 1871, 19; hours of, 88; economic effect of an Eight Hours Day upon, 125
Thompson, Dr. Dundas, quoted, 143
Timber trade, Hours in, 254
Tobacco factories, Maryland, Hours in, 51
Tobacco manufacturer against overtime, 162
Tobacco trade, Hours in, 254
Toronto, Movement in, 54; municipality and the tramways, 219
Tortellier, Anarchist delegate, 25
Trade, International effect of Eight Hours Day upon, 115
Trade option, Principle of, 11, 231; in Victorian Shop Hours Law, 228; in Fabian Society's Bill, 231; advantages of, 232; method of applying, 233
Trade Unions (see also Amalgamated Engineers and Amalgamated Carpenters), London bookbinders, 1780, 15; gas-workers, 26; general railway workers, 27
Trade Union Congresses, British, Birmingham, 1869, 18; London, 1871, 19; Swansea, 1888, 22; Dundee, 1889, 23, 177; Liverpool, 1890, 34, 178
Trade Union Congresses, International, London, 1889, 25; Paris, 1890, 32
Trade Unions, Evils of their action, 167; membership of, in United Kingdom, 167
Trades Councils, Views of, Accrington, 30; Birmingham, 37; Glasgow, 37; Hull, 37; Liverpool, 30, 37; London, 37; Wolverhampton, 30
Tramways, Effect of Eight Hours Day on, 132; hours on, 81, 82; Huddersfield, wages, hours, finances of, 23, 101, 102, 203; legislation on, in Maryland, 226; in Melbourne, 40; in New Jersey, 225; in New York, 226; legislative proposals for, 225, 226; London, 133; Melbourne, 40; profits of, 133; strike, evils of, 174
Trelawny, Mr., 201
Truck Acts, 207
Turkey red dyeing, Unlimited overtime in, 15

Unemployed, Number of, 169; effect on wages, 112; reduction of, 123; in Sheffield, 108; by shorter hours, 107
Unhealthiness of modern industry, 140
United States, Position of, 9; movement in, 44; Eight Hours Day in navy yard of, 48, 219
Unto this Last, by J. Ruskin, quoted, 150

Valentine making, Overtime in, 158
Van Buren, President M., Action of, 46, 217
Vermont, Legislation in, 48
Victoria, Eight Hours Day in, 38; Factory Act of, 11, 39, 42, 227; legislation in, 39, 42, 227; results of, 43, 150
Villey's *Traité d'Economie Politique*, 131
Voluntary concession of shorter hours, 165; closing of shops, breakdown of, 69

Wages, Effect of Eight Hours Day on, 111; effect of Ten Hours Day on, 95; piecework, how fixed, 113; of railway workers, effect on, 130; of tramway workers, 132; of coal miners, 128
Walker, General Francis A., Opinion of, 105, 109, 272
Ward, Sir H. G., 108, 202
Watering of capital, 131
Wealth and Progress, by George Gunton, quoted, 149
Westphalia, Hours in, 61
Williamson, Mr. S., M.P., 23
Wisconsin, Legislation in, 50
Women workers outside the English Factory Law, 4; restrictions on, 188, 235
Women's petticoats protecting men's labour, 20
Wood, Sir C., 201
Woolwich Arsenal, Hours at, 136; Overtime at, 155, 219
Working expenses of railways, 130; of mines, 127; of tramways, 133
Workman's Times, quoted, 154
Wright, Carroll D., 98, 109

THE WALTER SCOTT PRESS, NEWCASTLE-ON-TYNE.

SECOND EDITION, WITH PREFACE.

Crown 8vo, Cloth, Price 3s. 6d.

THE
CAREER OF A NIHILIST.
A NOVEL.
By STEPNIAK,

Author of " The Russian Storm Cloud," " The Russian Peasantry,' " Russia under the Tzars," etc., etc.

The large section of the English public now reading Russian fiction will be interested in the appearance of this work, the first novel written in English by a Russian. Intimately acquainted with the life of revolutionary Russia as the celebrated author is, he gives in this book a vivid picture of the manners and ways of the men and women engaged in the struggle against the system of despotism under which the subjects of the Tzar live, and lets us into the very heart and secret of Nihilism. Besides exhibiting that subtle psychology which we have learnt to look for as a special trait of Russian writers, this novel is full of stirring incident, and possesses one of the most powerful and pathetic plots to be found in the whole range of fiction.

"One expects a Nihilist romance by Stepniak to be full of the actualities of the situation, to display the genuine and intimate sentiments of revolutionary society in Russia, and to correct not a few of the impressions formerly gathered from novelists who only know that society by hearsay and at second-hand. The reader will not be disappointed in this expectation. No one can read this story . . . without deep interest."—*Athenæum.*

"A very brilliant and remarkable novel just published by Walter Scott, which will soon be the talk of literary London. We have seldom read a more fascinating book than Stepniak's *Career of a Nihilist.*"
— *The Star.*

London: WALTER SCOTT, 24 Warwick Lane, Paternoster Row.

Demy 8vo, Cloth, 420 Pages, Price 7s. 6d.

A SHORT HISTORY

OF

ANGLO-SAXON FREEDOM.

THE POLITY OF THE ENGLISH-SPEAKING RACE.

By JAMES K. HOSMER, Professor in Washington University; Author of "*A Life of Young Sir Harry Vane*," etc.

In this book an effort is made to compress a sketch of constitutional history for a period of nearly two thousand years, from the time of the Teutons of Cæsar and Tacitus to the British Empire and United States of 1890. Anglo-Saxon polity, in its long history, has shown adaptation to the needs of ever vaster multitudes and higher civilisations, manifold development and elaboration, one spirit, however, surviving throughout it all, apparent in the deliberations of the ancient folk-moots as in those of a modern Parliament. It is this unity which is traced in this highly interesting and brilliantly-written book.

"A volume in which Professor Hosmer ably propounds and justifies his well-known views. . . . The work might very properly be used in schools, but is also interesting to grown people, and may be strongly recommended to mechanics' institutes, workmen's clubs, and public libraries."—*Athenæum*.

London: WALTER SCOTT, 24 Warwick Lane, Paternoster Row.

Monthly Shilling Volumes.   *Cloth, cut or uncut edges.*

THE CAMELOT SERIES.

EDITED BY ERNEST RHYS.   VOLUMES ALREADY ISSUED—

ROMANCE OF KING ARTHUR.
THOREAU'S WALDEN.
ENGLISH OPIUM-EATER.
LANDOR'S CONVERSATIONS.
PLUTARCH'S LIVES.
RELIGIO MEDICI, &c.
SHELLEY'S LETTERS.
PROSE WRITINGS OF SWIFT.
MY STUDY WINDOWS.
GREAT ENGLISH PAINTERS.
LORD BYRON'S LETTERS.
ESSAYS BY LEIGH HUNT.
LONGFELLOW'S PROSE.
GREAT MUSICAL COMPOSERS.
MARCUS AURELIUS.
SPECIMEN DAYS IN AMERICA.
WHITE'S SELBORNE.
DEFOE'S SINGLETON.
MAZZINI'S ESSAYS.
PROSE WRITINGS OF HEINE.
REYNOLDS' DISCOURSES.
PAPERS OF STEELE AND ADDISON.
BURNS'S LETTERS.
VOLSUNGA SAGA.
SARTOR RESARTUS.
WRITINGS OF EMERSON.
SENECA'S MORALS.
DEMOCRATIC VISTAS.
LIFE OF LORD HERBERT.
ENGLISH PROSE.
IBSEN'S PILLARS OF SOCIETY.

IRISH FAIRY AND FOLK TALES.
EPICTETUS.
THE ENGLISH POETS.
ESSAYS OF DR. JOHNSON.
ESSAYS OF WILLIAM HAZLITT.
LANDOR'S PENTAMERON, &c.
POE'S TALES AND ESSAYS.
VICAR OF WAKEFIELD.
POLITICAL ORATIONS.
CHESTERFIELD'S LETTERS.
THOREAU'S WEEK.
STORIES FROM CARLETON.
AUTOCRAT OF THE BREAKFAST-TABLE
JANE EYRE.
ELIZABETHAN ENGLAND.
WRITINGS OF THOMAS DAVIS.
SPENCE'S ANECDOTES.
MORE'S UTOPIA.
SADI'S GULISTAN.
ENGLISH FAIRY TALES.
NORTHERN STUDIES.
FAMOUS REVIEWS.
ARISTOTLE'S ETHICS.
PERICLES AND ASPASIA.
ANNALS OF TACITUS.
ESSAYS OF ELIA.
BALZAC.
DE MUSSET'S PLAYS.
CORAL REEFS.
SHERIDAN'S PLAYS.
OUR VILLAGE.

London: WALTER SCOTT, 24 Warwick Lane, Paternoster Row.

GREAT WRITERS.

A NEW SERIES OF CRITICAL BIOGRAPHIES.
Edited by Professor ERIC S. ROBERTSON, M.A.

MONTHLY SHILLING VOLUMES.

VOLUMES ALREADY ISSUED—

LIFE OF LONGFELLOW. By Prof. Eric S. Robertson.
"A most readable little work."—*Liverpool Mercury.*

LIFE OF COLERIDGE. By Hall Caine.
"Brief and vigorous, written throughout with spirit and great literary skill."—*Scotsman.*

LIFE OF DICKENS. By Frank T. Marzials.
"Notwithstanding the mass of matter that has been printed relating to Dickens and his works . . . we should, until we came across this volume, have been at a loss to recommend any popular life of England's most popular novelist as being really satisfactory. The difficulty is removed by Mr. Marzials's little book."—*Athenæum.*

LIFE OF DANTE GABRIEL ROSSETTI. By J. Knight.
"Mr. Knight's picture of the great poet and painter is the fullest and best yet presented to the public."—*The Graphic.*

LIFE OF SAMUEL JOHNSON. By Colonel F. Grant.
"Colonel Grant has performed his task with diligence, sound judgment, good taste, and accuracy."—*Illustrated London News.*

LIFE OF DARWIN. By G. T. Bettany.
"Mr. G. T. Bettany's *Life of Darwin* is a sound and conscientious work."
—*Saturday Review.*

LIFE OF CHARLOTTE BRONTË. By A. Birrell.
"Those who know much of Charlotte Brontë will learn more, and those who know nothing about her will find all that is best worth learning in Mr. Birrell's pleasant book."—*St. James' Gazette.*

LIFE OF THOMAS CARLYLE. By R. Garnett, LL.D.
"This is an admirable book. Nothing could be more felicitous and fairer than the way in which he takes us through Carlyle's life and works."—*Pall Mall Gazette.*

LIFE OF ADAM SMITH. By R. B. Haldane, M.P.
"Written with a perspicuity seldom exemplified when dealing with economic science."—*Scotsman.*

LIFE OF KEATS. By W. M. Rossetti.
"Valuable for the ample information which it contains."—*Cambridge Independent.*

LIFE OF SHELLEY. By William Sharp.
"The criticisms . . . entitle this capital monograph to be ranked with the best biographies of Shelley."—*Westminster Review.*

LIFE OF SMOLLETT. By David Hannay.
"A capable record of a writer who still remains one of the great masters of the English novel."—*Saturday Review.*

LIFE OF GOLDSMITH. By Austin Dobson.
"The story of his literary and social life in London, with all its humorous and pathetic vicissitudes, is here retold, as none could tell it better."—*Daily News.*

LIFE OF SCOTT. By Professor Yonge.
"This is a most enjoyable book."—*Aberdeen Free Press.*

LIFE OF BURNS. By Professor Blackie.
"The editor certainly made a hit when he persuaded Blackie to write about Burns."—*Pall Mall Gazette.*

LIFE OF VICTOR HUGO. By Frank T. Marzials.
"Mr. Marzials's volume presents to us, in a more handy form than any English or even French handbook gives, the summary of what is known about the life of the great poet."—*Saturday Review.*

LIFE OF EMERSON. By Richard Garnett, LL.D.
"No record of Emerson's life could be more desirable."—*Saturday Review.*

LIFE OF GOETHE. By James Sime.
"Mr. James Sime's competence as a biographer of Goethe is beyond question."—*Manchester Guardian.*

LIFE OF CONGREVE. By Edmund Gosse.
"Mr. Gosse has written an admirable biography."—*Academy.*

LIFE OF BUNYAN. By Canon Venables.
"A most intelligent, appreciative, and valuable memoir."—*Scotsman.*

LIFE OF CRABBE. By T. E. Kebbel.
"No English poet since Shakespeare has observed certain aspects of nature and of human life more closely."—*Athenæum.*

LIFE OF HEINE. By William Sharp.
"An admirable monograph . . . more fully written up to the level of recent knowledge and criticism than any other English work."—*Scotsman.*

LIFE OF MILL. By W. L. Courtney.
"A most sympathetic and discriminating memoir."—*Glasgow Herald.*

LIFE OF SCHILLER. By Henry W. Nevinson.
"Presents the poet's life in a neatly rounded picture."—*Scotsman.*

LIFE OF CAPTAIN MARRYAT. By David Hannay.
"We have nothing but praise for the manner in which Mr. Hannay has done justice to him."—*Saturday Review.*

LIFE OF LESSING. By T. W. Rolleston.
"One of the best books of the series."—*Manchester Guardian.*

LIFE OF MILTON. By Richard Garnett, LL.D.
"Has never been more charmingly or adequately told."—*Scottish Leader.*

LIFE OF BALZAC. By Frederick Wedmore.
LIFE OF GEORGE ELIOT. By Oscar Browning.
LIFE OF JANE AUSTEN. By Goldwin Smith.
LIFE OF BROWNING. By William Sharp.
LIFE OF BYRON. By Hon. Roden Noel.
LIFE OF HAWTHORNE. By Moncure Conway.
LIFE OF SCHOPENHAUER. By Professor Wallace.
LIFE OF SHERIDAN. By Lloyd Sanders.
LIFE OF THACKERAY. By Herman Merivale and Frank T. Marzials.

Library Edition of "Great Writers," Demy 8vo, 2s. 6d.

London: WALTER SCOTT, 24 Warwick Lane, Paternoster Row.

The Canterbury Poets.

EDITED BY WILLIAM SHARP.   IN 1/- MONTHLY VOLUMES.

Cloth, Red Edges - 1s. | Red Roan, Gilt Edges 2s. 6d.
Cloth, Uncut Edges - 1s. | Pad. Morocco, Gilt Edges - 5s.

KEBLE'S CHRISTIAN YEAR.
COLERIDGE. Ed. by J. Skipsey.
LONGFELLOW. Ed. by E. Hope.
CAMPBELL. Ed. by J. Hogben.
SHELLEY. Edited by J. Skipsey.
WORDSWORTH.
   Edited by A. J. Symington.
BLAKE. Ed. by Joseph Skipsey.
WHITTIER. Ed. by Eva Hope.
POE. Edited by Joseph Skipsey.
CHATTERTON. By J. Richmond.
BURNS. Poems \} Edited by
BURNS. Songs / Joseph Skipsey.
MARLOWE. Ed. by P. E. Pinkerton.
KEATS. Edited by John Hogben.
HERBERT. Edited by E. Rhys.
HUGO. Trans. by Dean Carrington.
COWPER. Edited by Eva Hope.
SHAKESPEARE'S Poems, etc.
   Edited by William Sharp.
EMERSON. Edited by W. Lewin.
SONNETS of this CENTURY.
   Edited by William Sharp.
WHITMAN. Edited by E. Rhys.
SCOTT. Marmion, etc.
SCOTT. Lady of the Lake, etc.
   Edited by William Sharp.
PRAED. Edited by Fred. Cooper.
HOGG. By his Daughter, Mrs. Garden.
GOLDSMITH. Ed. by W. Tirebuck.
MACKAY'S LOVE LETTERS.
SPENSER. Edited by Hon. R. Noel.
CHILDREN OF THE POETS.
   Edited by Eric S. Robertson.
JONSON. Edited by J. A. Symonds.
BYRON (2 Vols.) Ed. by M. Blind.
THE SONNETS OF EUROPE.
   Edited by S. Waddington.
RAMSAY. Ed. by J. L. Robertson.
DOBELL. Edited by Mrs. Dobell.
DAYS OF THE YEAR.
   With Introduction by Wm. Sharp.
POPE. Edited by John Hogben.
HEINE. Edited by Mrs. Kroeker.
BEAUMONT & FLETCHER.
   Edited by J. S. Fletcher.
BOWLES, LAMB, &c.
   Edited by William Tirebuck.
EARLY ENGLISH POETRY.
   Edited by H. Macaulay Fitzgibbon.
SEA MUSIC. Edited by Mrs Sharp.
HERRICK. Edited by Ernest Rhys.

BALLADES AND RONDEAUS
   Edited by J. Gleeson White.
IRISH MINSTRELSY.
   Edited by H. Halliday Sparling.
MILTON'S PARADISE LOST.
   Edited by J. Bradshaw, M.A., LL.D.
JACOBITE BALLADS.
   Edited by G. S. Macquoid.
AUSTRALIAN BALLADS.
   Edited by D. B. W. Sladen, B.A.
MOORE. Edited by John Dorrian.
BORDER BALLADS.
   Edited by Graham R. Tomson.
SONG-TIDE. By P. B. Marston.
ODES OF HORACE.
   Translations by Sir S. de Vere, Bt.
OSSIAN. Edited by G. E. Todd.
ELFIN MUSIC. Ed. by A. Waite.
SOUTHEY. Ed. by S. R. Thompson.
CHAUCER. Edited by F. N. Paton.
POEMS OF WILD LIFE.
   Edited by Chas. G. D. Roberts, M.A.
PARADISE REGAINED.
   Edited by J. Bradshaw, M.A., LL.D.
CRABBE. Edited by E. Lamplough.
DORA GREENWELL.
   Edited by William Dorling.
FAUST. Edited by E. Craigmyle.
AMERICAN SONNETS.
   Edited by William Sharp.
LANDOR'S POEMS.
   Selected and Edited by E. Radford.
GREEK ANTHOLOGY.
   Edited by Graham R. Tomson.
HUNT AND HOOD.
   Edited by J. Harwood Panting.
HUMOROUS POEMS.
   Edited by Ralph H. Caine.
LYTTON'S PLAYS.
   Edited by R. F. Sharp.
GREAT ODES.
   Edited by William Sharp.
MEREDITH'S POEMS.
   Edited by M. Betham-Edwards.
PAINTER-POETS.
   Edited by Kineton Parkes.
WOMEN POETS.
   Edited by Mrs. Sharp.
LOVE LYRICS.
   Edited by Percy Hulburd.

WALTER SCOTT, 24 Warwick Lane, Paternoster Row.

POPULAR BOOKS IN 3 VOL. SETS
BY OLIVER WENDELL HOLMES, WALTER SAVAGE LANDOR, CHARLES LAMB, LEIGH HUNT, WILLIAM HAZLITT, ETC.

By OLIVER WENDELL HOLMES.

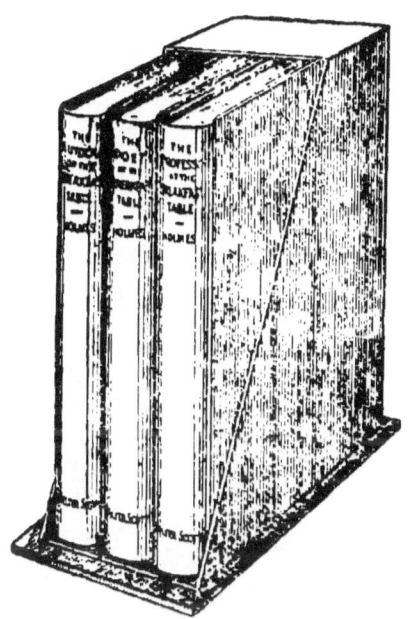

The Autocrat of the Breakfast-Table

The Poet at the Breakfast-Table

The Professor at the Breakfast-Table.

Reduced fac simile of HOLMES and LANDOR.
3 Vols., *Crown 8vo, Cloth, Gilt Top, in Shell Case. Price 4s. 6d.*
3 Vols., *Crown 8vo, Cloth, Gilt Top, in Cloth Pedestal Case. 5s.*
The Vols. may be had separately at 1/6 each.
Also in Half Polished Morocco, Gilt Top, Antique.

UNIFORM WITH ABOVE—
SELECTIONS FROM LANDOR (IN 3 VOLS.):—
1—IMAGINARY CONVERSATIONS.
2—PENTAMERON.   3—PERICLES AND ASPASIA.

IN THREE VOLUMES—
Essays of Charles Lamb, William Hazlitt, and Leigh Hunt.
IN THREE VOLUMES—
MEDITATIONS OF MARCUS AURELIUS.
TEACHING OF EPICTETUS.   MORALS OF SENECA.

London: WALTER SCOTT, 24 Warwick Lane, Paternoster Row.

*Crown 8vo, about 350 pp. each, Cloth Cover, 2s. 6d. per vol.
Half-polished Morocco, gilt top, 5s.*

COUNT TOLSTOÏ'S WORKS.

The following Volumes are already issued—

A RUSSIAN PROPRIETOR.
THE COSSACKS.
IVAN ILYITCH, AND OTHER STORIES.
THE INVADERS, AND OTHER STORIES.
MY RELIGION
LIFE.
MY CONFESSION.
CHILDHOOD, BOYHOOD, YOUTH.
THE PHYSIOLOGY OF WAR.
ANNA KARÉNINA. (2 VOLS.)
WHAT TO DO?
WAR AND PEACE. (4 VOLS.)
THE LONG EXILE, AND OTHER STORIES FOR CHILDREN.
SEVASTOPOL.
THE KREUTZER SONATA, AND FAMILY HAPPINESS.

Uniform with the above.
IMPRESSIONS OF RUSSIA.
BY DR. GEORG BRANDES.

London: WALTER SCOTT, 24 Warwick Lane, Paternoster Row.

NEW BOOKLETS.

Crown 8vo, Gilt Lettering, One Shilling each.

By COUNT LEO TOLSTOÏ.

WHERE LOVE IS, THERE GOD IS ALSO.

THE TWO PILGRIMS.

WHAT MEN LIVE BY.

THE GODSON.

IF YOU NEGLECT THE FIRE, YOU DON'T PUT IT OUT.

Published originally in Russia, as tracts for the people, these little stories possess all the grace, naïveté, and power which characterise the work of Count Tolstoï, and while inculcating in the most penetrating way the Christian ideas of love, humility, and charity, are perfect in their art form as stories pure and simple.

London : WALTER SCOTT, 24 Warwick Lane, Paternoster Row.

THE OXFORD LIBRARY.

Handsomely bound in Blue Cloth, Gilt Top, Uncut Edges,

PRICE 2s. EACH.

Comprises the most popular Works of SCOTT, DICKENS, LYTTON, MARRYAT, LEVER, OLIVER WENDELL HOLMES, SHERIDAN, etc., and original Novels by New Authors.

BARNABY RUDGE.
OLD CURIOSITY SHOP.
PICKWICK PAPERS.
NICHOLAS NICKLEBY.
OLIVER TWIST.
MARTIN CHUZZLEWIT.
SKETCHES BY BOZ.
RODERICK RANDOM.
PEREGRINE PICKLE.
IVANHOE.
KENILWORTH.
JACOB FAITHFUL.
PETER SIMPLE.
PAUL CLIFFORD.
EUGENE ARAM.
ERNEST MALTRAVERS.
ALICE; or, the Mysteries.
RIENZI.
PELHAM.
LAST DAYS OF POMPEII.
THE SCOTTISH CHIEFS.
WILSON'S TALES.
THE INHERITANCE.
ETHEL LINTON.
A MOUNTAIN DAISY.
HAZEL; or, Perilpoint Lighthouse.
VICAR OF WAKEFIELD.
PRINCE of the HOUSE of DAVID.
WIDE, WIDE WORLD.
VILLAGE TALES.
BEN-HUR.
UNCLE TOM'S CABIN.
ROBINSON CRUSOE.

THE WHITE SLAVE.
CHARLES O'MALLEY.
MIDSHIPMAN EASY.
BRIDE OF LAMMERMOOR.
HEART OF MIDLOTHIAN
LAST OF THE BARONS.
OLD MORTALITY.
TOM CRINGLE'S LOG.
CRUISE OF THE MIDGE.
COLLEEN BAWN.
VALENTINE VOX.
NIGHT AND MORNING.
BUNYAN.
FOXE'S BOOK OF MARTYRS
MANSFIELD PARK.
LAST OF THE MOHICANS.
POOR JACK.
THE LAMPLIGHTER.
JANE EYRE.
PILLAR OF FIRE.
THRONE OF DAVID.
DOMBEY AND SON.
VANITY FAIR.
INFELICE.
BEULAH.
HARRY LORREQUER.
BURNS'S POEMS.
SHERIDAN'S PLAYS.
WAVERLEY.
QUENTIN DURWARD.
TALISMAN.

London: WALTER SCOTT, 24 Warwick Lane, Paternoster Row.

RE-ISSUE IN 12 MONTHLY VOLUMES.
Commencing February 25th, 1891.
Strongly Bound in Cloth, Gilt Top, 2/6 each.

WILSON'S
TALES OF THE BORDERS
AND OF SCOTLAND:
HISTORICAL, TRADITIONARY, AND IMAGINATIVE.
REVISED BY ALEXANDER LEIGHTON.

No collection of tales published in a serial form ever enjoyed so great a popularity as "THE TALES OF THE BORDERS;" and the secret of their success lies in the fact that they are stories in the truest sense of the word, illustrating in a graphic and natural style the manners and customs, trials and sorrows, sins and backslidings, of the men and women of whom they treat. The heroes and heroines of these admirable stories belong to every rank of life, from the king and noble to the humble peasant.

"THE TALES OF THE BORDERS" have always been immensely popular with the young, and whether we view them in their moral aspect, or as vehicles for instruction and amusement, the collected series forms a repertory of healthy and interesting literature unrivalled in the language.

The *Scotsman* says:—"Those who have read the tales in the unwieldy tomes in which they are to be found in the libraries will welcome the publication of this neat, handy, and well-printed edition."

The *Dundee Advertiser* says:—"Considering how attractive are these tales, whether regarded as illustrating Scottish life, or as entertaining items of romance, there can be no doubt of their continued popularity. We last read them in volumes the size of a family Bible, and we are glad to have an opportunity to renew our acquaintance with them in a form so much more handy and elegant."

London: WALTER SCOTT, 24 Warwick Lane, Paternoster Row.

Quarto, cloth elegant, gilt edges, emblematic design on cover, 6s.
May also be had in a variety of Fancy Bindings.

THE
MUSIC OF THE POETS:
A MUSICIANS' BIRTHDAY BOOK.

Edited by Eleonore D'Esterre Keeling.

This is a unique Birthday Book. Against each date are given the names of musicians whose birthday it is, together with a verse-quotation appropriate to the character of their different compositions or performances. A special feature of the book consists in the reproduction in fac-simile of autographs, and autographic music, of living composers. The selections of verse (from before Chaucer to the present time) have been made with admirable critical insight. English verse is rich in utterances of the poets about music, and merely as a volume of poetry about music this book makes a charming anthology. Three sonnets by Mr. Theodore Watts, on the "Fausts" of Berlioz, Schumann, and Gounod, have been written specially for this volume. It is illustrated with designs of various musical instruments, etc.; autographs of Rubenstein, Dvorâk, Greig, Mackenzie, Villiers Stanford, etc., etc.

"To musical amateurs this will certainly prove the most attractive birthday book ever published."—*Manchester Guardian.*

"One of those happy ideas that seems to have been yearning for fulfilment. . . . The book ought to have a place on every music stand."—*Scottish Leader.*

London: Walter Scott, 24 Warwick Lane, Paternoster Row.

Windsor Series of Poetical Anthologies.

Printed on Antique Paper. Crown 8vo. Bound in Blue Cloth, each with suitable Emblematic Design on Cover, Price 3s. 6d. Also in various Calf and Morocco Bindings.

Women's Voices. An Anthology of the most Characteristic Poems by English, Scotch, and Irish Women. Edited by Mrs. William Sharp.

Sonnets of this Century. With an Exhaustive Essay on the Sonnet. Edited by Wm. Sharp.

The Children of the Poets. An Anthology from English and American Writers of Three Centuries. Edited by Professor Eric S. Robertson.

Sacred Song. A Volume of Religious Verse. Selected and arranged by Samuel Waddington.

A Century of Australian Song, Selected and Edited by Douglas B. W. Sladen, B.A., Oxon.

Jacobite Songs and Ballads. Selected and Edited, with Notes, by G. S. Macquoid.

Irish Minstrelsy. Edited, with Notes and Introduction, by H. Halliday Sparling.

The Sonnets of Europe. A Volume of Translations. Selected and arranged by Samuel Waddington.

Early English and Scottish Poetry. Selected and Edited by H. Macaulay Fitzgibbon.

Ballads of the North Countrie. Edited, with Introduction, by Graham R. Tomson.

Songs and Poems of the Sea. An Anthology of Poems Descriptive of the Sea. Edited by Mrs. William Sharp.

Songs and Poems of Fairyland. An Anthology of English Fairy Poetry, selected and arranged, with an Introduction, by Arthur Edward Waite.

Songs and Poems of the Great Dominion. Edited by W. D. Lighthall, of Montreal.

London: WALTER SCOTT, 24 Warwick Lane, Paternoster Row.

Cloth Elegant, Crown 8vo, 416 Pages, with 48 Illustrations. Price 2s. 6d.

THE CENTENARY LIFE OF WESLEY.

BEGINNING with the early home of the Wesleys at Epworth, this biography traces John Wesley's life at Charterhouse, and subsequently at Christ Church, Oxford, and his career as Fellow of Lincoln. It describes his doings as a missionary in the colony of Georgia; his meeting, after his return, with Böhler and his brother Moravians, and Wesley's conversion. It then deals with the period of his open-air preaching, first near Bristol, afterwards in London, where he was often listened to by crowds of five to twenty thousand, his itinerary as a preacher, and the gradual establishment of Methodism throughout the kingdom. Sympathetically and ably written, this volume, dealing with a man of such special gifts as Wesley possessed,—gifts which he employed with such effect during his extraordinary life, — will be read with interest by all who care for the history of a career devoted to great objects.

LONDON: WALTER SCOTT, 24 WARWICK LANE.

www.ingramcontent.com/pod-product-compliance
Lightning Source LLC
Chambersburg PA
CBHW022116230426
43672CB00008B/1406